Medieval People

MEDIEVAL PEOPLE

This is one of the great books of social history. Many writers have recounted the lives of the heroes of the Middle Ages. This book is about ordinary people who are so often left out of history. In it are described the lives of some typical people, ranging from Bodo, a Frankish peasant, to a housewife of fourteenth century Paris.

Medieval People

by

EILEEN POWER

M.A., D.Lit.

*Late Reader in History in the University of
London and sometime Fellow and Lecturer of
Girton College, Cambridge*

'I counsel thee, shut not thy heart nor thy library'

CHARLES LAMB

HarperCollins*Publishers*

First published by Methuen & Co., 1924

Published in the United States
in 1963
by Harper & Row, Publishers, Inc.

ISBN : 0-06-480694-4

Printed in the United States of America

To
my colleagues and students
at Girton College, Cambridge
1913–20

For if heuene be on this erthe . and ese to any soule,
It is in cloistere or in scole . by many skilles I fynde;
For in cloistre cometh no man . to chide ne to fiȝte,
But alle is buxomnesse there and bokes . to rede and to lerne,
In scole there is scorne . but if a clerke wil lerne,
And grete loue and lykynge . for eche of hem loueth other.

— LANGLAND, *Piers Plowman*

Author's Preface

SOCIAL HISTORY SOMETIMES suffers from the reproach that it is vague and general, unable to compete with the attractions of political history either for the student or for the general reader, because of its lack of outstanding personalities. In point of fact there is often as much material for reconstructing the life of some quite ordinary person as there is for writing a history of Robert of Normandy or of Philippa of Hainault; and the lives of ordinary people so reconstructed are, if less spectacular, certainly not less interesting. I believe that social history lends itself particularly to what may be called a personal treatment, and that the past may be made to live again for the general reader more effectively by personifying it than by presenting it in the form of learned treatises on the development of the manor or on medieval trade, essential as these are to the specialist. For history, after all, is valuable only in so far as it lives, and Maeterlinck's cry, 'There are no dead', should always be the historian's motto. It is the idea that history is about dead people, or, worse still, about movements and conditions which seem but vaguely related to the labours and passions of flesh and blood, which has driven history from bookshelves where the historical novel still finds a welcome place.

In the following series of sketches I have tried to illustrate at the same time various aspects of social life in the Middle Ages and various classes of historical material. Thus Bodo illustrates peasant life, and an early phase of a typical medieval estate; Marco Polo, Venetian trade with the East; Madame Eglentyne, monastic life; the Ménagier's wife, domestic life in a middle-class home, and medieval ideas about women; Thomas Betson, the wool trade, and the activities of the great English trading company of Merchants of the Staple; and Thomas Paycocke, the cloth industry in East Anglia. They are all quite ordinary people and unknown to fame, with the exception

Author's Preface

of Marco Polo. The types of historical evidence illustrated are the estate book of a manorial lord, the chronicle and traveller's tale, the bishop's register, the didactic treatise in household management, the collection of family letters, and houses, brasses, and wills. At the end of the book I have added a bibliography of the sources which form the raw material for my reconstructions, and a few additional notes and references. I hope that this modest attempt to bring to life again some of 'our fathers that begat us', may perhaps interest for an hour or two the general reader, or the teacher, who wishes to make more concrete by personification some of the general facts of medieval social and economic history.

My thanks are due to my publishers, Messrs. Methuen and Co., for allowing me to incorporate in Chapter VI the greater part of a chapter in my book 'The Paycockes of Coggeshall', and to the Cambridge University Press for similarly allowing me to repeat in Chapter III a few sentences from my study of 'Medieval English Nunneries'. I have also to thank my friends Miss M. G. Jones and Miss H. M. R. Murray of Girton College, Cambridge, for various suggestions and criticisms, and my sister Miss Rhoda Power for making the index.

May 1924   EILEEN POWER
London School of Economics and Political Science
University of London

Preface to the Tenth Edition

FOR YEARS after the first edition of *Medieval People* had come out, Eileen Power collected notes and made plans for several essays to be included in an enlarged edition of the book. Of these essays only one, "The Precursors", had been written out in full before she died; and it has now been added to the present edition. In its published form it is not in every respect identical with the author's original text.

The essay was taking shape as Munich came and went and as the war itself was drawing near. No historian writing at that time about Rome menaced by the barbarians – and least of all an historian as sensitive to the extra-mural world as Eileen Power was – could have helped noting the similarities between the Roman Empire in the fifth or sixth centuries and Europe in the nineteen-thirties. In the end, having finished the essay, she decided to withold it from publication for the time being and to present it instead to a friendly audience as a tract for the times. This she did at a meeting of the Cambridge History Club in the winter of 1938: and for that occasion she replaced the opening and concluding pages of the original essay with passages, or rather notes for passages, more suited to the purpose.

I am sure that she never intended these passages to be perpetuated in her *Medieval People* and I have therefore done what I could to replace them with a reconstructed version of her first draft. The reconstruction had to be done from somewhat disjointed notes and cannot therefore be word-faithful. The readers must therefore bear in mind that the first two and the last page of the essay are mere approximations to what Eileen Power in fact wrote.

April, 1963

M. M. POSTAN
Peterhouse, Cambridge.

Contents

xiii

List of Illustrations

List of Illustrations

Medieval People

Let us now praise famous men and our fathers that begat us. . . .

There be of them that have left a name behind them, that their praises might be reported.

And some there be which have no memorial; who are perished, as though they had never been; and are become as though they had never been born; and their children after them.

But these were merciful men, whose righteousness hath not been forgotten.

With their seed shall continually remain a good inheritance, and their children are within the covenant.

Their seed standeth fast, and their children for their sakes.

Their seed shall remain for ever, and their glory shall not be blotted out.

Their bodies are buried in peace; but their name liveth for evermore.

ECCLESIASTICUS xliv.

CHAPTER I

The Precursors

I. ROME IN DECLINE

Every schoolboy knows that the Middle Ages arose on the ruins of the Roman Empire. The decline of Rome preceded and in some ways prepared the rise of the kingdoms and cultures which composed the medieval system. Yet in spite of the self-evident truth of this historical preposition we know little about life and thought in the watershed years when Europe was ceasing to be Roman but was not yet medieval. We do not know how it felt to watch the decline of Rome; we do not even know whether the men who watched it knew what they saw, though we can be quite certain that none of them foretold, indeed could have foreseen, the shape which the world was to take in later centuries.

Yet the tragic story, its main themes and protagonists were for all to see. No observer should have failed to notice that the Roman Empire of the fourth and fifth centuries was no longer the Roman Empire of the great Antonine and Augustan age; that it had lost its hold over its territories and its economic cohesion and was menaced by the barbarians who were in the end to overwhelm it. The territory of the Roman Empire had at its height stretched from the lands bordering the North Sea to the lands on the northern fringes of the Sahara, and from the Atlantic coast of Europe to the central Asiatic Steppes; it comprised most of the regions of the former Hellenic, Iranian, and Phoenician empires, and it either ruled or kept in check great clusters of peoples and principalities beyond its Gallic and north African frontiers. From these farthest frontiers Rome of the fourth century had retreated and was still retreating.

Within its frontiers great currents of inter-regional commerce

I

had in earlier centuries flowed along the routes which bound all the provinces of the Empire to Rome and most of the provinces to each other. But from the third century onwards the economic unity of the Empire was in dissolution, and by the fifth century most of the great currents of inter-regional trade had ceased to flow, and provinces and districts had been thrown upon themselves and their own resources. And with the wealth of the provinces reduced, their commerce restricted, the great provincial cities also declined in population, wealth, political power.

Yet to its very last days the Empire endeavoured to defend its frontiers against the converging barbarians. Not only did the Barbarian Conquests, like all conquests, threaten destruction and ruin, but the way of life the barbarians stood for was the very denial of what Roman civilization had been, though alas, was gradually ceasing to be.

However, it was not in material things, that the contemporaries found, or should have found the sharpest conflict between Rome and the barbarian prospects before it. Above all Roman civilization was a civilization of the mind. It had behind it a long tradition of thought and of intellectual achievement, the legacy of Greece, to which it had in turn made its own contribution. The Roman world was a world of schools and universities, writers, and builders. The barbarian world was a world in which mind was in its infancy and its infancy was long. The battle sagas of the race, which have all but disappeared or have survived only as legends worked up in a later age; the few rude laws which were needed to regulate personal relationships, this was hardly civilization in the Roman sense. King Chilperic, trying to make verses in the style of Sedullus, though he could not distinguish between a long foot and a short and they all hobbled; Charlemagne himself, going to bed with his slate under his pillow in order to practice in the watches of the night that art of writing which he never mastered; what have they in common with Julius Caesar and Marcus Aurelius and that great Julian called the Apostate? They sum up in their very persons the whole wide gulf that yawned between Germany and Rome.

Rome and the barbarians were thus not only protagonists but two different attitudes to life, civilization and barbarism. We cannot here discuss in detail the question as to why, in the clash between the two, it was civilization which perished and barbarism which prevailed. But it is important to remember that while the Empire tried to defend its frontiers against the barbarian hosts, it gradually opened them to barbarian settlers.

This peaceful infiltration of barbarians which altered the whole character of the society which it invaded would have been impossible, of course, if that society had not been stricken by disease. The disease is plain enough to see by the third century. It shows itself in those internecine civil wars in which civilization rends itself, province against province and army against army. It shows itself in the great inflationary crisis from about 268 and in the taxation which gradually crushed out the smaller bourgeoisie while the fortunes of the rich escaped its net. It shows itself in the gradual sinking back of an economy based upon free exchange into more and more primitive conditions when every province seeks to be self-sufficient and barter takes the place of trade. It shows itself in the decline of farming and in the workless city population kept quiet by their dole of bread and their circuses, whose life contrasted so dramatically, so terribly with that of the haughty senatorial families and the great landowners in their palatial villas and town houses. It shows itself in the rise of mystical faiths on the ruins of philosophy, and of superstition (more especially astrology) on the ruins of reason. One religion in particular grew mighty, by clasping its sacred book and addressing itself with words of hope to the victims of social injustice, but although it was able to bring comfort to individuals it could do nothing, indeed it did not try, to give new strength or inspiration to the embattled civilization. True to its own ethos it was impartial as between Barbarian and Roman, or between the Romans who prospered and ruled and those outside the pale.

The most obvious manifestation of Roman society in decline was the dwindling numbers of Roman citizens. The Empire was being depopulated long before the end of the period of peace and prosperity which stretched from Augustus to Marcus Aurelius. Does not Augustus himself summon the poor man of Fiesole who has a family of eight children, thirty-six grandchildren and eighteen great grandchildren, and organize in his honour a fête in the

Capitol, accompanied by a great deal of publicity? Does not Tacitus, half-anthropologist and half-Rousseau, describing the noble savage with his eye on fellow citizens, remark that among the Germans it is accounted a shameful thing to limit the number of your children? The long duration of Augustus's legislation to raise the birthrate is significant; successful it was not, but the fact that it was maintained on the statute book and systematically revised and developed for three centuries shows that it was at least accounted necessary. It is true of course that the mortality rate was a far more important factor in those days than it is in our own, and the mortality from pestilence and civil war from Marcus Aurelius onwards was exceptional. And it is plain that the proportion of celibates was high in the Roman empire and that the fall in the fertility of marriages was going on. It is the childless marriage, the small family system that contemporary writers deplore. In Seeley's striking phrase: 'The human harvest was bad.' It was bad in all classes, but the decline was most marked in the upper ranks, the most educated, the most civilized, the potential leaders of the race. In the terrible words of Swift, facing his own madness, the Roman Empire might have cried: 'I shall die like a tree – from the top downwards.'

Why (the insistent question forces itself) did this civilization lose the power to reproduce itself? Was it, as Polybius said, because people preferred amusements to children or wished to bring their children up in comfort? Hardly, for it is more marked among the rich than the poor and the rich can have the best of both worlds. Was it because people had grown discouraged and disheartened, no longer believing in their own civilization and loath to bring children into the darkness and disaster of their war-shattered world? We do not know. But we can see the connection of the falling population with the other evils of the empire – the heavy cost of administration relatively heavier when the density of the population is low; the empty fields, the dwindling legions which did not suffice to guard the frontier.

To cure this sickness of population the Roman rulers knew no other way than to dose it with barbarian vigour. Just a small injection to begin with and then more and more till in the end the blood that flowed in its veins was not Roman but barbarian. In came

the Germans to settle the frontier, to till the fields, to enlist first in
the auxiliaries and then in the legions, to fill the great offices of state.
The army is barbarized, and a modern writer, Mr Moss, has quoted
most effectively the complaint of the Egyptian mother clamouring
to get back her son who (as she says) has gone off with the barbarians – he means that he has enlisted in the Roman legions. The
legions are barbarized and they barbarize the Emperor. For them
he is no longer the majestic embodiment of law, he is their leader,
their Führer, and they raise him on their shields. And side by side
with the barbarization of the army goes the barbarization of civil
manners too. In 397 Honorius has to pass an edict forbidding the
wearing of German fashions within the precincts of Rome. And in
the end, half barbarian themselves, they have only barbarians to
defend them against barbarism.

Such was the general picture of the great ruin of civilization
amidst which the Romans of the fourth, fifth, and sixth centuries
lived. What then did it feel like to live at a time when civilization
was going down before the forces of barbarism? Did people realize
what was happening? Did the gloom of the Dark Ages cast its
shadow before? It so happens that we can answer these questions
very clearly if we fix our eyes on one particular part of the Empire,
the famous and highly civilized province of Gaul. We can catch the
decline at three points because in three consecutive centuries, Gallo-
Roman writers have left us a picture of their life and times. In the
fourth century we have Ausonius, in the fifth Sidonius Apollinar-
ius, in the sixth Gregory of Tours and Fortunatus, a stranger from
Italy, who made his home in Poitiers. They show us Auvergne and
the Bordelais in the evening light. The fourth, the fifth, and the
sixth centuries – going, going, gone!

2. AUSONIUS

Going! This is the world of Ausonius, south-western France in the
latter half of the fourth century, 'an Indian summer between ages of
storm and wreckage'. Ausonius himself is a scholar and a gentleman, the friend alike of the pagan Symmachus and of St Paulinus
of Nela. He is for thirty years professor of rhetoric in the university

of Bordeaux, for some time tutor to a prince, praetorian prefect of Gaul, consul, and in his last years just an old man contentedly living on his estates. His most famous poem is a description of the Moselle, which for all its literary affectations evokes most magically the smiling countryside which was the background of his life. High above the river on either bank stand the villas and country houses, with their courts and lawns and pillared porticos, and the hot baths from which, if you will, you can plunge into the stream. The sunny hillside is covered with vines, and from slope to hill-top the husbandmen call to each other and the wayfarer on the towpath or the bargemen floating by, shout their rude jests to the loitering vine-dressers. Far out in midstream the fisherman trails his dripping net and on a rock by the shore the angler plies his rod. And, as twilight falls, the deepening shadow of the green hillside is reflected in the water and gazing downward the boatman can almost count the trembling vines and almost see the swelling of the grapes.

Equally peaceful, equally pleasant is life on Ausonius' own estate in the Bordelais, his little patrimony (he calls it) although he had a thousand acres of vineyard and tillage and wood. Miss Waddell has reminded us, on the authority of Saintsbury (whom else?) that 'to this day it boasts itself as Château-Ausone, one of the two best of the St Emilion clarets.' Here he tends his roses and sends his boy round to the neighbours to bid them to luncheon, while he interviews the cook. Six, including the host, is the right number – if more it is not a meal but a melée. Then there are all his relatives to be commemorated in verse, his grandfather and his grandmother and his sisters and his cousins and his aunts (especially his aunts).

And when the family circle palls there is the senior common room to fall back upon and the professors of Bordeaux to be celebrated in their turn. Professors were important people in the empire of the fourth century; Symmachus says that it is the mark of a flourishing state that good salaries should be paid to professors; though what exactly we are to deduce from that in the light of history I should hesitate to say. So Ausonius writes a collection of poems about the professors of Bordeaux. There are thirty-two of them and all are celebrated. There is Minervius the orator, who had a prodigious memory and after a game of backgammon was wont to conduct a post-mortem over every move. There is Anastasius the grammarian, who was so foolish as to leave Bordeaux for a provincial university and thenceforth languished in well-merited obscurity. There is Attius Tiro Delphidius, who retired from a legal career into the professorial chair, but could never be got to take any trouble with his men, to the disappointment of their parents. There is Jocundus the grammarian, who did not really deserve his title, but was such a kind man that we will commemorate him among men of worth, although he was, strictly speaking, unequal to the job. There is Exuperius, who was very good-looking and whose eloquence sounded superb until you examined it and found that it meant nothing. There is Dynamius, who slipped from the paths of virtue with a married lady in Bordeaux and left the place rather hastily, but fortunately fell on his feet in Spain. There is Victorius the usher, who liked only the most abstruse historical problems, such as what the pedigree of the sacrificial priest at Cureo was long before Numa's day, or what Castor had to say on all the shadowy kings, and who never got up as far as Tully or Virgil, though he might have done so if he had gone on reading long enough, but death cut him off too soon. They seem oddly familiar figures (except of course, Dynamius) and their chronicler contrives to make them live.

Such is the world depicted for us by Ausonius. But while this pleasant country house and senior common room life was going calmly on, what do we find happening in the history books? Ausonius was a man of nearly fifty when the Germans swarmed across the Rhine in 357, pillaging forty-five flourishing cities, and pitching their camps on the banks of the Moselle. He had seen the great Julian take up arms ('O Plato, Plato, what a task for a philosopher') and in a series of brilliant campaigns drive them out again. Ten years later when he was tutor to Gratian he had himself accompanied the emperor Valentinian on another campaign against the same foes. While he was preening himself on his consulship ten years later still, he must have heard of the disastrous battle of Adrianople in the east, when the Goths defeated a Roman army and slew an emperor. He died in 395 and within twelve years of his death the host of Germans had burst across the Rhine, 'all Gaul

was a smoking funeral pyre', and the Goths were at the gates of
Rome. And what have Ausonius and his correspondents to say
about this? Not a word. Ausonius and Symmachus and their set
ignore the barbarians as completely as the novels of Jane Austen
ignore the Napoleonic wars.

3. SIDONIUS APOLLINARIS

Going, going. . . . Some thirty-five years after the death of
Ausonius, in the midst of the disastrous sixth century, was born
Sidonius Apollinaris, Gallo-Roman aristocrat, father-in-law of an
emperor, sometime prefect of Rome and in the end Bishop of Clermont. Sidonius Apollinaris, 431 (or thereabouts) to 479 or perhaps
a few years later. Much had happened between the death of Ausonius and his birth. The lights were going out all over Europe. Barbarian kingdoms had been planted in Gaul and Spain, Rome herself had been sacked by the Goths; and in his lifetime the collapse
went on, ever more swiftly. He was a young man of twenty when
the ultimate horror broke upon the West, the inroad of Attila and
the Huns. That passed away, but when he was twenty-four the
Vandals sacked Rome. He saw the terrible German king-maker
Ricimer throne and unthrone a series of puppet emperors, he saw
the last remnant of Gallic independence thrown away and himself
become a barbarian subject, and he saw a few years before he died
the fall of the empire in the west.

They cannot, Sidonius and his friends, ignore as Ausonius and
his friends did, that something is happening to the empire. The men
of the fifth century are concerned at these disasters and they con-
sole themselves, each according to his kind. There are some who
think it cannot last. After all, they say, the empire has been in a
tight place before and has always got out of it in the end and risen
supreme over its enemies. Thus Sidonius himself, the very year
after they sacked the city; Rome has endured as much before – there
was Porsenna, there was Brennus, there was Hannibal. . . . Only
that time Rome did not get over it. Others tried to use the disasters
to castigate the sins of society. Thus Salvian of Marseilles who
would no doubt have been called the gloomy dean if he had not

been a bishop. For him all that the decadent Roman civilization needs is to copy some of the virtues of these fresh young barbarian people. There is the familiar figure of Orosius, defending the barbarians with the argument that when the Roman empire was founded it was founded in blood and conquest and can ill afford to throw stones at the barbarians; and after all the barbarians are not so bad. 'If the unhappy people they have despoiled will content themselves with the little that is left them, their conquerors will cherish them as friends and brothers.' Others, especially the more thoughtful churchmen are much concerned to explain why an empire which had flourished under paganism should be thus beset under Christianity. Others desert the Empire altogether and (like St Augustine) put their hope in a city not made with hands – though Ambrose, it is true, let fall the pregnant observation that it was not the will of God that his people should be saved by logic-chopping. 'It has not pleased God to save his people by dialectic.'

And how were they living? We have only to read the letters written by Sidonius during the period between 460 and 470, when he was living on his estate in Auvergne, to realize that on the surface all is going on exactly as before. Gaul is shrunk, it is true, to a mere remnant between three barbarian kingdoms, but save for that we might be back in the days of Ausonius. There is the luxurious villa, with its hot baths and swimming pool, its suites of rooms, its views over the lake; and there is Sidonius inviting his friends to stay with him or sending round his compositions to the professors and the bishops and the country-gentlemen. Sport and games are very popular – Sidonius rides and swims and hunts and plays tennis. In one letter he tells his correspondent that he has been spending some days in the country with his cousin and an old friend, whose estates adjoin each other. They had sent out scouts to catch him and bring him back for a week and took it in turns to entertain him. There are games of tennis on the lawn before breakfast or backgammon for the older men. There is an hour or two in the library before we sit down to an excellent luncheon followed by a siesta. Then we go out riding and return for a hot bath and a plunge in the river. I should like to describe our luscious dinner parties, he concludes, but I have no more paper. However, come and stay with us and you shall hear all about it. Clearly this is no Britain, where in the sixth century half-barbarian people camped in the abandoned villas and cooked their food on the floors of the principal rooms.

And yet . . . it had gone a long way downhill since the days of Ausonius, and Sidonius could not now ignore the very existence of the barbarians. He has indeed left notable protraits of them, especially of the king of the Visigoths and of the Burgundians who ruled Lyons, where he was born. Whenever he went to stay there, he complains, they flocked about him in embarrassing friendliness, breathing leeks and onions and dressing their hair with rancid butter (they were not, it appears, constrained to choose between spears and butter). How can he compose six foot metres, he asks, with so many seven foot patrons around him, all singing and all expecting him to admire their uncouth stream of non-Latin words? The shrug of the shoulder, the genial contempt of one conscious of an infinite superiority – how clear it is. One is reminded of a verse of Verlaine

> Je suis l'empire a la fin de la decadence
> qui regarde passer les grands barbares blancs

But Sidonius's good nature was to be rudely shaken. All barbarians were not friendly giants, and the Visigoths next door, under their new king Euric, turned covetous eyes upon Auvergne. Sidonius had not been two years bishop of Clermont before he had to organize the defence of the city against their attack. The Avernians stood out gallantly; they would fight and they would starve, but they would defend this last stronghold of Rome in Gaul. But they were a small people; to resist successfully they must have help from Rome itself. Lest anyone should suspect me of twisting the story, I give it in the words of Sidonius's editor, writing twenty years ago.

Julius Nepos was alive to the danger that Euric might cross the Rhône; but weak as his resources were he could only hope to secure peace by negotiation. The quaestor Licinianus had been sent into Gaul to investigate the condition of affairs on the spot. . . . He had now returned and it was soon only too clear that hopes based on his intervention were not likely to be fulfilled. We find Sidonius writing for information. . . . He began to fear that something was going on behind his back, and that the real danger to Auvergne came no longer from determined enemies but from pusillanimous friends. His suspicions were only too well founded. On receipt of the quaestor's report a Council was held to determine the policy of the Empire towards the Visigothic king. . . . The empire did not feel strong enough to support Auvergne and it was decided to cede the whole territory to Euric, apparently without condition.

The despair of Sidonius knew no bounds and he writes a nobly indignant letter to a bishop who had been concerned in the negotiations:

The state of our unhappy region is miserable indeed. Everyone declares that things were better in wartime than they are now after peace has been concluded. Our enslavement was made the price of security for a third party; the enslavement, ah – the shame of it!, of those Avernians . . . who in our own time stood forth alone to stay the advance of the common enemy. . . . These are the men whose common soldiers were as good as captains, but who never reaped the benefit of their victories: that was handed over for your consolation, while all the crushing burden of defeat they had to bear themselves. . . . This is to be our reward for braving destitution, fire, sword and pestilence, for fleshing our swords in the enemy's blood and going ourselves starved into battle. This is the famous peace we dreamed of, when we tore the grass from the crannies in the walls to eat. . . . For all these proofs of our devotion, it would seem that we are to be made a sacrifice. If it be so, may you live to blush for a peace without either honour or advantage.

Auvergne had been sacrificed to save Rome. But Rome was not to enjoy her peace with honour for long. These things took place in 475; and in 476 the last emperor was deposed by his barbarian bear-leader, and the empire in the west came to an end. As for Sidonius, the Goths imprisoned him for a time and before he could recover his estate he had to write a panegyric for King Euric (he who had written panegyrics for three Roman emperors). It is clear that the old country house life went on as before, though the men who exchanged letters and epigrams were now under barbarian rule. But in one letter shortly before his death there breaks from

Sidonius a single line in which he unpacks his heart. *O neccessitas abjecta nascendi, vivendi misera, dura moriendi.* 'O humiliating necessity of birth, sad necessity of living, hard necessity of dying.' Shortly after 479 he died and within twenty years Clovis had embarked upon his career of conquest and Theodoric was ruler of Italy.

4. FORTUNATUS AND GREGORY OF TOURS

Going, going, gone. . . . There is only the time and only the heart to look for a moment at the Frankish kingdom which once was Gaul, and to survey the world of Fortunatus and Gregory of Tours, born both of them just about a century later than Sidonius, in the 530s. For a moment when you look at Fortunatus you think the world of the sixth century is the same world as that in which Sidonius entertained his friends with epigrams and tennis. Fortunatus, that versatile, gentle, genial, boot-licking gourmet, who somehow managed to write two of the most magnificent hymns of the Christian church, came from Italy on a visit to Gaul in 565 and never left it again. He travelled all over the Frankish lands, in what had been Germania as well as in what had been Gaul. From Trier to Toulouse he made his way with ease by river and by road, and it might be Ausonius again. Fortunatus too writes a poem on the Moselle; and there is the same smiling countryside with terraced vineyards sloping down to the quiet stream and the smoke of villas rising from the woods. Fortunatus too made the round of the country houses, especially of the sumptuous villas belonging to Leontius bishop of Bordeaux, a great Gallo-Roman aristocrat, whose grandfather had been a friend of Sidonius. The hot baths, the pillared porticos, the lawns sloping to the river, are all there; the feasts are even more magnificent (they upset Fortunatus's digestion badly) and the talk is still of literature. The more intelligent of the barbarian lords have imitated this refined and luxurious life as best they may. The Franks as well as the Gallo-Romans welcome little eager Fortunatus; every count wants a set of Latin verses dedicated to himself. It is plain that some of the old country house life at least has survived. The Apollinaris set still enjoys its hot baths and its tennis; as Dill puts it, the barbarian might rule the land, but the laws of polite society would be administered as before.

But when you look again you realize that it is not the same. It is not merely because we know that even these remnants of the social and material civilization of Rome would soon themselves die away that the tragedy of the sixth century looms so dark. It is because when we look below the surface we see that the life has gone out of it all, the soul that inflamed it is dead, nothing is now left but the empty shell. These men welcome Fortunatus just because he comes from Italy, where the rot has gone less far, where there still survives some reputation for learning and for culture. They slake their nostalgia a little in the presence of that *enfant perdue* of a lost civilization.

For this is the world of Gregory of Tours, of which you may read in his *History of the Franks*. The rule under which it lives is the rule of the horrible Merovingian kings. Side by side with the villas barbarism spreads and flourishes like a jungle growth. Learning is dying – hardly the ghost of a university is left – and Gregory himself who came of a great Gallo-Roman family and was a bishop bewails his ignorance of grammar. The towns are shrinking, crouched behind their defences. The synagogues are flaming, and the first step has been taken in that tragic tale of proscription and tallage, tallage and expulsion which (it seems) must never end. As to politics, the will of the leader and his retinue is the rule of the Franks, and purge and bloodbath mark every stage in the rivalry of the Merovingian princes. The worst of them are devils like Chilperic and Fredegond, the best of them are still barbarians like that King Guntram, who fills so many indulgent pages in Gregory of Tours. He is a vaguely contemporary figure, a fat, voluble man, now purring with jovial good nature, now bursting into explosions of wrath and violence, a strange mixture of bonhomie and brutality. It is an ironic commentary on what has happened to civilization that Gregory should regard him with affection, that he should be known as 'Good King Guntram' and that the church should actually have canonized him after his death. Good.King Guntram; Michelet has summed him up in a phrase 'Ce bon roi à qui on ne reprochait que deux ou trois meurtres.'

CONCLUSION

These were the men who lived through the centuries of Roman fall and Barbarian triumph, and who by virtue of their elevated position, their learning, and talents, should have seen, if not foretold, the course of events. And yet as one contemplates the world of Ausonius and Sidonius (for by the time of Gregory of Tours it was already dead) one is, I think, impelled to ask oneself the question why they were apparently so blind to what was happening. The big country houses go on having their luncheon and tennis parties, the little professors in the universities go on giving their lectures and writing their books; games are increasingly popular and the theatres are always full. Ausonius has seen the Germans overrun Gaul once, but he never speaks of a danger that may recur. Sidonius lives in a world already half barbarian, yet in the year before the Western Empire falls he is still dreaming of the consulship for his son. Why did they not realize the magnitude of the disaster that was befalling them? This is indeed a question almost as absorbing as the question why their civilization fell, for *au fond* it is perhaps the same question. Several answers may be suggested in explanation.

In the first place the process of disintegration was a slow one, for the whole tempo of life was slow and what might take decades in our own time took centuries then. It is only because we can look back from the vantage point of a much later age that we can see the inexorable pattern which events are forming, so that we long to cry to these dead people down the corridor of the ages, warning them to make a stand before it is too late, hearing no answering echo, 'Physician, heal thyself!' They suffered from the fatal myopia of contemporaries. It was the affairs of the moment that occupied them; for them it was the danger of the moment that must be averted and they did not recognize that each compromise and each defeat was a link in the chain dragging them over the abyss.

At what point did barbarism within become a wasting disease? Yet from the first skinclad German taken into a legion to the great barbarian patricians of Italy, making and unmaking emperors, the chain is unbroken. At what point in the assault from without did the attack become fatal? Was it the withdrawal from Dacia in 270 –

allow the barbarians their sphere of influence in the east of Europe, fling them the last-won recruit to Romania and they will be satiated and leave the west alone? Was it the settlement of the Goths as *foederati* within the Empire in 382 and the beginning of that compromise between the Roman empire and the Germans which, as Bury says, masked the transition from the rule on one to the rule of the other, from federate states within the Empire to independent states replacing it? Was this policy of appeasement the fatal error? Was it the removal of the legions from Britain, a distant people (as a Roman senator might have said) of whom we know nothing? Or was it that fatal combination of Spain and Africa, when the Vandals ensconced themselves in both provinces by 428 and the Vandal fleet (with Majorca and the islands for its bases) cut off Rome from her corn supplies and broke the backbone of ancient civilization, which was the Mediterranean sea? Not once alone in the history of Europe has the triumph of a hostile rule in Africa and Spain spelt disaster to our civilization.

But if the gradualness of this process misled the Romans there were other and equally potent reasons for their blindness. Most potent of all was the fact that they mistook entirely the very nature of civilization itself. All of them were making the same mistake. People who thought that Rome could swallow barbarism and absorb it into her life without diluting her own civilization; the people who ran about busily saying that the barbarians were not such bad fellows after all, finding good points in their regime with which to castigate the Romans and crying that except ye become as little barbarians ye shall not attain salvation; the people who did not observe in 476 that one half of the Respublica Romanorum had ceased to exist and nourished themselves on the fiction that the barbarian kings were exercising a power delegated from the Emperor. All these people were deluded by the same error, the belief that Rome (the civilization of their age) was not a mere historical fact with a beginning and an end, but a condition of nature like the air they breathed and the earth they tread *Ave Roma immortalis*, most magnificent most disastrous of creeds!

The fact is that the Romans were blinded to what was happening to them by the very perfection of the material culture which they had created. All around them was solidity and comfort, a material existence which was the very antithesis of barbarism. How could they foresee the day when the Norman chronicler would marvel over the broken hypocausts of Caerleon? How could they imagine that anything so solid might conceivably disappear? Their roads grew better as their statesmanship grew worse and central heating triumphed as civilization fell.

But still more responsible for their unawareness was the educational system in which they were reared. Ausonius and Sidonius and their friends were highly educated men and Gaul was famous for its schools and universities. The education which these gave consisted in the study of grammar and rhetoric, which was necessary alike for the civil service and for polite society; and it would be difficult to imagine an education more entirely out of touch with contemporary life, or less suited to inculcate the qualities which might have enabled men to deal with it. The fatal study of rhetoric, its links with reality long since severed, concentrated the whole attention of men of intellect on form rather than on matter. The things they learned in their schools had no relation to the things that were going on in the world outside and bred in them the fatal illusion that tomorrow would be as yesterday, that everything was the same, whereas everything was different.

So we take our leave of them. Going . . . going . . . gone! Gone altogether? Perhaps not. Hundreds of years of barbarism were to elapse before a new society arose capable of matching or even excelling Rome in material wealth, in arts, in sciences, and in gentler modes of existence – the *douceur de la vie*. We cannot say what date marked the moment of final recovery, or who were the men who were to represent advancing civilization as fully as Ausonius or Gregory of Tours represented civilization in retreat: Dante, Shakespeare, Copernicus, Newton? But for many centuries, perhaps a whole millennium, before western Europe scaled the heights on which these men now stood, it had been gradually raising itself from the depths of post-Roman decline. The ascent was not only slow but also discontinuous, yet it was sufficient to establish within a few centuries of Gregory of Tours a social order different from Rome and less glorious to behold across a thousand years of history, but nevertheless sufficiently exalted to draw the interest, and even to command the admiration of other still later ages. In that culture and in that social order much of what Ausonius and Sidonius and even Fortunatus represented was brought to life again, albeit in a form they would not always have recognized as their own. To this extent, at least, they were not only the epigones of Rome but the true precursors of the Middle Ages.

CHAPTER II

The Peasant Bodo

LIFE ON A COUNTRY ESTATE IN THE TIME OF CHARLEMAGNE

Three slender things that best support the world: the slender stream of milk from the cow's dug into the pail; the slender blade of green corn upon the ground; the slender thread over the hand of a skilled woman.

Three sounds of increase: the lowing of a cow in milk; the din of a smithy; the swish of a plough.

— From *The Triads of Ireland* (9th century)

ECONOMIC HISTORY, as we know it, is the newest of all the branches of history. Up to the middle of the last century the chief interest of the historian and of the public alike lay in political and constitutional history, in political events, wars, dynasties, and in political institutions and their development. Substantially, therefore, history concerned itself with the ruling classes. 'Let us now praise famous men,' was the historian's motto. He forgot to add 'and our fathers that begat us'. He did not care to probe the obscure lives and activities of the great mass of humanity, upon whose slow toil was built up the prosperity of the world and who were the hidden foundation of the political and constitutional edifice reared by the famous men he praised. To speak of ordinary people would have been beneath the dignity of history. Carlyle struck a significant note of revolt: 'The thing I want to see,' he said, 'is not Redbook lists and Court Calendars and Parliamentary Registers, but the Life of Man in England: what men did, thought, suffered, enjoyed. . . . Mournful, in truth, it is to behold what the business called "History" in these so enlightened and illuminated times still continues to be. Can you gather from it, read till your eyes go out, any dimmest shadow of an answer to that great question: How men lived and had their being; were it but economically, as, what wages they got and what they bought with these? Unhappily you cannot. . . . History, as it stands all bound up in gilt volumes, is but a shade more instructive than the wooden volumes of a back-gammon-board.'

Carlyle was a voice crying in the wilderness. Today the new history, whose way he prepared, has come. The present age differs from the centuries before it in its vivid realization of that much-neglected person the man in the street; or (as it was more often in the earliest ages) the man with the hoe. Today the historian is interested in the social life of the past and not only in the wars and intrigues of princes. To the modern writer, the fourteenth century, for instance, is not merely the century of the Hundred Years' War and of the Black Prince and Edward III; more significantly it is for him the era of the slow decay of villeinage in England, a fact more epoch-making, in the long run, than the struggle over our French provinces. We still praise famous men, for he would be a poor historian who could spare one of the great figures who have shed glory or romance upon the page of history; but we praise them with due recognition of the fact that not only great individuals, but people as a whole, unnamed and undistinguished masses of people, now sleeping in unknown graves, have also been concerned in the story. Our fathers that begat us have come to their own at last. As Acton put it, 'The great historian now takes his meals in the kitchen.'

This book is chiefly concerned with the kitchens of History, and the first which we shall visit is a country estate at the beginning of the ninth century. It so happens that we know a surprising amount about such an estate, partly because Charlemagne himself issued a set of orders instructing the Royal stewards how to manage his own lands, telling them everything it was necessary for them to know, down to the vegetables which they were to plant in the garden. But our chief source of knowledge is a wonderful estate book which Irminon, the Abbot of St Germain des Prés near Paris, drew up so that the abbey might know exactly what lands belonged to it and who lived on those lands, very much as William I drew up an estate book of his whole kingdom and called it *Domesday Book*. In this estate book is set down the name of every little estate (or *fisc* as it was called) belonging to the abbey, with a description of the land which was worked under its steward to its own profit, and the land which was held by tenants, and the names of those tenants and of their wives and of their children, and the exact services and rents, down to a plank and an egg, which they had to do for their land. We know today the name of almost every man, woman, and child who was living on those little *fiscs* in the time of Charlemagne, and a great deal about their daily lives.

Consider for a moment how the estate upon which they lived was organized. The lands of the Abbey of St Germain were divided into a number of estates, called *fiscs*, each of a convenient size to be administered by a steward. On each of these *fiscs* the land was divided into seigniorial and tributary lands; the first administered by the monks through a steward or some other officer, and the second possessed by various tenants, who received and held them from the abbey. These tributary lands were divided into numbers of little farms, called manses, each occupied by one or more families. If you had paid a visit to the chief or seigniorial manse, which the monks kept in their own hands, you would have found a little house, with three or four rooms, probably built of stone, facing an inner court, and on one side of it you would have seen a special group of houses hedged round, where the women serfs belonging to the house lived and did their work; all round you would also have seen little wooden houses, where the household serfs lived, workrooms, a kitchen, a bakehouse, barns, stables, and other farm buildings, and round the whole a hedge carefully planted with trees, so as to make a kind of enclosure or court. Attached to this central manse was a considerable amount of land – ploughland, meadows, vineyards, orchards, and almost all the woods or forests on the estate. Clearly a great deal of labour would be needed to cultivate all these lands. Some of that labour was provided by servile workers who were attached to the chief manse and lived in the court. But these household serfs were not nearly enough to do all the work upon the monks' land, and far the greater part of it had to be done by services paid by the other land-owners on the estate.

January—Ploughing

March—Breaking Clods

August—Reaping

December—Threshing and Winnowing

I. BODO AT HIS WORK

II. EMBARKATION OF THE POLOS AT VENICE

The Peasant Bodo

Beside the seigniorial manse, there were a number of little dependent manses. These belonged to men and women who were in various stages of freedom, except for the fact that all had to do work on the land of the chief manse. There is no need to trouble with the different classes, for in practice there was very little difference between them, and in a couple of centuries they were all merged into one common class of medieval villeins. The most important people were those called *coloni*, who were personally free (that is to say, counted as free men by the law), but bound to the soil, so that they could never leave their farms and were sold with the estate, if it were sold. Each of the dependent manses was held either by one family or by two or three families which clubbed together to do the work; it consisted of a house or houses, and farm buildings, like those of the chief manse, only poorer and made of wood, with ploughland and a meadow and perhaps a little piece of vineyard attached to it. In return for these holdings the owner or joint owners of every manse had to do work on the land of the chief manse for about three days in the week. The steward's chief business was to see that they did their work properly, and from every one he had the right to demand two kinds of labour. The first was *field work*: every year each man was bound to do a fixed amount of ploughing on the domain land (as it was called later on), and also to give what was called a *corvée*, that is to say, an unfixed amount of ploughing, which the steward could demand every week when it was needed; the distinction corresponds to the distinction between *week work* and *boon work* in the later Middle Ages. The second kind of labour which every owner of a farm had to do on the monks' land was called handwork, that is to say, he had to help repair buildings, or cut down trees, or gather fruit, or make ale, or carry loads—anything, in fact, which wanted doing and which the steward told him to do. It was by these services that the monks got their own seigniorial farm cultivated. On all the other days of the week these hard-worked tenants were free to cultivate their own little farms, and we may be sure that they put twice as much elbow grease into the business.

But their obligation did not end here, for not only had they to pay services, they also had to pay certain rents to the big house.

There were no State taxes in those days, but every man had to pay an army due, which Charlemagne exacted from the abbey, and which the abbey exacted from its tenants; this took the form of an ox and a certain number of sheep, or the equivalent in money: 'He pays to the host two shillings of silver' comes first on every freeman's list of obligations. The farmers also had to pay in return for any special privileges granted to them by the monks; they had to carry a load of wood to the big house, in return for being allowed to gather firewood in the woods, which were jealously preserved for the use of the abbey; they had to pay some hogsheads of wine for the right to pasture their pigs in the same precious woods; every third year they had to give up one of their sheep for the right to graze upon the fields of the chief manse; they had to pay a sort of poll-tax of 4*d.* a head. In addition to these special rents every farmer had also to pay other rents in produce; every year he owed the big house three chickens and fifteen eggs and a large number of planks, to repair its buildings; often he had to give it a couple of pigs; sometimes corn, wine, honey, wax, soap, or oil. If the farmer were also an artisan and made things, he had to pay the produce of his craft; a smith would have to make lances for the abbey's contingent to the army, a carpenter had to make barrels and hoops and vine props, a wheelwright had to make a cart. Even the wives of the farmers were kept busy, if they happened to be serfs; for the servile women were obliged to spin cloth or to make a garment for the big house every year.

All these things were exacted and collected by the steward, whom they called *Villicus*, or *Major* (Mayor). He was a very hard-worked man, and when one reads the seventy separate and particular injunctions which Charlemagne addressed to his stewards one cannot help feeling sorry for him. He had to get all the right services out of the tenants, and tell them what to do each week and see that they did it; he had to be careful that they brought the right number of eggs and pigs up to the house, and did not foist off warped or badly planed planks upon him. He had to look after the household serfs too, and set them to work. He had to see about storing, or selling, or sending off to the monastery the produce of the estate and of the tenants' rents; and every year he had to present a full and detailed account of his stewardship to the abbot. He had a manse of his own, with services and rents due from it, and Charlemagne exhorted his stewards to be prompt in their payments, so as to set a good example. Probably his official duties left him very little time to work on his own farm, and he would have to put in a man to work it for him, as Charlemagne bade his stewards do. Often, however, he had subordinate officials called *deans* under him, and sometimes the work of receiving and looking after the stores in the big house was done by a special cellarer.

That, in a few words, is the way in which the monks of St Germain and the other Frankish landowners of the time of Charlemagne managed their estates. Let us try, now, to look at those estates from a more human point of view and see what life was like to a farmer who lived upon them. The abbey possessed a little estate called Villaris, near Paris, in the place now occupied by the park of Saint Cloud. When we turn up the pages in the estate book dealing with Villaris, we find that there was a man called Bodo living there.[1] He had a wife called Ermentrude and three children called Wido and Gerbert and Hildegard; and he owned a little farm of arable and meadow land, with a few vines. And we know very nearly as much about Bodo's work as we know about that of a smallholder in France today. Let us try and imagine a day in his life. On a fine spring morning towards the end of Charlemagne's reign Bodo gets up early, because it is his day to go and work on the monks' farm, and he does not dare to be late, for fear of the steward. To be sure, he has probably given the steward a present of eggs and vegetables the week before, to keep him in a good temper; but the monks will not allow their stewards to take big bribes (as is sometimes done on other estates), and Bodo knows that he will not be allowed to go late to work. It is his day to plough, so he takes his big ox with him and little Wido to run by its side with a goad, and he joins his friends from some of the farms near by, who are going to work at the big house too. They all assemble, some with horses and oxen, some with mattocks and hoes and spades and axes and scythes, and go off in gangs to work upon the fields and meadows and woods of the seigniorial manse, according as the steward orders them. The manse next door to Bodo is held by a group of families: Frambert and Ermoin and Ragenold, with their wives and children. Bodo bids them good morning as he passes. Frambert is going to make a fence round the wood, to prevent the rabbits from coming out and eating the young crops; Ermoin has been told off to cart a great load of firewood up to the house; and Ragenold is mending a hole in the roof of a barn. Bodo goes whistling off in the cold with his oxen and his little boy; and it is no use to follow him farther, because he ploughs all day and eats his meal under a tree with the other ploughmen, and it is very monotonous.

Let us go back and see what Bodo's wife, Ermentrude, is doing. She is busy too; it is the day on which the chicken-rent is due – a fat pullet and five eggs in all. She leaves her second son, aged nine, to look after the baby Hildegard and calls on one of her neighbours, who has to go up to the big house too. The neighbour is a serf and she has to take the steward a piece of woollen cloth, which will be sent away to St Germain to make a habit for a monk. Her husband is working all day in the lord's vineyards, for on this estate the serfs generally tend the vines, while the freemen do most of the ploughing. Ermentrude and the serf's wife go together up to the house. There all is busy. In the men's workshop are several clever workmen – a shoemaker, a carpenter, a blacksmith, and two silversmiths; there are not more, because the best artisans on the estates of St Germain live by the walls of the abbey, so that they can work for the monks on the spot and save the labour of carriage. But there were always some craftsmen on every estate, either attached as serfs to the big house, or living on manses of their own, and good landowners tried to have as many clever craftsmen as possible. Charlemagne ordered his stewards each to have in his district 'good workmen, namely, blacksmiths, goldsmiths, silversmiths, shoemakers, turners, carpenters, swordmakers, fishermen, foilers, soapmakers, men who know how to make beer, cider, perry, and all other kinds of beverages, bakers to make pasty for our table, netmakers who know how to make nets for hunting, fishing, and fowling, and others too many to be named'.[2] And some of these workmen are to be found working for the monks in the estate of Villaris.

But Ermentrude does not stop at the men's workshop. She finds the steward, bobs her curtsy to him, and gives up her fowl and eggs, and then she hurries off to the women's part of the house, to gossip with the serfs there. The Franks used at this time to keep the women of their household in a separate quarter, where they did the work which was considered suitable for women, very much as the Greeks of antiquity used to do. If a Frankish noble had lived at the big house, his wife would have looked after their work, but as no one lived in the stone house at Villaris, the steward had to oversee the women. Their quarter consisted of a little group of houses, with a workroom, the whole surrounded by a thick hedge with a strong bolted gate, like a harem, so that no one could come in without leave. Their workrooms were comfortable places, warmed by stoves, and there Ermentrude (who, being a woman, was allowed to go in) found about a dozen servile women spinning and dyeing cloth and sewing garments. Every week the harassed steward brought them the raw materials for their work and took away what they made. Charlemagne gives his stewards several instructions about the women attached to his manses, and we may be sure that the monks of St Germain did the same on their model estates. 'For our women's work,' says Charlemagne, 'they are to give at the proper time the materials, that is linen, wool, woad, vermilion, madder, wool combs, teasels, soap, grease, vessels, and other objects which are necessary. And let our women's quarters be well looked after, furnished with houses and rooms with stoves and cellars, and let them be surrounded by a good hedge, and let the doors be strong, so that the women can do our work properly.'[3] Ermentrude, however, has to hurry away after her gossip, and so must we. She goes back to her own farm and sets to work in the little vineyard; then after an hour or two goes back to get the children's meal and to spend the rest of the day in weaving warm woollen clothes for them. All her friends are either working in the fields on their husbands' farms or else looking after the poultry, or the vegetables, or sewing at home; for the women have to work just as hard as the men on a country farm. In Charlemagne's time (for instance) they did nearly all the sheep shearing. Then at last Bodo comes back for his supper, and as soon as the sun goes down they go to bed; for their hand-made candle gives only a flicker of light, and they both have to be up early in the morning. De Quincey once pointed out, in his inimitable manner, how the ancients everywhere went to bed, 'like good boys, from seven to nine o'clock'. 'Man went to bed early in those ages simply because his worthy mother earth could not afford him candles. She, good old lady . . . would certainly have shuddered to hear of any of her nations asking for candles. "Candles indeed!" she would have said; "who ever heard of such a thing? and with so much excellent daylight running to waste, as I have provided *gratis*! What will the wretches want next?"'[4] Something of the same situation prevailed even in Bodo's time.

This, then, is how Bodo and Ermentrude usually passed their working day. But, it may be complained, this is all very well. We know about the estates on which these peasants lived and about the rents which they had to pay, and the services which they had to do. But how did they feel and think and amuse themselves when they were not working? Rents and services are only outside things; an estate book only describes routine. It would be idle to try to picture the life of a university from a study of its lecture list, and it is equally idle to try and describe the life of Bodo from the estate book of his masters. It is no good taking your meals in the kitchen if you never talk to the servants. This is true, and to arrive at Bodo's thoughts and feelings and holiday amusements we must bid good-bye to Abbot Irminon's estate book, and peer into some very dark corners indeed; for though by the aid of Chaucer and Langland and a few Court Rolls it is possible to know a great deal about the feelings of a peasant six centuries later, material is scarce in the ninth century, and it is all the more necessary to remember the secret of the invisible ink.

Bodo certainly *had* plenty of feelings, and very strong ones. When he got up in the frost on a cold morning to drive the plough over the abbot's acres, when his own were calling out for work, he often shivered and shook the rime from his beard, and wished that the big house and all its land were at the bottom of the sea (which, as a matter of fact, he had never seen and could not imagine). Or else he wished he were the abbot's huntsman, hunting in the forest; or a monk of St Germain, singing sweetly in the abbey church; or a merchant, taking bales of cloaks and girdles along the high road to Paris; anything, in fact, but a poor ploughman ploughing other people's land. An Anglo-Saxon writer has imagined a dialogue with him:

'Well, ploughman, how do you do your work?' 'Oh, sir, I work very hard. I go out in the dawning, driving the oxen to the field and I yoke them to the plough. Be the winter never so stark, I dare not stay at home for fear of my lord; but every day I must plough a full acre or more, after having yoked the oxen and fastened the share and coulter to the plough!' 'Have you any mate?' 'I have a boy, who drives the oxen with a goad, who is now hoarse from cold and shouting.' (Poor little Wido!) 'Well, well, it is very hard work?' 'Yes, indeed it is very hard work.'[5]

Nevertheless, hard as the work was, Bodo sang lustily to cheer himself and Wido; for is it not related that once, when a clerk was singing the 'Allelulia' in the emperor's presence, Charles turned to one of the bishops, saying, 'My clerk is singing very well,' whereat the rude bishop replied, 'Any clown in our countryside drones as well as that to his oxen at their ploughing'?[6] It is certain too that Bodo agreed with the names which the great Charles gave to the months of the year in his own Frankish tongue; for he called January 'Winter-month', February 'Mud-month', March 'Spring-month', April 'Easter-month', May 'Joy-month', June 'Plough-month', July 'Hay-month', August 'Harvest-month', September 'Wind-month', October 'Vintage-month', November 'Autumn-month', and December 'Holy-month'.[7]

And Bodo was a superstitious creature. The Franks had been Christian now for many years, but Christian though they were, the peasants clung to old beliefs and superstitions. On the estates of the holy monks of St Germain you would have found the country people saying charms which were hoary with age, parts of the lay sung by the Frankish ploughman over his bewitched land long before he marched southwards into the Roman Empire, or parts of the spell which the bee-master performed when he swarmed his bees on the shores of the Baltic Sea. Christianity has coloured these charms, but it has not effaced their heathen origin; and because the tilling of the soil is the oldest and most unchanging of human occupations, old beliefs and superstitions cling to it and the old gods stalk up and down the brown furrows, when they have long vanished from houses and roads. So on Abbot Irminon's estates the peasant-farmers muttered charms over their sick cattle (and over their sick children too) and said incantations over the fields to make them fertile. If you had followed behind Bodo when he broke his first furrow you would have probably seen him take out of his jerkin a little cake, baked for him by Ermentrude out of different kinds of meal, and you would have seen him stoop and lay it under the furrow and sing:

> Earth, Earth, Earth! O Earth, our mother!
> May the All-Wielder, Ever-Lord grant thee
> Acres a-waxing, upwards a-growing,
> Pregnant with corn and plenteous in strength;
> Hosts of grain shafts and of glittering plants!
> Of broad barley the blossoms,
> And of white wheat ears waxing,
> Of the whole land the harvest. . . .
>
> .   .   .
>
> Acre, full-fed, bring forth fodder for men!
> Blossoming brightly, blessed become!
> And the God who wrought with earth grant us gift of growing
> That each of all the corns may come unto our need.[8]

Then he would drive his plough through the acre.

The Church wisely did not interfere with these old rites. It taught Bodo to pray to the Ever-Lord instead of to Father Heaven, and to the Virgin Mary instead of to Mother Earth, and with these changes let the old spell he had learned from his ancestors serve him still. It taught him, for instance, to call on Christ and Mary in his charm for bees. When Ermentrude heard her bees swarming, she stood outside her cottage and said this little charm over them:

> Christ, there is a swarm of bees outside,
> Fly hither, my little cattle,
> In blest peace, in God's protection,
> Come home safe and sound.
> Sit down, sit down, bee,
> St Mary commanded thee.

Thou shalt not have leave,
Thou shalt not fly to the wood.
Thou shalt not escape me,
Nor go away from me.
Sit very still,
Wait God's will![9]

And if Bodo on his way home saw one of his bees caught in a brier bush, he immediately stood still and wished – as some people wish today when they go under a ladder. It was the Church, too, which taught Bodo to add 'So be it, Lord', to the end of his charm against pain. Now, his ancestors for generations behind him had believed that if you had a stitch in your side, or a bad pain anywhere, it came from a worm in the marrow of your bones, which was eating you up, and that the only way to get rid of that worm was to put a knife, or an arrow-head, or some other piece of metal to the sore place, and then wheedle the worm out on to the blade by saying a charm. And this was the charm which Bodo's heathen ancestors had always said and which Bodo went on saying when little Wido had a pain: 'Come out, worm, with nine little worms, out from the marrow into the bone, from the bone into the flesh, from the flesh into the skin, from the skin into this arrow.' And then (in obedience to the Church) he added 'So be it, Lord'.[10] But sometimes it was not possible to read a Christian meaning into Bodo's doings. Sometimes he paid visits to some man who was thought to have a wizard's powers, or superstitiously reverenced some twisted tree, about which there hung old stories never quite forgotten. Then the Church was stern. When he went to confession the priest would ask him: 'Have you consulted magicians and enchanters, have you made vows to trees and fountains, have you drunk any magic philtre?'[11] And he would have to confess what he did last time his cow was sick. But the Church was kind as well as stern. 'When serfs come to you,' we find one bishop telling his priests, 'you must not give them as many fasts to perform as rich men. Put upon them only half the penance.'[12] The Church knew well enough that Bodo could not drive his plough all day upon an empty stomach. The hunting, drinking, feasting Frankish nobles could afford to lose a meal.

It was from this stern and yet kind Church that Bodo got his holidays. For the Church made the pious emperor decree that on Sundays and saints' days no servile or other works should be done. Charlemagne's son repeated his decree in 827. It runs thus:

We ordain according to the law of God and to the command of our father of blessed memory in his edicts, that no servile works shall be done on Sundays, neither shall men perform their rustic labours, tending vines, ploughing fields, reaping corn and mowing hay, setting up hedges or fencing woods, cutting trees, or working in quarries or building houses; nor shall they work in the garden, nor come to the law courts, nor follow the chase. But three carrying-services it is lawful to do on Sunday, to wit carrying for the army, carrying food, or carrying (if need be) the body of a lord to its grave. Item, women shall not do their textile works, nor cut out clothes, nor stitch them together with the needle, nor card wool, nor beat hemp, nor wash clothes in public, nor shear sheep: so that there may be rest on the Lord's day. But let them come together from all sides to Mass in the Church and praise God for all the good things He did for us on that day![13]

Unfortunately, however, Bodo and Ermentrude and their friends were not content to go quietly to church on saints' days and quietly home again. They used to spend their holidays in dancing and singing and buffoonery, as country folk have always done until our own gloomier, more self-conscious age. They were very merry and not at all refined, and the place they always chose for their dances was the churchyard; and unluckily the songs they sang as they danced in a ring were old pagan songs of their forefathers, left over from old Mayday festivities, which they could not forget, or ribald love-songs which the Church disliked. Over and over again we find the Church councils complaining that the peasants (and sometimes the priests too) were singing 'wicked songs with a chorus of dancing women,' or holding 'ballads and dancings and evil and wanton songs and such-like lures of the devil';[14] over and over again the bishops forbade these songs and dances; but in vain. In every country in Europe, right through the Middle Ages to the time of the Reformation, and after it, country folk continued to sing and dance in the churchyard. Two hundred years after Charlemagne's death there grew up the legend of the dancers of Kölbigk, who danced on

Christmas Eve in the churchyard, in spite of the warning of the priest, and all got rooted to the spot for a year, till the Archbishop of Cologne released them. Some men say that they were not rooted standing to the spot, but that they had to go on dancing for the whole year; and that before they were released they had danced themselves waist-deep into the ground. People used to repeat the little Latin verse which they were singing:

> Equitabat Bovo per silvam frondosam
> Ducebat sibi Merswindem formosam.
> Quid stamus? Cur non imus?[15]

> Through the leafy forest, Bovo went a-riding
> And his pretty Merswind trotted on beside him –
> Why are we standing still? Why can't we go away?

Another later story still is told about a priest in Worcestershire who was kept awake all right by the people dancing in his churchyard and singing a song with the refrain 'Sweetheart have pity', so that he could not get it out of his head, and the next morning at Mass, instead of saying 'Dominus vobiscum', he said 'Sweetheart have pity', and there was a dreadful scandal which got into a chronicle.[16]

Sometimes our Bodo did not dance himself, but listened to the songs of wandering minstrels. The priests did not at all approve of these minstrels, who (they said) would certainly go to hell for singing profane secular songs, all about the great deeds of heathen heroes of the Frankish race, instead of Christian hymns. But Bodo loved them, and so did Bodo's betters; the Church councils had sometimes even to rebuke abbots and abbesses for listening to their songs. And the worst of it was that the great emperor himself, the good Charlemagne, loved them too. He would always listen to a minstrel, and his biographer, Einhard, tells us that 'He wrote out the barbarous and ancient songs, in which the acts of the kings and their wars were sung, and committed them to memory';[17] and one at least of those old sagas, which he liked men to write down, has been preserved on the cover of a Latin manuscript, where a monk scribbled it in his spare time. His son, Louis the Pious, was very different; he rejected the national poems, which he had learnt in his youth, and would not have them read or recited or taught; he would not allow minstrels to have justice in the law courts, and he forbade idle dances and songs and tales in public places on Sundays; but then he also dragged down his father's kingdom into disgrace and ruin. The minstrels repaid Charlemagne for his kindness to them. They gave him everlasting fame; for all through the Middle Ages the legend of Charlemagne grew, and he shares with our King Arthur the honour of being the hero of one of the greatest romance-cycles of the Middle Ages. Every different century clad him anew in its own dress and sang new lays about him. What the monkish chroniclers in their cells could never do for Charlemagne, these despised and accursed minstrels did for him: they gave him what is perhaps more desirable and more lasting than a place in history – they gave him a place in legend. It is not every emperor who rules in those realms of gold of which Keats spoke, as well as in the kingdoms of the world; and in the realms of gold Charlemagne reigns with King Arthur, and his peers joust with the Knights of the Round Table. Bodo, at any rate, benefited by Charles's love of minstrels, and it is probable that he heard in the lifetime of the emperor himself the first beginnings of those legends which afterwards clung to the name of Charlemagne. One can imagine him round-eyed in the churchyard, listening to fabulous stories of Charles's Iron March to Pavia, such as a gossiping old monk of St Gall afterwards wrote down in his chronicle.[18]

It is likely enough that such legends were the nearest Bodo ever came to seeing the emperor, of whom even the poor serfs who never followed him to court or camp were proud. But Charles was a great traveller: like all the monarchs of the early Middle Ages he spent the time, when he was not warring, in trekking round his kingdom, staying at one of his estates, until he and his household had literally eaten their way through it, and then passing on to another. And sometimes he varied the procedure by paying a visit to the estates of his bishops or nobles, who entertained him royally. It may be that one day he came on a visit to Bodo's masters and stopped at the big house on his way to Paris, and then Bodo saw him plain; for Charlemagne would come riding along the road in his jerkin of otter skin, and his plain blue cloak (Einhard tells us that he hated

grand clothes and on ordinary days dressed like the common
people); [19] and after him would come his three sons and his body-
guard, and then his five daughters. Einhard has also told us that

He had such care of the upbringing of his sons and daughters that he
never dined without them when he was at home and never travelled without them. His sons rode along with him and his daughters followed in the
rear. Some of his guards, chosen for this very purpose, watched the end of
the line of march where his daughters travelled. They were very beautiful
and much beloved by their father, and, therefore, it is strange that he
would give them in marriage to no one, either among his own people or
of a foreign state. But up to his death he kept them all at home saying he
could not forgo their society. [20]

Then, with luck, Bodo, quaking at the knees, might even behold
a portent new to his experience, the emperor's elephant. Haroun
El Raschid, the great Sultan of the 'Arabian Nights' had sent it to
Charles, and it accompanied him on all his progresses. Its name was
'Abu-Lubabah', which is an Arabic word and means 'the father of
intelligence',* and it died a hero's death on an expedition against the
Danes in 810. [21] It is certain that ever afterwards Ermentrude quelled
little Gerbert, when he was naughty, with the threat, 'Abu-Lubabah will come with his long nose and carry you off.' But Wido, being aged eight and a bread-winner, professed to have felt no fear
on being confronted with the elephant; but admitted when pressed,
that he greatly preferred Haroun El Raschid's other present to the
emperor, the friendly dog, who answered to the name of 'Becerillo'.

It would be a busy time for Bodo when all these great folk came,
for everything would have to be cleaned before their arrival, the
pastry cooks and sausage-makers summoned and a great feast prepared; and though the household serfs did most of the work, it is
probable that he had to help. The gossipy old monk of St Gall has
given us some amusing pictures of the excitement when Charles
suddenly paid a visit to his subjects:

There was a certain bishopric which lay full in Charles's path when he
journeyed, and which indeed he could hardly avoid: and the bishop of

* *Abu-Lubabah.* – It is remarkable that the name should have suffered no corruption
in the chronicles.

this place, always anxious to give satisfaction, put everything that he had at Charles's disposal. But once the Emperor came quite unexpectedly and the bishop in great anxiety had to fly hither and thither like a swallow, and had not only the palaces and houses but also the courts and squares swept and cleaned: and then, tired and irritated, came to meet him. The most pious Charles noticed this, and after examining all the various details, he said to the bishop: 'My kind host, you always have everything splendidly cleaned for my arrival.' Then the bishop, as if divinely inspired, bowed his head and grasped the king's never-conquered right hand, and hiding his irritation, kissed it and said: 'It is but right, my lord, that, wherever you come, all things should be thoroughly cleansed.' Then Charles, of all kings the wisest, understanding the state of affairs said to him: 'If I empty I can also fill.' And he added: 'You may have that estate which lies close to your bishopric, and all your successors may have it until the end of time.' In the same journey, too, he came to a bishop who lived in a place through which he must needs pass. Now on that day, being the sixth day of the week, he was not willing to eat the flesh of beast or bird; and the bishop, being by reason of the nature of the place unable to procure fish upon the sudden, ordered some excellent cheese, rich and creamy, to be placed before him. And the most self-restrained Charles, with the readiness which he showed everywhere and on all occasions, spared the blushes of the bishop and required no better fare; but taking up his knife cut off the skin, which he thought unsavoury and fell to on the white of the cheese. Thereupon the bishop, who was standing near like a servant, drew closer and said: 'Why do you do that, lord emperor? You are throwing away the very best part.' Then Charles, who deceived no one, and did not believe that anyone would deceive him, on the persuasion of the bishop put a piece of the skin in his mouth, and slowly ate it and swallowed it like butter. Then approving of the advice of the bishop, he said: 'Very true, my good host,' and he added: 'Be sure to send me every year to Aix two cartloads of just such cheeses.' And the bishop was alarmed at the impossibility of the task and, fearful of losing both his rank and his office, he rejoined: 'My lord, I can procure the cheeses, but I cannot tell which are of this quality and which of another. Much I fear lest I fall under your censure.' Then Charles, from whose penetration and skill nothing could escape, however new or strange it might be, spoke thus to the bishop, who from childhood had known such cheeses and yet could not test them: 'Cut them in two,' he said, 'then fasten together with a skewer those that you find to be of the right quality and keep them in your cellar for a time and then send them to me. The rest you may keep for yourself and your clergy and your family.' This was done for two years, and the king ordered the present of cheeses to be taken in without remark: then in the third year the bishop brought in person his laboriously collected cheeses. But the most just Charles pitied his labour and anxiety and added to the bishopric an excellent estate whence he and his successors might provide themselves with corn and wine.[22]

We may feel sorry for the poor flustered bishop collecting his two cartloads of cheeses; but it is possible that our real sympathy ought to go to Bodo, who probably had to pay an extra rent in cheeses to satisfy the emperor's taste, and got no excellent estate to recompense him.

A visit from the emperor, however, would be a rare event in his life, to be talked about for years and told to his grandchildren. But there was one other event, which happened annually, and which was certainly looked for with excitement by Bodo and his friends. For once a year the king's itinerant justices, the *Missi Dominici*, came round to hold their court and to see if the local counts had been doing justice. Two of them would come, a bishop and a count, and they would perhaps stay a night at the big house as guests of the abbot, and the next day they would go on to Paris, and there they would sit and do justice in the open square before the church and from all the district round great men and small, nobles and freemen and *coloni*, would bring their grievances and demand redress. Bodo would go too, if anyone had injured or robbed him, and would make his complaint to the judges. But if he were canny he would not go to them empty-handed, trusting to justice alone. Charlemagne was very strict, but unless the *missi* were exceptionally honest and pious they would not be averse to taking bribes. Theodulf, Bishop of Orleans, who was one of the Emperor's *missi*, has left us a most entertaining Latin poem, in which he describes the attempts of the clergy and laymen, who flocked to his court, to buy justice.[23] Every one according to his means brought a present; the rich offered money, precious stones, fine materials, and Eastern carpets, arms, horses, antique vases of gold or silver chiselled with representations of the labours of Hercules. The poor brought skins of Cordova leather, tanned and untanned, excellent pieces of cloth and linen (poor Ermentrude must have worked hard for the month before the justices came!), boxes, and wax. 'With this battering-ram,' cries the shocked Bishop Theodulf, 'they hope to break down the wall of my soul. But they would not have thought that they could shake *me*, if they had not so shaken other judges before.' And indeed, if his picture be true, the royal justices must have been followed about by a regular caravan of carts and horses to carry their presents. Even Theodulf has to admit that, in order not to hurt people's feelings, he was obliged to accept certain unconsidered trifles in the shape of eggs and bread and wine and chickens and little birds, 'whose bodies' (he says, smacking his lips) 'are small, but very good to eat.' One seems to detect the anxious face of Bodo behind those eggs and little birds.

Another treat Bodo had which happened once a year; for regularly on the ninth of October there began the great fair of St Denys, which went on for a whole month, outside the gates of Paris.[24] Then for a week before the fair little booths and sheds sprang up, with open fronts in which the merchants could display their wares, and the Abbey of St Denys, which had the right to take a toll of all the merchants who came there to sell, saw to it that the fair was well enclosed with fences, and that all came in by the gates and paid their money, for wily merchants were sometimes known to burrow under fences or climb over them so as to avoid the toll. Then the streets of Paris were crowded with merchants bringing their goods, packed in carts and upon horses and oxen; and on the opening day all regular trade in Paris stopped for a month, and every Parisian shopkeeper was in a booth somewhere in the fair, exchanging the corn and wine and honey of the district for rarer goods from foreign parts. Bodo's abbey probably had a stall in the fair and sold some of those pieces of cloth woven by the serfs in the women's quarter, or cheeses and salted meat prepared on the estates, or wine paid in rent by Bodo and his fellow-farmers. Bodo would certainly take a holiday and go to the fair. In fact, the steward would probably have great difficulty in keeping his men at work during the month; Charlemagne had to give a special order to his stewards that they should 'be careful that our men do properly the work which it is lawful to exact from them, and that they do not waste their time in running about to markets and fairs'. Bodo and Ermentrude and the three children, all attired in their best, did not consider it waste of time to go to the fair even twice or three times. They pretended that they wanted to buy salt to salt down their winter meat, or some vermilion dye to colour a frock for the baby. What they really wanted was to wander along the little rows of booths and look at all the strange things assembled there; for merchants came to St Denys to sell their rich goods from the distant East to Bodo's betters, and wealthy Frankish nobles bargained there for purple and silken robes with orange borders, stamped leather jerkins, peacock's feathers, and the scarlet plumage of flamingos (which they called 'phoenix skins'), scents and pearls and spices, almonds and raisins, and monkeys for their wives to play with.[25] Sometimes these merchants were Venetians, but more often they were Syrians or crafty Jews, and Bodo and his fellows laughed loudly over the story of how a Jewish merchant had tricked a certain bishop, who craved for all the latest novelties, by stuffing a mouse with spices and offering it for sale to him, saying that 'he had brought this most precious never-before-seen animal from Judea,' and refusing to take less than a whole measure of silver for it.[26] In exchange for their luxuries these merchants took away with them Frisian cloth, which was greatly esteemed, and corn and hunting dogs, and sometimes a piece of fine goldsmith's work, made in a monastic workshop. And Bodo would hear a hundred dialects and tongues, for men of Saxony and Frisia, Spain and Provence, Rouen and Lombardy, and perhaps an Englishman or two, jostled each other in the little streets; and from time to time there came also an Irish scholar with a manuscript to sell, and the strange, sweet songs of Ireland on his lips:

> A hedge of trees surrounds me,
> A blackbird's lay sings to me;
> Above my lined booklet
> The thrilling birds chant to me.
>
> In a grey mantle from the top of bushes
> The cuckoo sings:
> Verily – may the Lord shield me! –
> Well do I write under the greenwood.[27]

Then there were always jugglers and tumblers, and men with performing bears, and minstrels to wheedle Bodo's few pence out of his pocket. And it would be a very tired and happy family that trundled home in the cart to bed. For it is not, after all, so dull in the kitchen, and when we have quite finished with the emperor, 'Charlemagne and all his peerage', it is really worth while to spend a few moments with Bodo in his little manse. History is largely made up of Bodos.

CHAPTER III

Marco Polo

Et por ce, veul ie que un et autre sachent a tos iors mais les euvres des Veneciens, et qui il furent, et dont il vindrent, et qui il sont, et comment il firent la noble Cite que l'en apele Venise, qui est orendroit la plus bele dou siecle. . . . La place de Monseignor Saint Marc est orendroit la plus bele place qui soit en tot li monde; que de vers li soleil levant est la plus bele yglise qui soit el monde, c'est l'Yglise de Monseignor Saint Marc. Et de les cele Yglise est li paleis de Monseignor li Dus, grant e biaus a mervoilles.

— MARTINO DA CANALE

And Kinsai [Hangchow] is the greatest city in the whole world, so great indeed that I should scarcely venture to tell of it, but that I have met at Venice people in plenty who have been there. . . . And if anyone should desire to tell of all the vastness and great marvels of this city, a good quire of paper would not hold the matter, I trow. For 'tis the greatest and noblest city, and the finest for merchandise, that the whole world containeth.

— ODORIC OF PORDENONE

LET US GO back in mind – as would that we could go back in body – to the year 1268. It is a year which makes no great stir in the history books, but it will serve us well. In those days, as in our own, Venice lay upon her lagoons, a city (as Cassiodurus long ago saw her*) like a sea-bird's nest afloat on the shallow waves, a city like a ship, moored to the land but only at home upon the seas, the proudest city in all the Western world. For only consider her position. Lying at the head of the Adriatic, half-way between East and West, on the one great sea thoroughfare of medieval commerce, a Mediterranean

* 'Hic vobis, aquatilium avium more, domus est.'

39

seaport, yet set so far north that she was almost in the heart of Europe, Venice gathered into her harbour all the trade routes overland and overseas, on which pack-horses could travel or ships sail. Merchants bringing silk and spices, camphor and ivory, pearls and scents and carpets from the Levant and from the hot lands beyond it, all came to port in Venice. For whether they came by way of Egypt sailing between the low banks of the Nile and jolting on camels to Alexandria, or whether they came through the rich and pleasant land of Persia and the Syrian desert to Antioch and Tyre, or whether they slowly pushed their way in a long, thin caravan across the highlands of Central Asia, and south of the Caspian Sea to Trebizond, and so sailed through the Black Sea and the Dardanelles, Venice was their natural focus. Only Constantinople might have rivalled her, and Constantinople she conquered. To Venice, therefore, as if drawn by a magnet, came the spoils of the East, and from Venice they went by horse across the Alps by the Brenner and St Gothard passes to Germany and France, or in galleys by way of the Straits of Gibraltar to England and Flanders;[1] and the galleys and pack-horses came back again to Venice, laden with the metals of Germany, the furs of Scandinavia, the fine wools of England, the cloth of Flanders, and the wine of France.

But if geography gave Venice an unrivalled site, the Venetians did the rest. Through all the early years of their history they defied Constantinople to the east of them, and Pope and Holy Roman Emperor to the west; sometimes turning to one, sometimes to the other, but stubbornly bent all the while upon independence, replying, when invited to become subjects: 'God, Who is our help and protector has saved us to dwell upon these waters. This Venice, which we have raised in the lagoons, is our mighty habitation, no power of emperor or of prince can touch us'; apt, if threatened, to retire to their islands and derisively to fire cannon balls of bread into the mainland force, which sought to starve them out.[2] Always they were conscious that their future lay upon the waters, and in that East, whose colour had crept into their civilization and warmed their blood. They were eastern and western both, the Venetians, hot hearts for loving and conquering, icy heads for scheming and ruling. Bit by bit they secured the ring of mainland behind them, all the while keeping at bay the Saracen and Slav sea rovers, whose ships were the terror of the Mediterranean. Then they descended upon the pirates of Dalmatia, who thus harassed their trading vessels, and took all the Dalmatian coast. The Doge of Venice became Duke of Dalmatia. 'True it is,' says their chronicles, 'that the Adriatic Sea is in the duchy of Venice,'[3] and they called it the 'Gulf of Venice'. Now it was that there was first instituted the magnificent symbolical ceremony of wedding the sea, with the proud words 'Desponsamus te mare in signum veri perpetuique domini'![4]

> She was a maiden city, bright and free,
> No guile seduced, no force could violate,
> And when she took unto herself a mate
> She must espouse the everlasting sea.

And truly it seemed as though the very sea had sworn to honour and obey her.

Then came the Crusades, when Europe forgot its differences and threw itself upon the paynim who held the holy places of its faith, when men from all lands marched behind the banner of the Cross and the towers of Jerusalem were more real than the Tower of Babel. Now, at last, Venice saw her dream within her hand. It was Venice who provided galleys and Venice who provided convoys and commissariat and soldiers, at a good round sum; and when time came for the division of the spoil, Venice demanded in every captured town of Palestine and Syria a church, a counting-house and the right to trade without tolls. Her great chance came in the Fourth Crusade, when her old blind Doge Enrico Dandolo (whose blindness had the Nelson touch) upon the pretext that the Crusaders could not pay the transport fees agreed upon, turned the whole Crusade to the use of Venice, and conquered first Zara, which had dared to revolt from her, and then her ancient – her only – rival, the immortal Byzantium itself. It is true that the Pope excommunicated the Venetians when they first turned the armies against Zara, but what matter? They looted Constantinople and brought back the four great gilded horses to St Mark's – St Mark's, which has been compared to a robbers' cave crowded with the booty of the Levant, and which held the sacred body of the saint, stolen from Alexandria by the Venetians, nearly four centuries before, concealed in a tub of pickled pork, in order to elude the Moslems. A Venetian patriarch now said Mass in St Sophia. Venice received the proud title of 'Ruler of a half and a quarter of the Roman Empire,' ('quartæ partis et dimidiæ totius imperii Romaniæ' – the words have a ring of trumpets), and the Doge, buskined in scarlet like the ancient Roman emperors, now ruled supreme over four seas – the Adriatic, the Aegean, the Sea of Marmora, and the Black Sea. Venetian factories studded all the Levantine coasts, in Tripoli and Tyre, Salonica, Adrianople, and Constantinople, in Trebizond on the Black Sea, even at Caffa in the far Crimea, whence ran the mysterious road into Russia. Crete and Rhodes and Cyprus were hers; her galleys swept the pirates from the seas and brooked no rivals; all trade with the East must pass through Venice, and Venice only. The other trading cities of Italy struggled against her, and Genoa came near to rivalling her, but in 1258, and again in 1284, she utterly defeated the Genoese fleet. Not for the city of 'sea without fish, mountains without woods, men without faith, and women without shame' was it to bit the horses on St Mark's.[5] In 1268 Venice seemed supreme. Byzantium was her washpot and over the Levant she had cast her shoe. Truly her chronicler might write of her:

Dalmatia, Albania, Rumania, Greece, Trebizond, Syria, Armenia, Egypt, Cyprus, Candia, Apulia, Sicily, and other countries, kingdoms and islands were the fruitful gardens, the proud castles of our people, where they found again pleasure, profit, and security. . . . The Venetians went about the sea, here and there and across the sea, and in all places wheresoever water runs, and bought merchandise and brought it to Venice from every side. Then there came to Venice Germans and Bavarians, French and Lombards, Tuscans and Hungarians, and every people that lives by merchandise and they took it to their countries.

Small wonder that (as a later traveller observed) the Venetians were proud of their great rule, and when a son was born to a Venetian were wont to say among themselves, 'A Signor is born into the world.'

Is it not true to say that Venice was the proudest city on earth, *la noble cite que l'en apele Venise, qui est orendroit la plus bele dou siecle?*[6] Life was a fair and splendid thing for those merchant princes, who held the gorgeous East in fee in the year of grace 1268. In that year traders in great stone counting-houses, lapped by the waters of the canals, were checking, book in hand, their sacks of cloves, mace and nutmegs, cinnamon and ginger from the Indies, ebony chessmen from Indo China, ambergris from Madagascar, and musk from Tibet. In that year the dealers in jewels were setting prices upon diamonds from Golconda, rubies and lapis lazuli from Badakhshan, and pearls from the fisheries of Ceylon; and the silk merchants were stacking up bales of silk and muslin and brocade from Bagdad and Yezd and Malabar and China. In that year young gallants on the Rialto (scented gallants, but each, like Shakespeare's Antonio, with a ship venturing into port somewhere in the Levant) rubbed elbows with men of all nations, heard travellers' tales of all lands, and at dawn slipped along the canals in gondolas (not black in those days, but painted and hung with silk), saluting the morning with songs; and the red-haired ladies of Venice whom centuries later Titian loved to paint, went trailing up and down the marble steps of their palaces, with all the brocades of Persia on their backs and all the perfumes of Arabia to sweeten their little hands.

It was in that year, too, that one Martino da Canale, a clerk in the customs house, began to busy himself (like Chaucer after him) less with his accounts than with writing in the delectable French language ('por ce que lengue franceise cort parmi le monde, et est la plus delitable a lire et a oir que nule autre') a chronicle of Venice. It is of the water, watery, Canale's chronicle, like Ariel's dirge; he has indeed, 'that intenseness of feeling which seems to resolve itself into the elements which it contemplates.' Here is nothing indeed, of 'the surge and thunder of the Odyssey', but the lovely words sparkle like the sun on the waters of the Mediterranean, and like a refrain, singing itself in and out of the narrative, the phrase recurs, 'Li tens estoit clers et biaus . . . et lors quant il furent en mer, li mariniers drecerent les voiles au vent, et lesserent core a ploine voiles les mes parmi la mer a la force dou vent';[7] for so much of the history of Venice was enacted upon deck. It is a passing proud chronicle, too, for Canale was, and well he knew it, a citizen of no mean city.

'Now would I,' he says, 'that every one and all know for ever the works of the Venetians, who they were and whence they came and what they are, and how they made the noble city which is called Venice, which is this day the fairest in the world. And I would that all those who are now living and those who are to come know how the noble city is builded and how all good things abound in her, and how the sire of the Venetians, the noble Doge, is powerful, and what nobility is found therein and the prowess of the Venetian people, and how they are all perfect in the faith of Jesu Christ and obedient to holy Church, and how they never disobey the commandment of holy Church. Within this noble Venice there dares to dwell neither heretic, nor usurer, murderer, thief nor robber. And I will tell you the names of all the Doges that have been in Venice, one after the other, and what they did to the honour of holy Church and of their noble City. And I will tell you the names of the noble captains whom the noble Doges sent in their time to lay low their enemies, and concerning the victories that they won I will have you know, for it is fitting. . . . In the year of the incarnation of our Lord Jesu Christ MCCLXVII years, in the time of Milord Renier Zeno, the high Doge of Venice, I laboured and strove until I found the ancient history of the Venetians, whence they came first and how they builded the noble city called Venice, which is today the fairest and the pleasantest in the world, full of beauty and of all good things. Merchandise flows through this noble city even as water flows from the fountains, and the salt water runs through it and round it and in all places save in the houses and the streets; and when the citizens go abroad they can return to their houses by land or by water, as they will. From all parts there come merchandise and merchants, who buy merchandise as they will and take it back to their own countries. Within this town is found food in great plenty, bread and wine, land fowl and river fowl, fresh meat and salt, and sea fish and river fish. . . . You may find within this fair town many men of gentle birth, both old men and young *damoisaus* in plenty, and merchants with them, who buy and sell, and money changers and citizens of all crafts, and therewith mariners of all sorts, and ships to carry them to all lands and galleys to lay low their enemies. And in this fair town is also great plenty of ladies and damsels and maidens, very richly apparelled.'[8]

It happened that there was a new Doge that year, our year 1268, Lorenzo Tiepolo by name, and a great procession of the gilds took place before the palace on the Piazza of St Mark to welcome his accession. Martino da Canale was watching it and wrote it all down

44

in his chronicle. First came the navy sailing past in the harbour, fifty galleys and other ships, with their crews cheering and shouting on deck. Then came the gilds on foot: first the master smiths, with garlands on their heads and banners and trumpets; then the furriers apparelled in samite and scarlet silk, with mantles of ermine and vair; then the weavers richly bedight, and the ten master tailors in white with crimson stars. Then the master clothworkers passed, carrying boughs of olive and wearing crowns of olive on their heads; then the fustian makers in furred robes of their own weaving, and the quilt makers with garlands of gilt beads and white cloaks sewn with fleurs-de-lis, marching two by two, with little children singing *chansonettes* and *cobles* before them. Then came the makers of cloth of gold, all in cloth of gold, and their servants in cloth of gold or of purple, followed by the mercers in silk and the butchers in scarlet, the fish sellers robed and furred and garlanded, and the master barbers, having with them two riders attired as knights-errant, and four captive damsels, strangely garbed. Then came the glass-workers in scarlet furred with vair, and gold-fringed hoods, and rich garlands of pearls, carrying flasks and goblets of the famous Venetian glass before them, and the comb and lantern makers, with a lantern full of birds to let loose in the Doge's presence, and the goldsmiths wearing wreaths and necklaces of gold and silver beads and sapphires, emeralds, diamonds, topazes, jacinths, amethysts, rubies, jasper, and carbuncles. Master and servants alike were sumptuously clad, and almost all wore gold fringes on their hoods, and garlands of gilded beads. Each craft was accompanied by its band of divers instruments, and bore with it silver cups and flagons of wine, and all marched in fair order, singing ballads and songs of greeting, and saluted the Doge and Dogaressa in turn, crying 'Long live our lord, the noble Doge Lorenzo Tiepolo!' Gild after gild they marched in their splendour, lovely alike to ear and eye; and a week fled before the rejoicings were ended and all had passed in procession. Canale surpasses himself here, for he loved State ceremonies; he gives a paragraph to the advance of each gild, its salutation and withdrawal, and the cumulative effect of all the paragraphs is enchanting, like a prose ballade, with a repeated refrain at the end of every verse.[9]

What, they lived once thus in Venice, where the merchants were the
   kings,
Where St Mark's is, where the Doges used to wed the sea with rings?

Listening to the magnificent salutation of the Doge by the priests of
St Mark's, 'Criste, vince, Criste regne, Criste inpere. Notre signor
Laurens Teuples, Des gracie, inclit Dus de Venise, Dalmace atque
Groace, et dominator de la quarte partie et demi de tot l'enmire de
Romanie, sauvement, honor, vie, et victoire. Saint Marc, tu le aie,'[10]
who, hearing, could have doubted that Venice, defier of Rome and
conqueror of Constantinople, was the finest, richest, most beauti-
ful, and most powerful city in the world?

But was she? Listen and judge. Thousands of miles away from
Venice, across the lands and seas of Asia, a little south of the Yangtze
River and close to the sea stood the city of Kinsai or Hangchow, the
capital of the Sung emperors, who ruled Southern China, not yet (in
1268) conquered by the Tartars.[11] Like Venice, Kinsai stood upon
lagoons of water and was intersected by innumerable canals. It was
a hundred miles in circuit, not counting the suburbs which stretched
round it, and there was not a span of ground which was not well
peopled. It had twelve great gates, and each of the twelve quarters
which lay within the gates was greater than the whole of Venice.
Its main street was two hundred feet wide, and ran from end to end
of the city, broken every four miles by a great square, lined with
houses, gardens, palaces, and the shops of the artisans, who were
ruled by its twelve great craft gilds. Parallel with the main street was
the chief canal, beside which stood the stone warehouses of the
merchants who traded with India. Twelve thousand stone bridges
spanned its waterways, and those over the principal canals were
high enough to allow ships with their tapering masts to pass below,
while the carts and horses passed overhead. In its market-places men
chaffered for game and peaches, sea-fish, and wine made of rice and
spices; and in the lower part of the surrounding houses were shops,
where spices and drugs and silk, pearls and every sort of manufactured article were sold. Up and down the streets of Kinsai moved
lords and merchants clad in silk, and the most beautiful ladies in the
world swayed languidly past in embroidered litters, with jade pins

in their black hair and jewelled earrings swinging against their smooth cheeks.[12]

On one side of this city lay a beautiful lake (famous in Chinese history, and still one of the fairest prospects upon earth), studded with wooded islands, on which stood pavilions with charming names: 'Lake Prospect', 'Bamboo Chambers', 'The House of the Eight Genii', and 'Pure Delight'. Here, like the Venetians, the men of Kinsai came for pleasure parties in barges, nobly hung and furnished, the cabins painted with flowers and mountain landscapes, and looking out they saw on one side the whole expanse of the city, its palaces, temples, convents, and gardens, and on the other the stretch of clear water, crowded with coloured pleasure boats, over which came echoing the high, clear voices and the tinkling instruments of the revellers. There is no space in which to tell of the King's palace, with its gardens and orchards, its painted pavilions, and the groves where the palace ladies coursed the game with dogs, and, tired of the pastime, flung off their robes and ran to the lake, where they disported themselves like a shoal of silver fishes. But a word must be said of the junks, which came sailing into the harbour four and twenty miles away, and up the river to the city; and of the great concourse of ships which came to Zaiton (perhaps the modern Amoy), the port of the province. Here every year came a hundred times more pepper than came to the whole of Christendom through the Levantine ports. Here from Indo China and the Indies came spices and aloes and sandalwood, nutmegs, spikenard and ebony, and riches beyond mention. Big junks laded these things, together with musk from Tibet, and bales of silk from all the cities of Mansi,* and sailed away in and out of the East India Archipelago, with its spice-laden breezes billowing their sails, to Ceylon. There merchants from Malabar and the great trading cities of southern India took aboard their cargoes and sold them in turn to Arab merchants, who in their turn sold them to the Venetians in one or other of the Levantine ports. Europeans who saw Zaiton and the other Chinese seaports in after years were wont to say that no one, not even a

---

* Mansi or Manji was southern China and Cathay was northern China, the boundary between them lying along the River Hoang-Ho on the east and the southern boundary of Shen-si on the west.

Venetian, could picture to himself the multitude of trading vessels which sailed upon those eastern seas and crowded into those Chinese harbours. They said also with one accord that Kinsai was without doubt the finest and richest and noblest city in the world. To the men of Kinsai, Venice would have been a little suburb and the Levant a backyard. The whole of the east was their trading field, and their wealth and civilization were already old when Venice was a handful of mud huts peopled by fishermen.

Nor was Kinsai alone and unmatched in all its wonder and beauty, for a three days' journey from it stood Sugui, which today we call Suchow, lying also on the great canal, with its circumference of twenty miles, its prodigious multitudes swarming the streets, its physicians, philosophers, and magicians; Sugui, with the ginger which was so common that forty pounds of it might be bought for the price of a Venetian silver groat, the silk which was manufactured in such vast quantities that all the citizens were dressed in it and still ships laden with it sailed away; Sugui under whose jurisdiction were sixteen wealthy cities, where trade and the arts flourished. If you had not seen Hangchow, you would have said that there was no city in the world, not Venice nor Constantinople nor another worthy to be named in the same breath with Sugui. The Chinese indeed, seeing the riches and beauty of these two cities, doubted whether even the pleasant courts of heaven could show their equal and proudly quoted the proverb:

> *Shang yeu t'ien t'ang,*
> *Hia yeu Su Hang.*

> (There's Paradise above, 'tis true,
> But here below we've Hang and Su.)[13]

Kinsai seems far enough away in all conscience from Venice in the year 1268, and Venice was all unwitting of its existence, far beyond the sunrise. Yet there was in the city of the lagoons that year, watching the same procession of the gilds which Canale watched, a boy who was destined to link them for ever in the minds of men — a lean lad of fourteen, Marco Polo by name, who was always kicking his heels on the quay and bothering foreign sailors for tales of dis-

48

tant lands. He heard all they had to tell him very willingly, storing it up in that active brain of his, for his curiosity was insatiable; but always the tales that he heard most willingly were about the Tartars.

At this time the Tartars were at the height of their power in the West and the East. Tartars ruled at Peking all over northern China, Corea, Mongolia, Manchuria, and Tibet, and took tribute from Indo-China and Java. Tartars were spread over central Asia, holding sway in Turkestan and Afghanistan. The Golden Horde ruled the Caucasus, a large part of Russia, and a piece of Siberia. Tartars held sway in Persia, Georgia, Armenia, and a part of Asia Minor. When the great Mangu Khan died in 1259, one empire lay spread across Asia and Europe, from the Yellow River to the Danube. There had been nothing like it in the world before, and there was nothing like it again, until the Russian Empire of modern times. By 1268 it was beginning to split up into the four kingdoms of China, central Asia, Russia, and Persia, but still it was one people. Now, the attitude of the West to the Tartars at this time was very interesting. At first it feared them as a new scourge of God, like Attila and his Huns; they overran Poland, ravaged Hungary, and seemed about to break like a great flood upon the West, and overwhelm it utterly. Then the tide rolled back. Gradually the West lost its first stupefaction and terror and began to look hopefully towards the Tartars as a possible ally against its age-old foe, the Moslem. The Christians of the West knew that the Tartars had laid the Moslem power low through the length and breadth of Asia, and they knew too, that the Tartars had no very sharply defined faith and were curious of all beliefs that came their way. Gradually the West became convinced that the Tartars might be converted to Christianity, and fight side by side beneath the Cross against the hated Crescent. There grew up the strange legend of Prester John, a Christian priest-king, ruling somewhere in the heart of Asia; and indeed little groups of Nestorian Christians did still survive in eastern Asia at this time.[14] Embassies began to pass between Tartar khans and western monarchs, and there began also a great series of missions of Franciscan friars to Tartary, men who were ethnologists and geographers at heart as well as missionaries, and have left us priceless accounts of the lands which they visited. In the year of grace 1268, much was known about central Asia, for in 1245 the Pope had sent the Italian friar John of Plano Carpini thither, and in 1251 another friar, William of Rubruck, a French Fleming, had been sent by the saintly Louis, King of France. Both got as far as Karakorum, the Tartar camp on the borders of northern China, though they did not enter China itself. They had brought back innumerable stories about the nomad conquerors, who carried their tents on carts, and drank fermented mares' milk, about the greatness of the khan and his welcome to the strangers from the West, and the interest with which he listened to their preaching.[15] These tales were common property now, and Marco Polo must have listened to them.

Marco Polo was always talking of the Tartars, always asking about them. Indeed, he had reason to be interested in them. This (as we have said) was the year of grace 1268, and eight years before (some, indeed, say fifteen years) his father, Nicolo Polo, and his uncle Maffeo had vanished into Tartary. They were rich merchants, trading with their own ship to Constantinople, and there they had decided to go on a commercial venture into the lands of the Golden Horde, which lay to the north of the Black Sea. So they had sailed over to the Crimea, where they had a counting-house at Soldaia, and taking with them a store of costly jewels, for they were jewel merchants, they had set off on horseback to visit the Khan of the West Tartars. So much the Venetians knew, for word had come back from Soldaia of their venture; but they had never returned. And so Marco, kicking his heels upon the quay, caught sailor-men by the sleeve and asked them about those wild horsemen with their mares' milk and their magicians and their droves of cattle; and as he asked he wondered about his father and his uncle, and whether they were dead and lost for ever in the wilds of Tartary. But even while he asked and wondered and kicked his heels on the quay, while the Doge Tiepolo was watching the procession of the gilds and the clerk Canale was adding up customs dues or writing the ancient history of the Venetians, at that very moment the two Polos were slowly and wearily making their way across the heights of central Asia with a caravan of mules and camels, drawing near to golden Samarcand with its teeming bazaars, coming nearer and nearer to the West; and in the following year, 1269, they reached Acre, and took ship there for Venice, and so at last came home.

They had a strange story to tell, stranger and better than anything the lean, inquisitive boy had heard upon the quays. They had soon disposed of their jewels and they had spent a year at the camp of the Khan of the Golden Horde of Kipchak on the mighty River Volga. Then war broke out between that ruler and the Khan who ruled the Persian Khanate, and it cut off their way back. But Marco's curiosity was inherited; and no Venetian was ever averse to seeing strange lands and seeking out new opportunities for trade; so the Polos decided to go on and visit the Khan of central Asia or Chagatai, and perhaps make their way back to Constantinople by some unfrequented route. They struggled over plains peopled only by tent-dwelling Tartars and their herds, until at last they reached the noble city of Bokhara. They must have followed the line of the Oxus River, and if we reverse the marvellous description which Matthew Arnold wrote of that river's course in *Sohrab and Rustum*, we shall have a picture of the Polos' journey:

> But the majestic River floated on,
> Out of the mist and hum of that low land,
> Into the frosty starlight, and there moved,
> Rejoicing, through the hush'd Chorasmian waste
> Under the solitary moon; he flow'd
> Right for the Polar Star, past Orgunjè,
> Brimming and bright and large: then sands begin
> To hem his watery march, and dam his streams,
> And split his currents; that for many a league
> The shorn and parcell'd Oxus strains along
> Through beds of sand and matted rushy isles –
> Oxus, forgetting the bright speed he had
> In his high mountain cradle in Pamere,
> A foil'd circuitous wanderer: – till at last
> The long'd-for dash of waves is heard, and wide
> His luminous home of waters opens, bright
> And tranquil, from whose floor the new-bathed stars
> Emerge and shine upon the Aral Sea.

For three years the Polos remained at Bokhara, until one day it happened that an embassy came to the city, on its way back from the khan in Persia to the great Khan Kublai, who ruled in far-off China, and to whom all the Tartar rulers owed allegiance. The chief ambassador was struck with the talents and charm of the brothers, who had now become proficient in the Tartar language, and persuaded them to accompany him on his journey to the presence of the Great Khan, who had never yet set eyes on a man of the West, and would, he assured them, receive them honourably. They would not have been Venetians had they refused such an opportunity, and, taking their Venetian servants with them, they journeyed for a year with the Tartar embassy across the heart of Asia, and so reached the great Kublai Khan. Many years later Marco himself described their reception, as they had told it to him:

Being introduced to the presence of the Grand Khan Kublai, the travellers were received by him with the condescension and affability that belonged to his character, and as they were the first Latins who had made their appearance in that country, they were entertained with feasts and honoured with other marks of distinction. Entering graciously into conversations with them, he made earnest inquiries on the subject of the western parts of the world, of the Emperor of the Romans, and of other christian kings and princes . . . and above all he questioned them particularly respecting the Pope, the affairs of the Church, and the religious worship and doctrine of the Christians. Being well instructed and discreet men, they gave appropriate answers upon all these points, and as they were perfectly acquainted with the Tartar language, they expressed themselves always in becoming terms; insomuch that the Grand Khan, holding them in high estimation, frequently commanded their attendance.[16]

The Great Khan finally decided to send these two intelligent strangers back to their own land on a mission from himself to the Pope, asking for a hundred men of learning to be sent to teach and preach to his Tartars, and for some holy oil from the lamp which burned over Christ's sepulchre in Jerusalem. He provided them with a golden tablet of honour, which acted as a passport and secured that they should be entertained and their journey facilitated from city to city in all his dominions, and so they set forth once more

III. PART OF A LANDSCAPE BY CHAO MÊNG-FU

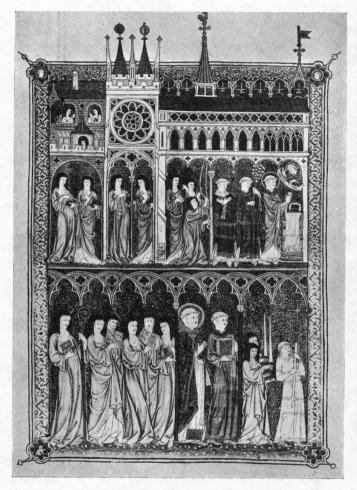

IV. MADAME EGLENTYNE AT HOME

upon their homeward journey. But they were delayed by the dangers and difficulties of travel, 'the extreme cold, the snow, the ice, and the flooding of the rivers', and it was three years before they at last reached Acre in the April of 1269, and finding that the Pope had died the year before, and that no election had yet been made, so that they could not immediately accomplish their mission, they decided to visit their home again, and so went back to Venice. There Nicolo found that his wife, who had been with child at his departure, was dead, leaving behind her a son Marco, our young haunter of quays.

This was the marvellous tale which the same Marco drank in from the lips of his new-found father and uncle. But more marvels were to come. For two years the Venetians remained at home, awaiting the election of a Pope in order to deliver the Great Khan's letters; but no election was made, and at last, fearing that Kublai might suspect them of playing him false, they decided to return to the East, and this time they took with them Marco, now a well-grown lad of sixteen or seventeen years with a bright eye that looked everywhere and took in everything, observant and sober beyond his age. But when they got as far as Ayas on the Gulf of Scanderoon, news was brought them of the election of Tebaldo di Piacenza as Pope Gregory X, and as Tebaldo had already interested himself in their mission, they returned with all speed to Acre, and obtained from him letters to the Khan (they had already visited Jerusalem and provided themselves with some of the holy oil), and two Dominican friars, 'men of letters and science as well as profound theologians,' though not the hundred men of learning for whom the Khan had asked; and so they set out again from Acre in November 1271. The Dominicans may have been profound theologians, but they were somewhat chicken-hearted adventurers, and when rumours reached them of wars in the district of Armenia, through which they had to pass, they hastily handed over their letters to the Venetians, put themselves under the protection of the Knights Templars, and scuttled back to the coast and safety as fast as they could go, leaving the Polos, 'undismayed by perils and difficulties, to which they had long been inured,' to proceed alone. Assuredly, St Francis crows over St Dominic somewhere in the courts of

53

Heaven; his friars never feared for their skins, as they travelled blithely into the heat of India and the cold of central Asia; and it is easy to imagine the comments of fat William of Rubruck upon the flight of the profound theologians.

The account of this second journey of the Polos may be read in the wonderful book which Marco afterwards wrote to describe the wonders of the world. They went from Lajazzo through Turcomania, past Mount Ararat, where Marco heard tell that Noah's ark rested, and where he first heard also of the oil wells of Baku and the great inland sea of Caspian. Past Mosul and Bagdad they went, through Persia, where brocades are woven and merchants bring caravan after caravan of treasures, to Hormuz, on the Persian Gulf, into which port put the ships from India, laden with spices, drugs, scented woods, and jewels, gold tissues and elephants' teeth. Here they meant to take ship, but they desisted, perhaps because they feared to trust themselves to the flimsy nailless vessels in which the Arabs braved the dangers of the Indian Ocean. So they turned north again and prepared to make the journey by land. They traversed the salt desert of Kerman, through Balk and Khorassan to Badakhshan, where there are horses bred from Alexander the Great's steed Bucephalus, and ruby mines and lapis lazuli. It is a land of beautiful mountains and wide plains, of trout streams and good hunting, and here the brothers sojourned for nearly a year, for young Marco had fallen ill in the hot plains: a breath of mountain air blows through the page in which he describes how amid the clean winds his health came back to him. When he was well, they went on again, and ascended the upper Oxus to the highlands of Pamir, 'the roof of the world' as it has been called in our own time, a land of icy cold, where Marco saw and described the great horned sheep which hunters and naturalists still call after him the *Ovis Poli*,[17] a land which no traveller (save Benedict Goës, about 1604) described again, until Lieutenant John Wood of the Indian Navy went there in 1838. Thence they descended upon Kashgar, Yarkand, and Khotan, where jade is found, regions which no one visited again until 1860. From Khotan they pushed on to the vicinity of Lake Lob, never to be reached again until a Russian explorer got there in 1871. They halted there to load asses and camels with provisions, and then, with sinking hearts, they began the terrible thirty days' journey across the Gobi Desert. Marco gives a vivid description of its terrors, voices which seem to call the traveller by name, the march of phantom cavalcades, which lures them off the road at night, spirits which fill the air with sounds of music, drums and gongs and the clash of arms – all those illusions which human beings have heard and seen and feared in every desert and in every age.

> What might this be? A thousand fantasies
> Begin to throng into my memory,
> Of calling shapes, and beckoning shadows dire,
> And airy tongues that syllable men's names
> On sands and shores and desert wildernesses.

At last they arrived safely at Tangut in the extreme north-west of China, and, skirting the frontier across the great steppes of Mongolia, they were greeted by the Khan's people, who had been sent forward to meet them at the distance of forty days' journey, and so at last they reached his presence in the May of 1275, having journeyed for three years and a half.

The Great Khan received the Polos kindly, listened attentively to the account which they gave of their mission, commended them for their zeal and fidelity, and received the holy oil and the Pope's gifts with reverence. He then observed the boy Marco, now a 'young gallant' and personable enough, no doubt, and inquired who he was, and Nicolo made answer, 'Sire, this is your servant, and my son,' to which the Khan replied, 'He is welcome, and much it pleases me,' and enrolled Marco among his own attendants. It was the beginning of a long and close association, for Kublai Khan soon found that Marco Polo was both discreet and intelligent, and began to employ him on various missions. Moreover, Marco, for his part, found that the Great Khan was always desirous of learning the manners and customs of the many tribes over whom he ruled. Kublai had to the full that noble curiosity which is the beginning of wisdom, and it irked him exceedingly that his envoys, good conscientious men, followed their noses upon his business, looking neither to right nor to left, and as like as not never even noticed that among the aboriginal hill tribes of the interior called Miaotzu there prevailed the peculiar and entertaining custom of the *couvade*, wherein

> Chinese go to bed
> And lie in, in their ladies' stead.[18]

'The Prince, in consequence,' says Marco, 'held them for no better than fools and dolts and would say, "I had far liever hearken about the strange things and the manners of the different countries you have seen than merely be told of the business you went upon."'

Very different was the habit of the Venetian, who as a lad, had lent ear so readily to swarthy sailors on the Rialto. He quickly picked up several of the languages current in the Great Khan's empire, and here is his account of his proceedings when on a mission to foreign parts:

Perceiving that the Great Khan took a pleasure in hearing accounts of whatever was new to him respecting the customs and manners of people, and the peculiar circumstances of distant countries, he endeavoured, wherever he went, to obtain correct information on these subjects and made notes of all he saw and heard, in order to gratify the curiosity of his master. In short, during seventeen years that he continued in his service, he rendered himself so useful, that he was employed on confidential missions to every part of the empire and its dependencies; and sometimes also he travelled on his own private account, but always with the consent and sanctioned by the authority of the Grand Khan. In such circumstances it was that Marco Polo had the opportunity of acquiring a knowledge, either by his own observation or by what he collected from others, of so many things until his time unknown, respecting the Eastern parts of the world, and these he diligently and regularly committed to writing. . . . And by this means he obtained so much honour that he provoked the jealousy of other officers of the court.[19]

It is small wonder that when first the lad came back with his reports the Great Khan and his courtiers marvelled and exclaimed, 'If this young man live he will assuredly be a person of great worth and ability.'

It was while on these various public missions that Marco Polo journeyed through the provinces of Shansi, Shensi, and Szechuen, and skirted the edge of Tibet to Yunnan, and entered Northern Burma, lands unknown again to the West until after 1860. For three years he was himself governor of the great city of Yangchow, which had twenty-four towns under its jurisdiction, and was full of traders and makers of arms and military accoutrements.[20] He visited Karakorum in Mongolia, the old Tartar capital, and with his Uncle Maffeo spent three years in Tangut. On another occasion he went on a mission to Cochin China, and by sea to the southern states of India, and he has left a vivid picture of the great trading cities of Malabar. He might indeed have pondered with Ulysses,

> I am become a name
> For always roaming with a hungry heart,
> Much have I seen and known, cities of men,
> And manners, climates, countries, governments,
> Myself not least, but honoured of them all.

He describes the great capital Cambaluc (Peking) in the north, and the beautiful Kinsai (Hangchow) in the south. He describes the Khan's summer palace at Shandu, with its woods and gardens, its marble palace, its bamboo pavilion swung like a tent from two hundred silken cords, its stud of white mares, and its wonder-working magicians. Indeed his description of the summer palace is better known to Englishmen than any other part of his work, for Shandu is Xanadu, which Coleridge saw in a dream after he had been reading Marco's book and wove into wonderful verse:

> In Xanadu did Kubla Khan
> A stately pleasure dome decree,
> Where Alph the sacred river ran,
> Past caverns measureless to man,
> Down to a sunless sea.

> And there were gardens bright with sinuous rills
> Where blossomed many an incense bearing tree,
> And here were forests, ancient as the hills
> Enfolding sunny spots of greenery.

Nor is it only palaces which Marco Polo describes, for he tells of the great canal and inland river trade of China, the exports and imports at its harbours, the paper money, the system of posts and caravanserais, which linked it together. He gives an unsurpassed picture of that huge, rich, peaceful empire, full of wealth and commerce and learned men and beautiful things, and of its ruler Kublai Khan, one of the noblest monarchs who ever sat upon a throne, who, since 'China is a sea that salts all the rivers that flow into it,'[21] was far more than a barbarous Mongol khan, was in very truth a Chinese emperor, whose house, called by the Chinese the 'Yuan Dynasty', takes its place among the great dynasties of China.

Even more than Marco Polo tells us he must, indeed, have seen. The impersonality of the greater part of the book is its one blemish, for we would fain know more of how he lived in China. There is some evidence that he consorted with the Mongol conquerors rather than with the Chinese, and that Chinese was not one of the languages which he learned. He makes no mention of several characteristic Chinese customs, such as the compressed feet of the women, and fishing with cormorants (both of which are described by Ordoric of Pordenone after him); he travelled through the tea districts of Fo-kien, but he never mentions tea-drinking, and he has no word to say even of the Great Wall.[22] And how typical a European he is, in some ways, for all his keen interest in new and strange things. 'They are,' he says of the peaceful merchants and scholars of Suchow, 'a pusillanimous race and solely occupied with their trade and manufactures. In these indeed they display considerable ability, and if they were as enterprising, manly, and warlike as they are ingenious, so prodigious is their number that they might not only subdue the whole of the province, but carry their rule further still.'[23] Nearly five hundred years later we find the same judgement expressed in different words: 'Better fifty years of Europe than a cycle of Cathay.' The answer is a question: Would you rather be the pusillanimous Chinese, who painted the landscape roll of which a portion is reproduced opposite page 52, or the enterprising, manly, and warlike European of the same period, whose highest achievement in pictorial art is the picture of Marco Polo's embarkation, reproduced opposite page 21? What is civilization and what progress? Yet Marco Polo shows himself throughout his book far from unable to appreciate other standards than those of his own land and religion, for of Sakya-muni Buddha he says that, 'had he been a Christian he would have been a great saint of our Lord Jesus Christ,' and he could honour Kublai as that great Khan deserved.

Nevertheless, although Marco Polo shows less knowledge of the Chinese than one might expect from the extraordinary detail and fidelity of his observation in other directions, he must have known many of these charming and cultivated people, at Kinsai or Cambaluc, or at the city which he governed. Among others, he must have known the great artist who painted the roll mentioned above, Chao Mêng-fu, whom the Chinese called '*Sung ksüeh Tao jen*', or the 'Apostle of Pine Trees and Snow'. He was a lineal descendant of the founder of the Sung dynasty and a hereditary official. When that dynasty at last fell before the Tartars, he and his friend Ch'ien Hsüan, 'the Man of the Jade Pool and Roaring Torrent', retired into private life. But in 1286 Chao Mêng-fu was summoned to court by Kublai Khan, and, to the indignation of his friend, returned and became secretary in the Board of War, occupying his time in this post (what must Marco Polo have thought of him!) in painting his marvellous pictures. He became a great favourite of the Khan and was always about the court, and Marco Polo must have known him well and perhaps have watched him at work painting those matchless landscapes, and those pictures of horses and men for which he was famous. Marco loved horses, as, indeed, he loved all kinds of sport (of which he had plenty, for the Khan was a great hunter and hawker), and he has left a word picture of the white brood mares at Shansi, which may be set beside Chao Mêng-fu's brush picture of the 'Eight Horses in the Park of Kublai Khan'.[24] He knew, too, perhaps Chao Mêng-fu's wife, the Lady Kuan, who painted most exquisitely the graceful bamboo and the peony, so loved by Chinese artists, and of whom it is related that 'she would watch the moving shadows of the sprays thrown by the moon on the paper windows, and transfer the fugitive outlines to paper with a few strokes of her supple brush, so that every smallest scrap of her work was mounted in albums as models for others to copy'.[25] Chao Mêng-fu and the Lady Kuan had a son, Chao Yung, who is of special interest to us, for he painted a picture of a Tangut hunter, and Marco Polo has also given a description of the Tartar horsemen and of the province of Tangut, where he saw and described the musk deer and the yak.

But we must return to the history of the Polos in China. From time to time in Marco's book we hear also of his father and uncle, travelling about the empire, growing rich by trade, and amassing a store of those jewels, in the value of which they were so skilled, even helping the Khan to reduce a rebel town, by constructing siege engines for him on the European model, handy Venetians that they were, who could lay their hands to anything.[27] Without doubt they were proud of their Marco, who from an inquisitive lad had grown to so wise and observant a man, and had risen to so high a position. So for seventeen years the three Polos abode in the Khan's service in China. The long months slipped by; and at last they began to feel upon them a longing to see Venice and the lagoons again, and to hear Mass once more beneath the majestic roof of St Mark's before they died. Moreover, Kublai Khan was growing old himself, and the favour which he had always shown to them had excited some jealousy among his own people, and they feared what might happen when he died. But the old Khan was adamant to all their prayers; wealth and honours were theirs for the asking, but he would not let them go. They might, indeed, have died in China, and we of the West might never have heard of Marco Polo or of Kublai Khan, but for a mere accident, a stroke of fate, which gave them their chance. In 1286 Arghun, the Khan of Persia, lost by death his favourite wife Bolgana, and, according to her dying wish, he sent ambassadors to the Court of Peking to ask for another bride from her own Mongol tribe. Their overland route home again was endangered by a war, and they therefore proposed to return by sea. Just at that moment, Marco Polo happened to return from a voyage on which he had been sent, and spoke with such assurance of the ease with which it had been accomplished, that the three ambassadors conceived a strong desire to take with them all three of these ingenious Venetians, who seemed to know so much about ships. Thus it was that the great Khan was prevailed upon, very reluctantly, to let them go.

Early in 1292 they set sail from the busy port of Zaiton in four-

teen big Chinese junks (of which Marco, writing of the shipping of
the Indian and China seas, has left an excellent description),[28] with
the three envoys, the princess, a beautiful girl of seventeen, 'moult
bèle dame at avenant,' says Marco, who had an eye for pretty ladies,
and a large suite of attendants. One version of Marco's book says
that they took with them also the daughter of the king of Mansi, one
of those Sung princesses who in happier days had wandered beside
the lake in Hangchow, and who had no doubt been brought up at
Cambaluc by the care of Kublai Khan's favourite queen, the Lady
Jamui. The voyage was a long and difficult one; they suffered
lengthy delays in Sumatra, Ceylon, and Southern India, occupied
by Marco in studying the sea charts of the coast of India which
the Arab pilots showed him, and adding to his knowledge of these
parts, which he had already visited. Thus it was over two years
before the junks reached Persia, and two of the three envoys and a
large number of their suite had died by the way. When at last they
landed, it was found that Arghun, the prospective bridegroom, had
meanwhile died too, leaving his throne in the charge of a regent for
his young son. But on the regent's advice a convenient solution of
the difficulty was found by handing the princess over to this prince,
and Marco and his uncles duly conducted her to him in the province
of Timochain, where Marco Polo noticed that the women were 'in
my opinion the most beautiful in the world', where stood the famed
and solitary *arbor secco*, and where men still told tales of great
Alexander and Darius. There they took leave of their princess, who
had come on the long voyage to love them like fathers, so Marco
says, and wept sorely when they parted. It was while they were
still in Persia, where they stayed for nine months after handing
over the princess, that the Polos received news of the death of the
Great Khan whom they had served so faithfully for so many years.
He died at the ripe age of eighty, and with his death a shadow fell
over central Asia, darkening the shining yellow roofs of Cambaluc,

> the barren plains
> Of Sericana, where Chineses drive
> With sails and wind their cany waggons light,

the minarets of Persia, and the tents of wild Kipchak Tartars, gal-
loping over the Russian steppes. So wide had been the sway of

Kublai Khan. A shadow fell also upon the heart of Marco Polo. It was as though a door had clanged to behind him, never to open again. 'In the course of their journey,' he says, 'our travellers received intelligence of the Great Khan having departed this life, which entirely put an end to all prospects of their revisiting those regions.' So he and his elders went on by way of Tabriz, Trebizond, and Constantinople to Venice, and sailed up to the city of the lagoons at long last at the end of 1295.

A strange fairy-tale legend has come down to us about the return of the Polos. 'When they got thither,' says Ramusio, who edited Marco's book in the fifteenth century, 'the same fate befell them as befell Ulysses, who when he returned after his twenty years' wanderings to his native Ithaca was recognized by nobody.' When, clad in their uncouth Tartar garb, the three Polos knocked at the doors of the Ca' Polo, no one recognized them, and they had the greatest difficulty in persuading their relatives and fellow-Venetians that they were indeed those Polos who had been believed dead for so many years. The story goes that they satisfactorily established their identity by inviting all their kinsmen to a great banquet, for each course of which they put on a garment more magnificent than the last, and finally, bringing in their coarse Tartar coats, they ripped open the seams and the lining thereof, 'upon which there poured forth a great quantity of precious stones, rubies, sapphires, carbuncles, diamonds, and emeralds, which had been sewn into each coat with great care, so that nobody could have suspected that anything was there. . . . The exhibition of such an extraordinary and infinite treasure of jewels and precious stones, which covered the table, once more filled all present with such astonishment that they were dumb and almost beside themselves with surprise: and they at once recognized these honoured and venerated gentlemen in the Ca' Polo, whom at first they had doubted and received them with the greatest honour and reverence.[29] Human nature has changed little since the thirteenth century. The precious stones are a legend, but no doubt the Polos brought many with them, for they were jewel merchants by trade; they had had ample opportunities for business in China, and the Great Khan had loaded them with 'rubies and other handsome jewels of great value' to boot. Jewels were the most convenient form in which they could have brought home their wealth. But the inquiring Marco brought other things also to tickle the curiosity of the Venetians, as he lets fall from time to time in his book. He brought, for example, specimens of the silky hair of the Tangut yak, which his countrymen much admired, the dried head and feet of a musk deer, and the seeds of a dye plant (probably indigo) from Sumatra, which he sowed in Venice, but which never came up, because the climate was not sufficiently warm.[30] He brought presents also for the Doge; for an inventory made in 1351 of things found in the palace of Marino Faliero includes among others a ring given by Kublai Khan, a Tartar collar, a three-bladed sword, an Indian brocade, and a book 'written by the hand of the aforesaid Marco,' called *De locis mirabilibus Tartarorum.*[31]

The rest of Marco Polo's life is quickly told. The legend goes that all the youth of Venice used to resort to the Ca' Polo in order to hear his stories, for not even among the foreign sailors on the quays, where once the boy Marco had wandered and asked about the Tartars, were stories the like of his to be heard. And because he was always talking of the greatness of Kublai Khan's dominions, the millions of revenue, the millions of junks, the millions of riders, the millions of towns and cities, they gave him a nickname and jestingly called him Marco *Milione*, or *Il Milione*, which is, being interpreted, 'Million Marco'; and the name even crept into the public documents of the Republic, while the courtyard of his house became known as the *Corte Milione*. To return from legend to history, the ancient rivalry between Venice and Genoa had been growing during Marco Polo's absence, nor had Venice always prevailed. Often as her galleys sailed,

> dipping deep
> For Famagusta and the hidden sun
> That rings black Cyprus with a lake of fire, . . .
> Questing brown slaves or Syrian oranges,
> The pirate Genoese
> Hell raked them till they rolled
> Blood, water, fruit, and corpses up the hold.

At last in 1298, three years after Marco's return, a Genoese fleet under Lamba Doria sailed for the Adriatic, to bate the pride of Venice in her own sea. The Venetians fitted out a great fleet to meet it, and Marco Polo, the handy man who knew so much about navigation, albeit more skilled with Chinese junks than with western ships, went with it as gentleman commander of a galley. The result of the encounter was a shattering victory for the Genoese off Curzola. Sixty-eight Venetian galleys were burnt, and seven thousand prisoners were haled off to Genoa, among them Marco Polo, who had now a taste of the results of that enterprise, manliness, and warfare, whose absence he so deprecated in the men of Suchow.

But soon there began to run through the streets and courtyards of Genoa a rumour that in prison there lay a certain Venetian captain, with tales so wonderful to beguile the passing hours that none could tire of hearing them; and anon the gallants and sages and the bold ladies of Genoa were flocking, just as the men of the Rialto had flocked before, to hear his stories of Kublai Khan.

> Lord of the fruits of Tartary
>> Her rivers silver-pale,
> Lord of the hills of Tartary,
>> Glen, thicket, wood, and dale,
> Her flashing stars, her scented breeze,
> Her trembling lakes, like foamless seas,
> Her bird-delighting citron-trees
>> In every purple vale.

'Messer Marco,' so runs Ramusio's account of the tradition which lingered in Venice in his day, 'finding himself in this position, and witnessing the general eagerness to hear all about Cathay and the Great Khan, which indeed compelled him daily to repeat his story till he was weary, was advised to put the matter in writing, so he found means to get a letter written to his father in Venice, in which he desired the latter to send those notes and memoranda which he had brought home with him.'

It happened that in prison with Marco Polo there lay a certain Pisan writer of romances, Rusticiano by name,[32] who had probably been taken prisoner before at the battle of Melaria (1284), when so many Pisan captives had been carried to Genoa, that the saying arose 'He who would see Pisa let him go to Genoa.' Rusticiano was skilled in the writing of French, the language *par excellence* of romances, in which he had written versions of the Round Table Tales, and in him Marco Polo found a ready scribe, who took down the stories as he told them, in the midst of the crowd of Venetian prisoners and Genoese gentlemen, raptly drinking in all the wonders of Kublai Khan. It was by a just instinct that, when all was written, Rusticiano prefixed to the tale that same address to the lords and gentlemen of the world, bidding them to take heed and listen, which he had been wont to set at the beginning of his tales of Tristan and Lancelot and King Arthur: 'Ye Lords, Emperors and Kings, Dukes and Marquises, Counts, Knights and Burgesses and all ye men who desire to know the divers races of men and the diversities of the different regions of the world, take ye this book and cause it to be read, and here shall ye find the greatest marvels.' But he adds, 'Marco Polo, a wise and learned citizen of Venice, states distinctly what things he saw and what things he heard from others, for this book will be a truthful one.' Marco Polo's truthful marvels were more wonderful even than the exploits of Arthur's knights, and were possibly better suited to the respectable Rusticiano's pen, for his only other claim to distinction in the eyes of posterity seems to be that in his abridgment of the Romance of Lancelot he entirely omits the episode (if episode it can be called) of the loves of Lancelot and Guinevere. 'Alas,' remarks his French editor, 'that the copy of Lancelot which fell into the hands of poor Francesca of Rimini was not one of those expurgated by Rusticiano!'[33]

Marco Polo was released from prison (there must have been mourning in the palaces of Genoa) and returned to Venice at the end of a year. Sometimes hereafter his name occurs in the records of Venice, as he moves about on his lawful occasions.[34] In 1305 we find 'Nobilis Marchus Polo Milioni' standing surety for a wine smuggler; in 1311 he is suing a dishonest agent who owes him money on the sale of musk (he, Marco, had seen the musk deer in its lair); and in 1323 he is concerned in a dispute about a party wall. We know too, from his will, that he had a wife named Donata, and three daughters, Fantina, Bellela, and Moreta. Had he loved before, under the alien skies where his youth was spent, some languid, exquisite lady of China, or hardy Tartar maid? Had he profited himself from the strange marriage customs of Tibet, of which he remarks (with one of his very rare gleams of humour), 'En cele contree aurent bien aler les jeume de seize anz en vingt quatre'? Had Fantina, Bellela, and Moreta half-brothers, flying their gerfalcons at the quails by the shores of the 'White Lake' where the Khan hunted, and telling tales of the half legendary father, who sailed away for ever when they were boys in the days of Kublai Khan? These things we cannot know, nor can we ever guess whether he regretted that only daughters sprang from his loins in the city of the lagoons, and no Venetian son to go venturing again to the far-distant country where assuredly he had left a good half of his heart. Perhaps he talked of it sometimes to Peter, his Tartar servant, whom he freed at his death 'from all bondage as completely as I pray God to release mine own soul from all sin and guilt'. Some have thought that he brought Peter the Tartar with him from the East, and the thought is a pleasant one; but it is more likely that he bought him in Italy, for the Venetians were inveterate slave-owners, and captive Tartars were held of all the slaves the strongest and best. So his life passed; and in 1324 Marco Polo died, honoured much by his fellow-citizens, after making a will which is still preserved in the library of St Mark's.

A characteristic story of his death-bed is related by a Dominican friar, one Jacopo of Acqui, who wrote some time later. 'What he told in the book,' says Jacopo, 'was not as much as he had really seen, because of the tongues of detractors, who being ready to impose their own lies on others, are over hasty to set down as lies what they in their perversity disbelieve or do not understand. And because there are many great and strange things in that book, which are reckoned past all credence, he was asked by his friends on his death-bed to correct the book, by removing everything that went beyond the facts. To which his reply was that he had not told *one half* of what he had really seen.'[35] How well one can see that last indignant flash of the dying observer, who in the long years of his youth had taken notes of strange tribes and customs for the wise and gracious Kublai Khan, and whom little men now dared to doubt. Indeed, modern discovery has entirely confirmed the exactitude of

Marco Polo's observation. It is true that he sometimes repeated some very tall stories which had been told to him, of dog-faced men in the Andaman Islands and of the 'male and female islands' so beloved of medieval geographers. These were sailors' yarns, and where Marco Polo reports what he has seen with his own eyes, he reports with complete accuracy, nor does he ever pretend to have seen a place which he had not visited. The explorers of our own day, Aurel Stein, Ellsworth Huntington, and Sven Hedin, travelling in central Asia, have triumphantly vindicated him. 'It is,' says an eminent French historian, 'as though the originals of very old photographs had been suddenly rediscovered: the old descriptions of things which were unchanged could be perfectly superimposed upon present reality,'[36] and Huntington and Aurel Stein took with them to the inaccessible districts of central Asia as guide-books the book of the Chinese pilgrim Hiwen Thsang (seventh century) and the book of Marco Polo, and over and over again found how accurate were their descriptions.

It is indeed almost impossible to exaggerate the extent of Marco Polo's accomplishment. It is best estimated in the often-quoted words of Sir Henry Yule, whose edition of his book is one of the great works of English scholarship:

He was the first traveller to trace a route across the whole longitude of Asia, naming and describing kingdom after kingdom, which he had seen with his own eyes, the desert of Persia, the flowering plateaux and wild gorges of Badakhshan, the jade-bearing rivers of Khotan, the Mongol steppes, cradle of the power that had so lately threatened to swallow up Christendom, the new and brilliant court that had been established at Cambaluc: the first Travellers to reveal China in all its wealth and vastness, its mighty rivers, its huge cities, its rich manufactures, its swarming population, the inconceivably vast fleets that quickened its seas and inland waters; to tell us of the nations on its borders with all their eccentricities of manners and worship; of Tibet with its sordid devotees; of Burma with its golden pagodas and their tinkling crowns; of Laos, of Siam, of Cochin China, of Japan, the Eastern Thule, with its rosy pearls and golden-roofed palaces; the first to speak of that Museum of Beauty and Wonder, still so imperfectly ransacked, the Indian Archipelago, source of those aromatics then so highly prized and whose origin was so dark; of Java the Pearl of Islands; of Sumatra with its many kings, its strange costly products, and

Genoa

Venice

R. Dnieper

R. Volga

KHANATE OF KIPCHAK

URAL MTS

R. Danube

Constantinople

Trebizond

CASPIAN

ARAL SEA

KHANAT OF CHAGA

Lajazzo

Mosul

Bokhara

Kashi

Alexandria

Acre

Bagdad

Samarkand

PAMIR

Ya

Jerusalem

KHORASAN

Balkh

Khot

KHANATE OF PERSIA

KIRMAN

Ormuz

IND

J.F.H.

MALABAR

Calicut

Extent of Tartar domin-
ions in Marco Polo's day.

×××××××××× First journey of the two
elder Polos.

•—•—• Outward route of Marco Polo
& some of his journeys
in China.

←—•—• Homeward route of Marco Polo

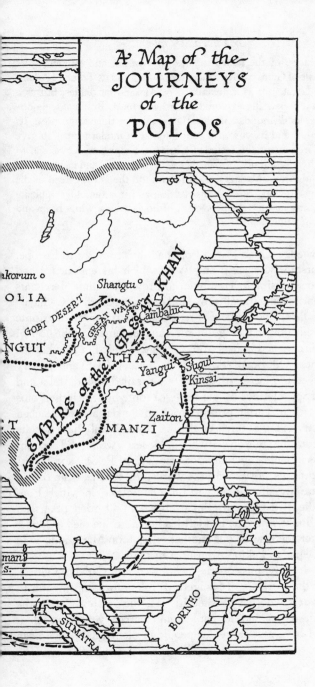

A Map of the
JOURNEYS
of the
POLOS

its cannibal races; of the naked savages of Nicobar and Andaman; of Ceylon, the Isle of Gems, with its Sacred Mountain and its Tomb of Adam; of India the Great, not as a dreamland of Alexandrian fables, but as a country seen and partially explored, with its virtuous Brahmans, its obscene ascetics, its diamonds and the strange tales of their acquisition, its sea-beds of pearl and its powerful sun; the first in modern times to give any distinct account of the secluded Christian Empire of Abyssinia, to speak, though indeed dimly, of Zanzibar with its negroes and its ivory and of the vast and distant Madagascar, bordering on the Dark Ocean of the South, with its Ruc and other monstrosities; and in a remotely opposite region, of Siberia and the Arctic Ocean, of dog-sledges, white bears and reindeer-riding Tunguses.[37]

The knowledge which Marco Polo had thus brought to Europe, the intercourse between East and West which his experience had shown to be so desirable, continued to grow after him. Merchants and missionaries alike travelled by land or sea eastward to Cathay.[38] Another of those indomitable Franciscan friars, John of Monte Corvino, went out at the age of fifty and became Archbishop of Peking. Churches and houses of friars were founded in some of the Chinese cities. Odoric of Pordenone, another friar, and a very good observer too, set forth in 1316 and sailed round India and through the Spice Islands by the same sea route by which the Polos had brought their Tartar princess back to Persia, and so reached Canton, 'a city as big as three Venices . . . and all Italy hath not the amount of craft that this one city hath.' He left a wonderful account of his travels in China, including descriptions of Peking and Hangchow, and ends his stories with the words, 'As for me, from day to day I prepare myself to return to those countries, in which I am content to die, if it pleaseth Him from whom all good things do come' – no doubt where he had left his heart, but he died at Udine in Italy. Later there went out another friar, John Marignolli, who was Papal Legate to Peking from 1342 to 1346.

Nor was it only missionaries who went to Cathay. Odoric, speaking of the wonders of Hangchow, refers for confirmation to Venetian traders who have visited it: "Tis the greatest city in the whole world, so great indeed that I should scarcely venture to tell of it, but that I have met at Venice people in plenty who have been there'; John of Monte Corvino was accompanied by Master Peter of Lucolongo, 'a great merchant,' and John Marignolli mentions a *fondaco* for the use of Christian merchants, which was attached to one of the Franciscan convents at Zaiton. Above all, there is Francis Balducci Pegolotti, that intrepid factor who served the great commercial house of the Bardi of Florence, and who wrote a priceless handbook for the use of merchants about 1340. In this he gives detailed instructions for the guidance of a merchant, who wishes to proceed from Tana on the Black Sea by the overland route across Asia to Cathay and back again with £12,000 worth of silk in his caravan, and remarks casually, in passing, 'The road you travel from Tana to Cathay is perfectly safe, whether by day or night, according to what merchants say who have used it' – 'il chanmino dandare dalla Tana al Ghattajo è *sichurissimo!*'[39] Think only of what it all means. Marco Polo travelling where no man set foot again till the twentieth century. The bells of the Christian church ringing sweetly in the ears of the Great Khan in Peking. The long road across central Asia perfectly safe for merchants. The 'many persons at Venice' who have walked in the streets of Hangchow. This is in the late thirteenth and early fourteenth centuries, in the despised and hidebound Middle Ages. *È sichurissimo!* It takes some of the gilt off Columbus and Vasco da Gama and the age (forsooth) of 'discovery'.

But a change came over everything in the middle of the fourteenth century. Darkness fell again and swallowed up Peking and Hangchow, the great ports, the crowding junks, the noble civilization. No longer was the great trade route *sichurissimo*, and no longer did Christian friars chant their Masses in Zaiton. The Tartar dynasty fell and the new rulers of China reverted to the old anti-foreign policy; moreover, Islam spread its conquests all over central Asia and lay like a rampart between the far east and west, a great wall of intolerance and hatred stronger by far than the great wall of stone which the Chinese had once built to keep out the Tartars. All Marco Polo's marvels became no more than a legend, a traveller's tale.

But that great adventurer was not done for yet. Nearly a century and a half after Marco's death a Genoese sea captain sat poring over one of the new printed books, which men were beginning to buy

and to hand about among themselves. The book which he was reading was the Latin version of Marco Polo's travels. He was reading
it with intentness and indeed with passion. As he read he made
notes in the margin; on over seventy pages he made his notes.[40]
From time to time he frowned and turned back and read again the
tale of those great ports of Cathay and the gold-roofed palaces of
Cipangu; and always he wondered how those lands might be
reached, now that the wall of darkness covered central Asia, and
anarchy blocked the road to the Persian Gulf. One day (may we not
see him?) he lifted his head and smote his hand upon the table. 'I
will sail west', he said. 'Maybe I shall find the lost island of Antilha
in the western ocean, but maybe on its far rim I shall indeed come to
Cipangu, for the world is round, and somewhere in those great seas
beyond the coast of Europe must lie Marco Polo's rich Cathay. I
will beseech the kings of England and of Spain for a ship and a ship's
company, and the silk and the spices and the wealth shall be theirs.
I will sail west,' said the Genoese sea captain, and he smote his
thigh. 'I will sail west, west, west!' And this was the last of Messer
Marco's marvels; he discovered China in the thirteenth century,
when he was alive, and in the fifteenth, when he was dead, he discovered America!

CHAPTER IV

Madame Eglentyne

Ther was also a Nonne, a Prioresse,
That of her smyling was ful simple and coy;
Hir grettest ooth was ne but by sëynt Loy;
And she was cleped madame Eglentyne.
Ful wel she song the service divyne,
Entuned in hir nose ful semely;
And Frensh she spak ful faire and fetisly,
After the scole of Stratford atte Bowe,
For Frensh of Paris was to hir unknowe.
At mete wel y-taught was she with-alle;
She leet no morsel from hir lippes falle,
Ne wette hir fingres in hir sauce depe.
Wel coude she carie a morsel and wel kepe,
That no drope ne fille up-on hir brest.
In curteisye was set ful muche hir lest.
Hir over lippe wyped she so clene,
That in hir coppe was no ferthing sene
Of grece, whan she dronken haddie hir draughte
Ful semely after hir mete she raughte,
And sikerly she was of greet disport,
And ful plesaunt and amiable of port,
And peyned hir to countrefete chere
Of court, and been estatlich of manere,
And to be holden digne of reverence.
But, for to speken of hir conscience,
She was so charitable and so pitous,
She wolde wepe, if that she sawe a mous
Caught in a trap, if it were deed or bledde.
Of smale houndes had she, that she fedde
With rosted flesh, or milk and wastel-breed,
But sore weep she if oon of hem were deed,
Or if men smoot it with a yerde smerte:

73

And al was conscience and tendre herte
Ful semely hir wimpel pinched was:
Hir nose tretys; her eyen greye as glas;
Hir mouth ful smal, and ther-to softe and reed;
But sikerly she hadde a fair foreheed;
It was almost a spanne brood, I trowe;
For, hardily, she was nat undergrowe.
Ful fetis was hir cloke, as I was war.
Of smal coral aboute hir arm she bar
A peire of bedes, gauded al with grene;
And ther-on heng a broche of gold ful shene,
On which ther was first write a crowned A,
And after, *Amor vincit omnia!*

— GEOFFREY CHAUCER
Prologue to the *Canterbury Tales*

EVERY ONE KNOWS Chaucer's description of the Prioress, Madame Eglentyne, who rode with that very motley and talkative company on the way to Canterbury. There is no portrait in his gallery which has given rise to more diverse comment among critics. One interprets it as a cutting attack on the worldliness of the Church; another thinks that Chaucer meant to draw a charming and sympathetic picture of womanly gentleness; one says that it is a caricature, another an ideal; and an American professor even finds in it a psychological study of thwarted maternal instinct, apparently because Madame Eglentyne was fond of little dogs and told a story about a schoolboy. The mere historian may be excused from following these vagaries. To him Chaucer's Prioress, like Chaucer's monk and Chaucer's friar, will simply be one more instance of the almost photographic accuracy of the poet's observation. The rippling undercurrent of satire is always there; but it is Chaucer's own peculiar satire – mellow, amused, uncondemning, the most subtle kind of satire, which does not depend upon exaggeration. The literary critic has only Chaucer's words and his own heart, or sometimes (low be it spoken) his own desire to be original, by which to guide his judgement. But the historian knows; he has all sorts of historical sources in which to study nunneries, and there he meets Chaucer's Prioress at every turn. Above all, he has the bishop's registers.

For a long time historians foolishly imagined that kings and wars and parliaments and the jury system alone were history; they liked chronicles and Acts of Parliament, and it did not strike them to go and look in dusty episcopal archives for the big books in which medieval bishops entered up the letters which they wrote and all the complicated business of running their dioceses. But when historians did think of looking there, they found a mine of priceless information about almost every side of social and ecclesiastical life. They had to dig for it of course, for almost all that is worth knowing has to be mined like precious metals out of a rock; and for one nugget the miner often has to grub for days underground in a mass of dullness; and when he has got it he has to grub in his own heart, or else he will not understand it. The historians found fine gold in the bishops' registers, when once they persuaded themselves that it was not beneath their dignity to grub there. They found descriptions of vicarages, with all their furniture and gardens; they found marriage disputes; they found wills full of entertaining legacies to people dead hundreds of years ago; they found ex-communications; they found indulgences to men for relieving the poor, repairing roads, and building bridges, long before there was any poor law, or any county council; they found trials for heresy and witchcraft; they found accounts of miracles worked at the tombs of saints and even of some quite unsaintly people, such as Thomas of Lancaster, and Edward II, and Simon de Montfort; they found lists of travelling expenses when the bishops rode round their dioceses; in one they even found a minute account of the personal appearance of Queen Philippa, then a little girl at her father's Court at Hainault, whom the Bishop of Exeter had been sent to inspect, in order to see if she were pretty and good enough to marry Edward III: she was nine years old, and the bishop said that her second teeth were whiter than her first teeth and that her nose was broad but not snub, which was reassuring for Edward.[1] Last, but not least, the historians found a multitude of documents about monasteries, and among these documents they found visitation records, and among visitation records they found Chaucer's Prioress, smiling full simple and coy, fair forehead, well-pinched wimple, necklace, little dogs, and all, as though she had stepped into a stuffy register by mistake for the *Canterbury Tales* and was longing to get out again.

This was the reason that Madame Eglentyne got into the register. In the Middle Ages all the nunneries of England, and a great many of the monasteries, used to be visited at intervals by the bishop of their diocese – or by somebody sent by him – in order to see whether they were behaving properly. It was rather like the periodical visitation of a school by one of Her Majesty's inspectors, only what happened was very different. When Her Majesty's inspector comes he does not sit in state in the hall, and call all the inmates in front of him one after another, from the head mistress to the smallest child in the first form, and invite them to say in what way they think the school is not being properly run, and what complaints they have to make against their mistresses and which girl habitually breaks the rules – all breathed softly and privately into his ear, with no one to overhear them. But when the bishop came to visit a nunnery, that is precisely what happened. First of all, he sent a letter to say he was coming, and to bid the nuns prepare for him. Then he came, with his clerks and a learned official or two, and was met solemnly by the prioress and all the nuns, and preached a sermon in their church, and was entertained, perhaps, to dinner. And then he prepared to examine them, and one by one they came before him, in order of rank, beginning with the prioress, and what they had to do was to tell tales about each other. He wanted to find out if the prioress were ruling well, and if the services were properly performed, and if the finances were in good order, and if discipline were maintained; and if any nun had a complaint, then was the time to make it.

And the nuns were full of complaints. A modern schoolgirl would go pale with horror over their capacity for tale-bearing. If one nun had boxed her sister's ears, if another had cut church, if another were too much given to entertaining friends, if another went out without a licence, if another had run away with a wandering fluteplayer, the bishop was sure to hear about it; that is, unless the whole convent were in a disorderly state, and the nuns had made a compact to wink at each other's peccadilloes; and not to betray them to the bishop, which occasionally happened. And if the prioress were at all unpopular he was quite certain to hear all about her. 'She fares splendidly in her own room and never invites us,' says one nun;

'She has favourites,' says another, 'and when she makes corrections she passes lightly over those whom she likes, and speedily punishes those whom she dislikes'; 'She is a fearful scold,' says a third; 'She dresses more like a secular person than a nun, and wears rings and necklaces,' says a fourth; 'She goes out riding to see her friends far too often,' says a fifth; 'She-is-a-very-bad-business-woman-and-she-has-let-the-house-get-into-debt-and-the-church-is-falling-about-our-ears-and-we-don't-get-enough-food-and-she-hasn't-given-us-any-clothes-for-two-years-and-she-has-sold-woods-and-farms-without-your-licence-and-she-has-pawned-our-best-set-of-spoons; and no wonder, when she never consults us in any business as she ought to do.' They go on like that for pages, and the bishop must often have wanted to put his fingers in his ears and shout to them to stop; especially as the prioress had probably spent half an hour, for her part, in telling him how disobedient and ill-tempered, and thoroughly badly behaved the nuns were.

All these tales the bishop's clerk solemnly wrote down in a big book, and when the examination was over the bishop summoned all the nuns together again. And if they had answered 'All is well', as they sometimes did, or only mentioned trivial faults, he commended them and went his way; and if they had shown that things really were in a bad way, he investigated particular charges and scolded the culprits and ordered them to amend, and when he got back to his palace, or the manor where he was staying, he wrote out a set of injunctions, based on the complaints, and saying exactly how things were to be improved; and of these injunctions one copy was entered in his register and another was sent by hand to the nuns, who were supposed to read it aloud at intervals and to obey everything in it. We have in many bishops' registers these lists of injunctions, copied into them by the bishops' clerks, and in some, notably in a splendid fifteenth-century Lincoln register, belonging to the good bishop Alnwick, we have also the evidence of the nuns, just as it was taken down from their chattering mouths, and these are the most human and amusing of all medieval records. It is easy to see what important historical documents visitation reports are, especially in a diocese like Lincoln, which possesses an almost unbroken series of registers, ranging over the three centuries before the Dissolution, so that one can trace the whole history of some of the nunneries by the successive visitations.

Let us see what light the registers will throw upon Madame Eglentyne, before Chaucer observed her mounting her horse outside the Tabard Inn. Doubtless she first came to the nunnery when she was quite a little girl, because girls counted as grown up when they were fifteen in the Middle Ages; they could be married out of hand at twelve, and they could become nuns for ever at fourteen. Probably Eglentyne's father had three other daughters to marry, each with a dowry, and a gay young spark of a son, who spent a lot of money on fashionable suits.

> Embroidered . . . as it were a mede
> All ful of fresshe flowers white and rede.

So he thought he had better settle the youngest at once; and he got together a dowry (it was rarely possible to get into a nunnery without one, though Church law really forbade anything except voluntary offerings), and, taking Eglentyne by the hand one summer day, he popped her into a nunnery a few miles off, which had been founded by his ancestors. We may even know what it cost him; it was rather a select, aristocratic house, and he had to pay an entrance fee of £200 in modern money; and then he had to give Eglentyne her new habit and a bed, and some other furniture; and he had to make a feast on the day she became a nun, and invite all the nuns and all his own friends; and he had to tip the friar, who preached the sermon; and, altogether, it was a great affair.² But the feast would not come at once, because Eglentyne would have to remain a novice for some years, until she was old enough to take the vows. So she would stay in the convent and be taught how to sing and to read, and to talk French of the school of Stratford-atte-Bowe with the other novices. Perhaps she was the youngest, for girls often did not enter the convent until they were old enough to decide for themselves whether they wanted to be nuns; but there were certainly some other quite tiny novices learning their lessons; and occasionally there would be a little girl like the one whose sad fate is recorded in a dull law-book, shut up in a nunnery by a wicked stepfather who wanted her inheritance (a nun could not inherit land, because she was supposed to be dead to the world), and told by the nuns that the devil would fly away with her if she tried to set foot outside the door.[3] However, Eglentyne had a sunny disposition and liked life in the nunnery, and had a natural aptitude for the pretty table manners which she learnt there, as well as for talking French, and though she was not at all prim and liked the gay clothes and pet dogs which she used to see at home in her mother's bower, still she had no hesitation at all about taking the veil when she was fifteen, and indeed she rather liked the fuss that was made of her, and being called *Madame* or *Dame*, which was the courtesy title always given to a nun.

The years passed and Eglentyne's life jogged along peacefully enough behind the convent walls. The great purpose for which the nunneries existed, and which most of them fulfilled not unworthily, was the praise of God. Eglentyne spent a great deal of her time singing and praying in the convent church, and, as we know,

> Ful wel she song the service divyne,
> Entuned in hir nose ful semely.

The nuns had seven monastic offices to say every day. About 2 a.m. the night office was said; they all got out of bed when the bell rang, and went down in the cold and the dark to the church choir and said Matins, followed immediately by Lauds. Then they went back to bed, just as the dawn was breaking in the sky, and slept again for three hours, and then got up for good at six o'clock and said Prime. After that there followed Tierce, Sext, None, Vespers, and Compline, spread at intervals through the day. The last service, compline, was said at 7 p.m. in winter, and at 8 p.m. in summer, after which the nuns were supposed to go straight to bed in the dorter, in which connexion one Nun's Rule ordains that 'None shall push up against another wilfully, nor spit upon the stairs going up and down, but if they tread it out forthwith'![4] They had in all about eight hours' sleep, broken in the middle by the night service. They had three meals, a light repast of bread and beer after prime in the morning, a solid dinner to the accompaniment of reading aloud in the middle of the day, and a short supper immediately after vespers at 5 or 6 p.m.

From 12 to 5 p.m. in winter and from 1 to 6 p.m. in summer Eglentyne and her sisters were supposed to devote themselves to manual or brain work, interspersed with a certain amount of sober and godly recreation. She would spin, or embroider vestments with the crowned monogram M of the Blessed Virgin in blue and gold thread, or make little silken purses for her friends and finely sewn bands for them to bind round their arms after a bleeding. She would read too, in her psalter or in such saints' lives as the convent possessed, written in French or English; for her Latin was weak, though she could construe *Amor vincit omnia*. Perhaps her convent took in a few little schoolgirls to learn their letters and good manners with the nuns, and when she grew older she helped to teach them to read and sing; for though they were happy, they did not receive a very extensive education from the good sisters. In the summer Eglentyne was sometimes allowed to work in the convent garden, or even to go out haymaking with the other nuns; and came back round-eyed to confide in her confessor that she had seen the cellaress returning therefrom seated behind the chaplain on his nag,[5] and had thought what fun it must be to jog behind stout Dan John.

Except for certain periods of relaxation strict silence was supposed to be observed in the convent for a large part of the day, and if Eglentyne desired to communicate with her sisters, she was urged to do so by means of signs. The persons who drew up the lists of signs which were in use in medieval monastic houses, however, combined a preternatural ingenuity with an extremely exiguous sense of humour, and the sort of dumb pandemonium which went on at Eglentyne's dinner table must often have been more mirth-provoking than speech. The sister who desired fish would 'wag her hands displayed sidelings in manner of a fish tail'; she who wanted milk would 'draw her left little finger in manner of milking'; for mustard one would 'hold her nose in the upper part of her right fist and rub it'; another for salt would 'fillip with her right thumb and forefinger over the left thumb'; another desirous of wine would 'move her forefinger up and down the end of her thumb afore her eye'; and the guilty sacristan, struck by the thought that she had not provided incense for the Mass, would 'put her two fingers into her nostrils'. In one such table drawn up for nuns there are no less than 106 signs, and on the whole it is not surprising that the rule of the same nuns enjoins that 'it is never lawful to use them without some reason and profitable need, for oft-times more hurt hath an evil word, and more offence it may be to God'. [6]

The nuns, of course, would not have been human if they had not sometimes grown a little weary of all these services and this silence; for the religious life was not, nor was it intended to be, an easy one. It was not a mere means of escape from work and responsibility. In the early golden age of monasticism only men and women with a vocation, that is to say a real genius for monastic life, entered convents. Moreover, when there they worked very hard with hand and brain, as well as with soul, and so they got variety of occupation, which is as good as a holiday. The basis of wise St Benedict's Rule was a nicely adjusted combination of variety with regularity; for he knew human nature. Thus monks and nuns did not find the services monotonous, and indeed regarded them as by far the best part of the day. But in the later Middle Ages, when Chaucer lived, young people had begun to enter monastic houses rather as a profession than as a vocation. Many truly spiritual men and women still took the vows, but with them came others who were little suited to monastic life, and who lowered its standard, because it was hard and uncongenial to them. Eglentyne became a nun because her father did not want the trouble and expense of finding her a husband, and because being a nun was about the only career for a well-born lady who did not marry. Moreover, by this time, monks and nuns had grown more lazy, and did little work with their hands and still less with their heads, particularly in nunneries, where the early tradition of learning had died out and where many nuns could hardly understand the Latin in which their services were written. The result was that monastic life began to lose that essential variety which St Benedict had designed for it, and as a result the regularity sometimes became irksome, and the series of services degenerated into a mere routine of peculiar monotony, which many of the singers could no longer keep alive with spiritual fervour. Thus sometimes (it must not be imagined that this happened in all or even in the majority of houses) the services became empty forms, to be hurried through with scant devotion and occasionally with scandalous irreverence. It was the almost inevitable reaction from too much routine.

Carelessness in the performance of the monastic hours was an exceedingly common fault during the later Middle Ages, though the monks were always worse about it than the nuns. Sometimes they 'cut' the services. Sometimes they behaved with the utmost levity, as at Exeter in 1330, where the canons giggled and joked and quarrelled during the services and dropped hot candle wax from the upper stalls on to the shaven heads of the singers in the stalls below![7] Sometimes they came late to matins, in the small hours after midnight. This fault was common in nunneries, for the nuns always would insist on having private drinkings and gossipings in the evening after compline, instead of going straight to bed, as the rule demanded – a habit which did not conduce to wakefulness at 1 a.m. Consequently they were somewhat sleepy at matins and found an almost Johnsonian difficulty in getting up early. Wise St Benedict foresaw the difficulty, when he wrote in his rule: 'When they rise for the Divine Office, let them gently encourage one another, because of the excuses made by those that are drowsy.'[8] At the nunnery of Stainfield in 1519 the bishop discovered that half an hour sometimes elapsed between the last stroke of the bell and the beginning of the service, and that some of the nuns did not sing, but dozed, partly because they had not enough candles, but chiefly because they went late to bed;[9] and whoever is without sin among us, let him cast the first stone! There was a tendency also among both monks and nuns to slip out before the end of the service on any good or bad excuse: they had to see after the dinner or the guest-house, their gardens needed weeding, or they did not feel well. But the most common fault of all was to gabble through the services as quickly as they could in order to get them over. They left out the syllables at the beginning and end of words, they omitted the dipsalma or pause between two verses, so that one side of the choir was beginning the second half before the other side had finished the first; they skipped sentences, they mumbled and slurred what should have been 'entuned in their nose ful semely', and altogether they made a terrible mess of the stately plainsong.

So prevalent was the fault of gabbling that the Father of Evil was obliged to charter a special Devil called Tittivillus, whose sole business it was to collect all these dropped syllables and carry them back to his master in a big bag. In one way or another, we have a good deal of information about him, for he was always letting himself be seen by holy men, who generally had a sharp eye for devils. One Latin rhyme distinguishes carefully between the contents of his sack: 'These are they who wickedly corrupt the holy psalms: the dangler, the gasper, the leaper, the galloper, the dragger, the mumbler, the fore-skipper, the fore-runner and the over-leaper: Tittivillus collecteth the fragments of these men's words.'[10] Indeed, a holy Cistercian abbot once interviewed the poor little devil himself and heard about his alarming industry; this is the story as it is told in *The Myroure of Oure Ladye*, written for the delectation of the nuns of Syon in the fifteenth century: 'We read of a holy Abbot of the order of Citeaux that while he stood in the choir at matins he saw a fiend that had a long and great poke hanging about his neck and went about the choir from one to another and waited busily after all letters and syllables and words and failings that any made; and them he gathered diligently and put them in his poke. And when he came before the Abbot, waiting if aught had escaped him that he might have gotten and put in his bag, the Abbot was astonied and afeard of the foulness and misshape of him and said unto him: What art thou? And he answered and said, I am a poor devil and my name is Tittivillus and I do mine office that is committed unto me. And what is thine office? said the Abbot. He answered: I must each day, he said, bring my master a thousand pokes full of failings and of negligences and syllables and words, that are done in your order in reading and singing and else I must be sore beaten.'[11] But there is no reason to suppose that he often got his beating, though one may be sure that Madame Eglentyne, busily chanting through her nose, never gave him the slightest help. In his spare moments, when he was not engaged in picking up those unconsidered trifles which the monks let fall from the psalms, Tittivillus used to fill up odd corners of his sack with the idle talk of people who gossiped in church; and he also sat up aloft and collected all the high notes of vain tenors, who sang to their own glory, instead of to the glory of God, and pitched the chants three notes higher than the cracked voices of their elders could rise.

But the monotony of convent life sometimes did more than make the nuns unconscious contributors to Tittivillus's sack. It sometimes played havoc with their tempers. The nuns were not chosen for convent life because they were saints. They were no more immune from tantrums than was the Wife of Bath, who was out of all charity when other village wives went into church before her; and sometimes they got terribly on each others' nerves. Readers of *Piers Plowman* will remember that when the seven deadly sins come in, Wrath tells how he was cook to the prioress of a convent and, says he,

> Of wycked wordes I, Wrath . here wordes imade,
> Til 'thow lixte' and 'thow lixte' . lopen oute at ones,
> And eyther hitte other . vnder the cheke;
> Hadde thei had knyves, by Cryst . her eyther had killed other.

To be sure, it is not often that we hear of anything so bad as that fifteenth-century prioress, who used to drag her nuns round the choir by their veils in the middle of the service, screaming 'Liar!' and 'Harlot!' at them;[12] or that other sixteenth-century lady who used to kick them and hit them on the head with her fists and put them in the stocks.[13] All prioresses were not 'ful plesaunt and amiable of port', or stately in their manner. The records of monastic visitations show that bad temper and petty bickering sometimes broke the peace of convent life.

But we must be back at Eglentyne. She went on living for ten or twelve years as a simple nun, and she sang the services very nicely and had a sweet temper and pretty manners and was very popular. Moreover, she was of good birth; Chaucer tells us a great deal about her beautiful behaviour at table and her courtesy, which shows that she was a lady born and bred; indeed, his description of this might have been taken straight out of one of the feudal books of deportment for girls; even her personal beauty – straight nose, grey eyes, and little red mouth – conforms to the courtly standard. The convents were apt to be rather snobbish; ladies and rich burgesses' daughters got into them, but poor and low-born girls never. So the nuns probably said to each other that what with her pretty ways and her good temper and her aristocratic connexions, wouldn't it be a good thing to choose her for prioress when the old prioress died? And so they did, and she had been a prioress for some years when Chaucer met her. At first it was very exciting, and Eglentyne liked being called 'Mother' by nuns who were older than herself, and having a private room to sit in and all the visitors to entertain. But she soon found that it was not by any means all a bed of roses; for there was a great deal of business to be done by the head of a house – not only looking after the internal discipline of the convent, but also superintending money matters and giving orders to the bailiffs on her estates, and seeing that the farms were paying well, and the tithes coming in to the churches which belonged to the nunnery, and that the Italian merchants who came to buy the wool off her sheeps' backs gave a good price for it. In all this business she was supposed to take the advice of the nuns, meeting in the chapter-house, where all business was transacted. I am afraid that sometimes Eglentyne used to think that it was much better to do things by herself, and so she would seal documents with the convent seal without telling them. One should always distrust the head of an office or school or society who says, with a self-satisfied air, that it is much more satisfactory to do the thing herself than to depute it to the proper subordinates; it either means that she is an autocrat, or else that she cannot organize. Madame Eglentyne was rather an autocrat, in a good-natured sort of way, and besides she hated bother. So she did not always consult the nuns; and I fear too (after many researches into that past of hers which Chaucer forgot to mention) that she often tried to evade rendering an account of income and expenditure to them every year, as she was supposed to do.

The nuns, of course, objected to this; and the first time the bishop came on his rounds they complained about it to him. They said, too, that she was a bad business woman and got into debt; and that when she was short of money she used to sell woods belonging to the convent, and promise annual pensions to various people in return for lump sums down, and lease out farms for a long time at low rates, and do various other things by which the convent would lose in the long run. And besides, she had let the roof of the church get into such ill repair that rain came through the holes on to their heads when they were singing; and would my lord bishop please to look at the holes in their clothes and tell her to provide them with new ones? Other wicked prioresses used sometimes even to pawn the plate and jewels of the convent, to get money for their own private purposes. But Eglentyne was not at all wicked or dishonest, though she was a bad manager; the fact was that she had no head for figures. I am *sure* that she had no head for figures; you have only got to read Chaucer's description of her to know that she was not a mathematician. Besides the nuns were exaggerating: their clothes were not in holes, only just a little threadbare. Madame Eglentyne was far too fastidious to allow ragged clothes about her; and as to the roof of the church, she had meant to save enough money to have some tiles put on to it, but it really *was* very hard to make two ends meet in a medieval nunnery, especially if (as I repeat) you had no head for figures. Probably the bishop saw how the land lay, so he ordered her never to do anything without consulting the convent, and he shut up the common seal in a box with three different sorts of locks, to which Madame Eglentyne and two of the senior nuns had the keys, so that she could not open it alone and so could not seal any business agreement without their consent. And he ordered her to keep accounts and present them every year (there are bundles of her accounts still preserved in the Record Office). Finally he deputed a neighbouring rector to act as custodian of the business affairs of the house so that she should always have his help. Things went better after that.

Eglentyne, it seems, was never really interested in business, and was quite pleased to have her time taken up with looking after internal affairs and entertaining visitors, with an occasional jaunt outside to see how the estates were getting on. And she began to find that she could lead a much freer and gayer life now that she was a prioress; for the prioress of a convent had rooms of her own, instead of sharing the common dormitory and refectory; sometimes she even had a sort of little house with a private kitchen. The abbess of one great nunnery at Winchester in the sixteenth century had her own staff to look after her, a cook, and an under cook, and a housemaid and a gentlewoman to wait upon her, like any great lady in the world, and never dined with the nuns except on state occasions. But a superior generally had with her one nun to act as her companion and assist her in the choir and be a witness to her good behaviour; this nun was called her chaplain, and was supposed to be changed every year, to prevent favouritism. It will be remembered that when Madame Eglentyne went on her pilgrimage she took her nun chaplain with her, as well as three priests; that was because no nun was ever allowed to go out alone. One of Madame Eglentyne's duties as prioress was to entertain visitors with her celebrated cheer of court, and we may be sure that she had a great many. Her sisters, who were now grand ladies with husbands and manors of their own, and her old father, and all the great people of the county came to congratulate her; and after that they used often to drop in for a dinner of chickens and wine and wastel bread if they passed the house on a journey, and sometimes they spent the night there. One or two ladies, whose husbands were away at the wars or on a pilgrimage to Rome, even came as paying guests to the convent and lived there for a whole year, for nothing pleased the country gentlemen or wealthy burgesses better than to use nunneries as boarding-houses for their women-kind.

All this was very disturbing to the peace and quiet of the nuns, and especially disturbing were the boarders, for they wore gay clothes, and had pet dogs and callers, and set a very frivolous example to the nuns. At one nunnery we find a bishop ordering: 'Let Felmersham's wife, with her whole household and other women, be utterly removed from your monastery within one year, seeing that they are a cause of disturbance to the nuns and an occasion to bad example, by reason of their attire and of those who come to visit them.'[14] It can be easily imagined *why* the bishops objected so much to the reception of these worldly married women as boarders. Just substitute for 'Felmersham's wife' 'the Wife of Bath' and all is explained. That lady was not a person whom a prioress would lightly refuse; the list of her pilgrimages alone would give her the *entrée* into any nunnery. Smiling her gap-toothed smile and riding easily upon her ambler, she would enter the gates, and what a month of excitement would pass before she rode away again. I am sure that it was she who taught Madame Eglentyne the most fashionable way to pinch a wimple; and she certainly introduced hats 'as broad as is a buckler or a targe' and scarlet stockings into some nunneries. The bishops disliked it all very much, but they never succeeded in turning the boarders out for all their efforts, because the nuns always needed the money which they paid for their board and lodging.

It is easy to understand that this constant intercourse with worldly visitors would give rise to the spread of worldly habits in Madame Eglentyne's nunnery. Nuns, after all, were but women, and they had the amiable vanities of their sex. But Authority (with a large A) did not consider their vanities amiable at all. It was the view of Authority that the Devil had dispatched three lesser D's to be the damnation of nuns, and those three D's were Dances, Dresses, and Dogs. Medieval England was famous for dancing and mumming and minstrelsy; it was Merry England because, however plague and pestilence and famine and the cruelties of man to man might darken life, still it loved these things. But there were no two views possible about what the Church thought of dancing; it was accurately summed up by one moralist in the aphorism, 'The Devil is the inventor and governor and disposer of dances and dancing.' Yet when we look into those accounts which Madame Eglentyne rendered (or did not render) to her nuns at the end of every year, we shall find payments for wassail at New Year and Twelfth Night, for May games, for bread and ale on bonfire nights, for harpers and players at Christmas, for a present to the Boy Bishop on his rounds, and perhaps for an extra pittance when the youngest schoolgirl was allowed to dress up and act as abbess of the convent for the whole of Innocents' Day. And when we look in the bishops' registers we shall find Madame Eglentyne forbidden 'all manner of minstrelsy, interludes, dancing or revelling within your holy place'; and she would be fortunate indeed if her bishop would make exception for Christmas, 'and other honest times of recreation among yourselves used in absence of seculars in all wise'. Somehow one feels an insistent conviction that her cheer of court included dancing.[15]

Then, again, there were the fashionable dresses which the visitors introduced into nunneries. It is quite certain that Madame Eglentyne was not unmoved by them; and it is a sad fact that she began to think the monastic habit very black and ugly, and the monastic life very strict; and to decide that if some little amenities were imported into it no one would be a penny the worse, and perhaps the bishop would not notice. That is why, when Chaucer met her,

> Ful fetis was hir cloke, as I was war,
> Of smal coral aboute hir arm she bar
> A peire of bedes, gauded al with grene,
> And ther-on heng a broche of gold ful shene.

Unfortunately, however, the bishop did notice; the registers are indeed full of those clothes of Madame Eglentyne's, and of the even more frivolous ones which she wore in the privacy of the house. For more than six weary centuries the bishops waged a holy war against fashion in the cloister, and waged it in vain; for as long as nuns mingled freely with secular women, it was impossible to prevent them from adopting secular modes. Occasionally a wretched bishop would find himself floundering unhandily, in masculine bewilderment, through something like a complete catalogue of contemporary fashions, in order to specify what the nuns were *not* to wear. Synods sat solemnly, bishops and archbishops shook their grey heads, over golden hairpins and silver belts, jewelled rings, laced shoes, slashed tunics, low necks and long trains, gay colours, costly cloth, and valuable furs. The nuns were supposed to wear their veils pinned tightly down to their eyebrows, so that their foreheads were completely hidden; but high foreheads happened to be fashionable among worldly ladies, who even shaved theirs to make them higher, and the result was that the nuns could not resist lifting up and spreading out their veils, for how otherwise did Chaucer *know* that Madame Eglentyne had such a fair forehead ('almost a spanne broad, I trowe')? If she had been wearing her veil properly, it would have been invisible, and the father of English poetry may be observed discreetly but plainly winking the other eye when he puts in that little touch; his contemporaries would see the point very quickly. And that brooch and that fetis cloak of hers. . . . Here is what some tale-bearing nuns told the Bishop of Lincoln about their Prioress, fifty years after Chaucer wrote the *Canterbury Tales*.

'The Prioress,' they said with their most sanctimonious air, 'wears golden rings exceeding costly, with divers precious stones and also girdles silvered and gilded over and silken veils and she carries her veil too high above her forehead, so that her forehead, being entirely uncovered, can be seen of all, and she wears furs of vair. Also she wears shifts of cloth of Rennes, which costs sixteen pence the ell. Also she wears kirtles laced with silk and tiring pins of silver and silver gilt and has made all the nuns wear the like. Also she wears above her veil a cap of estate, furred with budge. Item, she has on her neck a long silken band, in English a lace, which hangs down below her breast and there on a golden ring with one diamond.'[16] Is it not Madame Eglentyne to the life? Nothing escaped our good Dan Chaucer's eye, for all that he rode always looking on the ground.

Moreover, it was not only in her dress that the Prioress and her sister nuns aped the fashions of the world. Great ladies of the day loved to amuse themselves with pet animals; and nuns were quick to follow their example. So,

> Of smale houndes had she, that she fedde
> With rosted flesh, or milk and wastel-breed.
> But sore weep she if oon of hem were deed,
> Or if men smoot it with a yerde smerte.

The visitation reports are full of those little dogs and other animals; and how many readers of the Prologue know that the smale houndes, like the fair forehead and the brooch of gold full sheen, were strictly against the rules? For the bishops regarded pets as bad for discipline, and century after century they tried to turn the animals out of the convents, without the slightest success. The nuns just waited till the bishop had gone and then whistled their dogs back again. Dogs were easily the favourite pets, though monkeys, squirrels, rabþits, birds and (very rarely) cats were also kept. One archbishop had to forbid an abbess whom he visited to keep *monkeys and a number of dogs* in her own chamber and charged her at the same time with stinting her nuns in food; one can guess what became of the roasted flesh or milk and wastel-breed! It was a common medieval practice to bring animals into church, where ladies often attended service with dog in lap and men with hawk on wrist; just as the highland farmer brings his collie with him today. This happened in the nunneries too. Sometimes it was the lay-boarders in the convents who brought their pets with them; there is a pathetic complaint by the nuns of one house 'that Lady Audley, who boards there, has a great abundance of dogs, insomuch that whenever she comes to church there follow her twelve dogs, who make a great uproar in church, hindering the nuns in their psalmody and the nuns thereby are terrified!'[17] But often enough the nuns themselves transgressed. Injunctions against bringing pet dogs into choir occur in several visitation reports, the most amusing instance being contained in those sent to Romsey Abbey by William of Wykeham in 1387, just about the same year that Chaucer was writing the *Canterbury Tales*: 'Item,' runs the injunction, 'whereas we have convinced ourselves by clear proofs that some of the nuns of your house bring with them to church birds, rabbits, hounds and such like frivolous things, whereunto they give more heed than to the offices of the church, with frequent hindrance to their own psalmody and to that of their fellow nuns and to the grievous peril of their souls – therefore we strictly forbid you all and several, in virtue of the obedience due to us that ye presume henceforward to bring to church no birds, hounds, rabbits or other frivolous things that promote indiscipline. . . . Item, whereas through hunting dogs and other hounds abiding within your monastic precincts, the alms that should be given to the poor are devoured and the church and cloister . . . are foully defiled . . . and whereas, through their inordinate noise divine service is frequently troubled – therefore we strictly command and enjoin you, Lady Abbess, that you remove the dogs altogether and that you suffer them never henceforth, nor any other such hounds, to abide within the precincts of your nunnery.'[18] But it was useless for any bishop to order Madame Eglentyne to give up her dogs, she could not even be parted from them on a pilgrimage, though they must have been a great nuisance in the inns, especially as she was so fussy about their food.

For Chaucer's prioress, we must admit, was rather a worldly lady, though her pretty clothes and little dogs were harmless enough on modern standards and one's sympathies are all against the bishops. She probably became more worldly as time went on, because she had so many opportunities for social intercourse. Not only had she to entertain visitors in the convent, but often the business of the house took her away upon journeys and these offered many opportunities for hobnobbing with her neighbours. Sometimes she had to go to London to see after a law-suit and that was a great excursion with another nun, or perhaps two, and a priest and several yeomen to look after her. Sometimes she had to go and see the bishop, to get permission to take in some little schoolgirls. Sometimes she went to the funeral of a great man, whom her father knew and who left her twenty shillings and a silver cup in his will. Sometimes she went to the wedding of one of her sisters, or to be godmother to their babies; though the bishops did not like these worldly ties, or the dances and merry-makings which accompanied weddings and christenings. Indeed her nuns occasionally complained about her journeys and said that though she pretended it was all on the business of the house, they had their doubts; and would the bishop please just look into it. At one nunnery we find the nuns complaining that their house is £20 in debt 'and this principally owing to the costly expenses of the prioress, because she frequently rides abroad and pretends that she does so on the common business of the house although it is not so, with a train of attendants much too large and tarries too long abroad and she feasts sumptuously, both when abroad and at home and she is very choice in her dress, so that the fur trimmings of her mantle are worth 100s'![19]

As a matter of fact there was nothing of which the church disapproved more than this habit, shared by monks and nuns, of wandering about outside their cloisters; moralists considered that intercourse with the world was at the root of all the evil which crept into the monastic system. The orthodox saying was that a monk out of his cloister was like a fish out of water; and it will be remembered that Chaucer's monk thought the text not worth an oyster. Indeed most of the monks managed to swim very well in the air, and the nuns too persisted in taking every sort of excuse for wandering in the world. Right through the Middle Ages council after council, bishop after bishop, reformer after reformer, tried in vain to keep them shut up. The greatest attempt of all began in

1300, when the pope published a Bull ordering that nuns should never, save in very exceptional circumstances, leave their convents and that no secular person should be allowed to go in and visit them, without a special licence and a good reason. This will make the modern reader pity the poor nuns, but there is no need, for nobody ever succeeded in putting it into force for more than five minutes, though the bishops spent over two centuries in trying to do so and were still trying in vain when King Henry VIII dissolved the nunneries and turned all the nuns out into the world for ever, whether they liked it or not. At one nunnery in the Lincoln diocese, when the bishop came and deposited a copy of the Bull in the house and ordered the nuns to obey it, they ran after him to the gate when he was riding away and threw the Bull at his head, screaming that they would never observe it.[20] The more practical bishops indeed, soon stopped trying to enforce the Bull as it stood and contented themselves with ordering that nuns were not to go out or pay visits too often, or without a companion, or without licence, or without a good reason. But even in this they were not very successful, because the nuns were most prolific in excellent reasons why they should go out. Sometimes they said that their parents were ill; and then they would go away to smooth the pillow of the sick. Sometimes they said that they had to go to market to buy herrings. Sometimes they said that they had to go to confession at a monastery. Sometimes it is really difficult to imagine *what* they said. What are we to think, for instance, of that giddy nun 'who on Monday night did pass the night with the Austin friars at Northampton and did dance and play the lute with them in the same place until midnight, and on the night following she passed the night with the Friars' preachers at Northampton, luting and dancing in like manner'?[21] Chaucer told us how the friar loved harping and how his eyes twinkled like stars in his head when he sang, but failed perhaps to observe that he had lured Madame Eglentyne into a dance.

It is indeed difficult to see what 'legitimate' excuses the nuns can have made for all their wandering about in the streets and the fields and in and out of people's houses, and it is sorely to be feared that either they were too much of a handful for Madame Eglentyne, or else she winked at their doings. For somehow or other one suspects that she had no great opinion of bishops. After all Chaucer would never have met her, if she had not managed to circumvent her own, since if there was one excuse for wandering of which the bishops thoroughly disapproved, it was precisely the excuse of pilgrimages. Madame Eglentyne was not quite as simple and coy as she looked. How many of the literary critics, who chuckle over her, know that she never ought to have got into the Prologue at all? The Church was quite clear in its mind that pilgrimages for nuns were to be discouraged. As early as 791 a council had forbidden the practice and in 1195 another at York decreed, 'In order that the opportunity of wandering may be taken from nuns we forbid them to take the path of pilgrimage.' In 1318 an archbishop of York strictly forbade the nuns of one convent to leave their house 'by reason of any vow of pilgrimage which they might have taken. If any had taken such vows she was to say as many psalters as it would have taken days to perform the pilgrimage so rashly vowed.'[22] One has a melancholy vision of poor Madame Eglentyne saying psalters interminably through her tretys nose, instead of jogging along so gaily with her motley companions and telling so prettily her tale of little St Hugh. Such prohibitions might be multiplied from medieval records; and indeed it is unnecessary to go further than Chaucer to understand why it was that bishops offered such strenuous opposition to pilgrimages for nuns; one has only to remember some of the folk, in whose company the prioress travelled and some of the tales they told. If one could only be certain, for instance, that she rode all the time with her nun and her priests, or at least between the Knight and the poor Parson of a town! But there were also the Miller and the Summoner and (worst of all) that cheerful and engaging sinner, the Wife of Bath. It is really quite disturbing to think what additional details the Wife of Bath may have given the prioress about her five husbands.

This then was Chaucer's prioress in real life, for the poet who drew her was one of the most wonderful observers in the whole of English literature. We may wade through hundreds of visitation reports and injunctions and everywhere the grey eyes of his prioress will twinkle at us out of their pages, and in the end we must always go to Chaucer for her picture, to sum up everything that historical records have taught us. As the bishop found her, so he saw her, aristocratic, tender-hearted, worldly, taking pains to 'countrefete chere of court'; liking pretty clothes and little dogs; a lady of importance, attended by a nun and three priests; spoken to with respect by the none too mealy-mouthed host – no 'by Corpus Dominus' or 'cokkes bones' or 'tel on a devel wey' for her, but 'cometh neer, my lady prioress,' and

> My lady Prioresse, by your leve
> If that I wiste I sholde yow nat greve,
> I wolde demen that ye tellen sholde
> A tale next, if so were that ye wolde.
> Now wol ye vouche-sauf, my lady dere?

He talks to no one else like that, save perhaps to the knight. Was she religious? Perhaps; but save for her singing the divine service and for her lovely address to the Virgin, at the beginning of her tale, Chaucer can find but little to say on the point;

> But for speken of hir conscience (he says)
> She was so charitable and so pitous,

and then, as we are waiting to hear of her almsgiving to the poor – that she would weep over a mouse in a trap, or a beaten puppy, says Chaucer. A good ruler of her house? again, doubtless. But when Chaucer met her the house was ruling itself somewhere at the 'shire's ende'. The world was full of fish out of water in the fourteenth century, and, by sëynt Loy, said Madame Eglentyne, swearing her greatest oath, like Chaucer's monk, she held that famous text not worth an oyster. So we take our leave of her, characteristically on the road to Canterbury.

CHAPTER V

The Ménagier's Wife

A PARIS HOUSEWIFE IN THE FOURTEENTH CENTURY

The sphere of woman is the home.

— Homo Sapiens

THE MEN OF the middle, as indeed of all ages, including our own, were very fond of writing books of deportment telling women how they ought to behave in all the circumstances of their existence, but more particularly in their relations with their husbands. Many of these books have survived, and among them one which is of particular interest, because of the robust good sense of its writer and the intimate and lively picture which it gives of a bourgeois home. Most books of deportment were written, so to speak, in the air, for women in general, but this was written by a particular husband for a particular wife, and thus is drawn from life and full of detail, showing throughout an individuality which its compeers too often lack. If a parallel be sought to it, it is perhaps to be found not in any other medieval treatise but in those passages of Xenophon's *Economist*, in which Isomachus describes to Socrates the training of a perfect Greek wife.

The Ménagier de Paris (the Householder or Goodman of Paris, as we might say) wrote this book for the instruction of his young wife between 1392 and 1394. He was a wealthy man, not without learning and of great experience in affairs, obviously a member of that solid and enlightened *haute bourgeoisie*, upon which the French monarchy was coming to lean with ever-increasing confidence. When he wrote he must have been approaching old age, and he was certainly over sixty, but he had recently married a young wife of higher birth than himself, an orphan from a different province. He speaks several times of her 'very great youth', and kept a sort of duenna-housekeeper with her to help and direct her in the management of his house; and indeed, like the wife of Isomachus, she was only fifteen years old when he married her. Modern opinion is shocked by a discrepancy in age between husband and wife, with which the Middle Ages, a time of *mariages de convenance*, was more familiar. 'Seldom,' the Ménagier says, 'will you see ever so old a man who will not marry a young woman.' Yet his attitude towards his young wife shows us that there may have been compensations, even in a marriage between May and January. Time after time in his book there sounds the note of a tenderness which is paternal rather than marital, a sympathetic understanding of the feelings of a wedded child, which a younger man might not have compassed. Over all the matter-of-fact counsels there seems to hang something of the mellow sadness of an autumn evening, when beauty and death go ever hand in hand. It was his wife's function to make comfortable his declining years; but it was his to make the task easy for her. He constantly repeats the assurance that he does not ask of her an overweening respect, or a service too humble or too hard, for such is not due to him; he desires only such care as his neighbours and kinswomen take of their husbands, 'for to me belongeth none save the common service, or less'.

In his Prologue, addressed to her, he gives a charming picture of the scene which led him to write his book: 'You, being of the age of fifteen years and in the week that you and I were wed, did pray me that I would please to be indulgent to your youth and to your small and ignorant service mewards, until that you should have seen and learned more, to the hastening whereof you did promise me to set all care and diligence, ... praying me humbly, in our bed as I remember, that for the love of God I would not correct you harshly before strangers nor before our own folk, 'but that I would correct you each night or from day to day in our chamber and show you the unseemly or foolish things done in the day or days past, and chastise you, if it pleased me, and then you would not fail to amend yourself according to my teaching and correction, and would do all in your power according to my will, as you said.

And I thought well of, and praise and thank you for, what you said to me and I have often remembered it since. And know, dear sister,* that all that I know you have done since we were wed up to this day, and all that you shall do hereafter with good intent has been and is good and well hath pleased, pleases and shall please me. For your youth excuses you from being very wise, and will still excuse you in everything that you do with good intent to please me. And know that it doth not displease, but rather pleases me that you should have roses to grow and violets to care for and that you should make chaplets and dance and sing, and I would well that you should so continue among our friends and those of our estate, and it is but right and seemly thus to pass the time of your feminine youth, provided that you desire and offer not to go to the feasts and dances of too great lords, for that is not seemly for you, nor suitable to your estate nor mine.'[1]

Meanwhile he has not forgotten her request that he would teach and correct her in private, and so he writes a little book (but it was a big book before he had finished) to show her how to comport herself; for he is sorry for this child, who has for long had neither father nor mother, and who is far from kinswomen who might counsel her, having 'me only' he says, 'for whom you have been taken from your kinsfolk and from the land of your birth.' He has often deliberated the matter and now here is 'an easy general introduction' to the whole art of being a wife, a housewife, and a perfect lady. One characteristic reason, apart from his desire to help her and to be comfortable himself (for he was set in his ways), he gives for his trouble and recurs to from time to time, surely the strangest ever given by a husband for instructing his wife. He is old, he says, and must die before her, and it is positively essential that she should do him credit with her second husband. What a reflection upon him if she accompanied his successor to Mass with the collar of her *cotte* crumpled, or if she knew not how to keep fleas from the blankets, or how to order a supper for twelve in Lent! It is characteristic of the Ménagier's reasonableness and solid sense that he regards his young wife's second marriage with equanimity. One of his sections is headed, 'That you should be loving to your husband

* He addresses her throughout as 'sister', a term of affectionate respect.

(whether myself or another), by the example of Sarah, Rebecca, Rachel.' How different from those husbands (dog-in-the-manger, or anxious for the future of their children under a possibly harsh stepfather) whose wills so often reveal them trying to bind their wives to perpetual celibacy after their deaths, such husbands as William, Earl of Pembroke, who died in 1469, admonishing his lady: 'And wyfe, ye remember your promise to me to take the ordere of wydowhood, as ye may be the better mastre of your owne to performe my wylle.'

The plan of the book 'in three sections, containing nineteen principal articles', is most exhaustive. The first section deals with religious and moral duties. In the words of the Ménagier, 'the first section is necessary to gain for you the love of God and the salvation of your soul, and also to win for you the love of your husband and to give you in this world that peace which ought to be had in marriage. And because these two things, to wit the salvation of your soul and the comfort of your husband, are the two things most chiefly necessary, therefore are they here placed first.' Then follows a series of articles telling the lady how to say her morning prayer when she rises, how to bear herself at Mass, and in what form to make her confession to the priest, together with a long and some-what alarming discursus upon the seven deadly sins, which it assuredly never entered into her sleek little head to commit, and another, on the corresponding virtues.[2] But the greater part of the section deals with the all-important subject of the wife's duty to her husband. She is to be loving, humble, obedient, careful and thought-ful for his person, silent regarding his secrets, and patient if he be foolish and allow his heart to stray towards other women. The whole section is illustrated by a series of stories (known as *exempla* in the Middle Ages), culled from the Bible, from the common stock of anecdotes possessed by jongleur and preacher alike, and (most interesting of all) from the Ménagier's own experience. Among the Ménagier's longer illustrations is the favourite but intolerably dull moral tale of Melibeu and Prudence, by Albertano of Brescia, translated into French by Renault de Louens, whose version the Ménagier copied, and adapted by Jean de Meung in the *Roman de la Rose*, from which in turn Chaucer took it to tell to the Canterbury

Pilgrims. Here also are to be found Petrarch's famous tale of patient Griselda, which Chaucer also took and gave a wider fame, and a long poem written in 1342 by Jean Bruyant, a notary of the Châtelet at Paris, and called 'The Way of Poverty and Wealth', inculcating diligence and prudence.[3]

The second section of the book deals with household management and is far the most interesting. The range of the Ménagier's knowledge leaves the reader gasping. The man is a perfect Mrs Beeton! The section comprises a detailed treatise on gardening and another on the principles which should govern the engagement of servants and the method by which they should be managed when hired; the modern problem of servants who leave does not seem to have presented itself to him. There are instructions how to mend, air, and clean dresses and furs, get out grease spots, catch fleas and keep flies out of the bedroom, look after wine, and superintend the management of a farm.

At one point he breaks off, addressing his wife thus: 'Here will I leave you to rest or to play and will speak no more to you; and while you disport yourself elsewhere I will speak to Master John, the Steward, who looks after our possessions, so that if there is anything wrong with any of our horses, whether for the plough or for riding, or if it is necessary to buy or exchange a horse, he may know a little of that it behoves him to know in this matter.' There follow several pages of wise advice as to the good points of horses, how to examine them and to find their ages and defects under the eye of the horse dealer, the practical 'tips' of a man who evidently knew and loved his horses, together with advice upon the treatment of their various diseases. Among the various recipes which the Ménagier gives to this intent are two charms; for instance, 'when a horse has glanders, you must say to him these three words, with three paternosters: ✠ *abgla*, ✠ *abgly*, ✠ *alphard*, ✠ *asy*, ✠ *pater noster*, etc.'[4]

Last, but not least, there is a magnificent cookery book, arranged in the form sacred to cookery books from that day to this, beginning with a list of specimen menus for dinners and suppers, hot or cold, fast or feast, summer or winter, giving hints on the choice of meat, poultry, and spices, and ending with a long series of recipes for all manner of soups, stews, sauces, and other viands, with an excursus on invalid's cookery!

The third section of the book was intended by the Ménagier to contain three parts: first of all, a number of parlour games for indoor amusement; secondly, a treatise on hawking, the favourite outdoor amusement of ladies; and thirdly, a list of amusing riddles and games of an arithmetical kind ('concerning counting and numbering, subtle to find out or guess'), presumably of the nature of our old friend, 'If a herring and a half cost three ha'pence.' Unfortunately, the Ménagier seems never to have finished the book, and of this section only the treatise on hawking has survived. It is a great pity, for we have several such treatises, and how interesting an account of indoor games and riddles might have been we may guess from a passage in the Ménagier's version of the story of Lucrece, when he describes the Roman ladies 'some gossiping, others playing at *bric*, others at *qui féry*, others at *pince merille*, others at cards or other games of pleasure with their neighbours; others, who had supped together, were singing songs and telling fables and stories and wagers; others were in the street with their neighbours, playing at blind man's buff or at *bric* and at several other games of the kind.'[5] In those days, before the invention of printing had made books plentiful, medieval ladies were largely dependent for amusement upon telling and listening to stories, asking riddles, and playing games, which we have long ago banished to the nursery; and a plentiful repertoire of such amusements was very desirable in a hostess. The Ménagier was clearly anxious that his wife should shine in the amenities as well as in the duties of social life.

Such was the monumental work which the Ménagier de Paris was able to present to his awed but admiring wife; and though it has been sadly neglected by historians it deserves to be well known, for it gives us a picture of a medieval housewife which it would be hard indeed to surpass. There is hardly a side of her daily life upon which it does not touch, and we may now with advantage look more closely upon her, and see in turn the perfect lady, whose deportment and manners do credit to her breeding; the perfect wife, whose submission to her husband is only equalled by her skill in ministering to his ease; the perfect mistress, whose servants love her and run her house like clockwork; and the perfect housewife, the Mrs Beeton of the fifteenth century.

The Ménagier's views on deportment are incongruously sandwiched into his section on spiritual duties, under the general headings of getting up in the morning and going to church. His ideas on the subject of clothes are very clearly defined: a sweet disorder in the dress was in no way to his taste:

Know, dear sister, that if you wish to follow my advice you will have great care and regard for what you and I can afford to do, according to our estate. Have a care that you be honestly clad, without new devices and without too much or too little frippery. And before you leave your chamber and house, take care first that the collar of your shift, and of your *blanchet, cotte* and *surcotte*, do not hang out one over the other, as happens with certain drunken, foolish or witless women, who have no care for their honour, nor for the honesty of their estate or of their husbands, and who walk with roving eyes and head horribly reared up like a lion (*la teste espoventablement levée comme un lyon!*), their hair straggling out of their wimples, and the collars of their shifts and *cottes* crumpled the one upon the other, and who walk mannishly and bear themselves uncouthly before folk without shame. And if one speaks to them about it, they excuse themselves on the ground of their industry and humility, saying that they are so diligent, hardworking, and humble that they care not for themselves. But they lie; they care so much for themselves that if they were in an honourable company, never would they be willing that men should wait less upon them than upon the wiser ladies of like lineage with themselves, nor that they should have fewer salutations, bows, reverences and speech than the rest, but rather they desire more. And they are unworthy of it, for they know not how to maintain their own honourable fame, nay, nor the fame of their husbands and of their lineage, which they bring to shame. Therefore, fair sister, have a care that your hair, wimple, kerchief and hood and all the rest of your attire be well arranged and decently ordered, that none who see you can laugh or mock at you, but that all the others may find in you an example of fair and simple and decent array. . . . When you go to town or to church go suitably accompanied by honourable women according to your estate, and flee suspicious company, never allowing any ill famed woman to be seen in your presence. And as you go bear your head upright and your eyelids low and without fluttering, and look straight in front of you about four rods ahead, without looking round at any man or woman to the right or to the left, nor looking up, nor glancing from place to place, nor stopping to speak to anyone on the road.[6]

Such was the model of female deportment in the Middle Ages.

Let us pass from the lady to the wife. On the attitude of wife to husband the Ménagier's ideas are much the same as those of the rest of his age. They may be summed up as submission, obedience, and constant attention. She must be buxom at bed and at board, even in circumstances when buxomness hides a heavy heart. The good sense of the burgess does not prevent him from likening the wife's love for her husband to the fidelity of domestic animals towards their masters: 'Of the domestic animals you see how a greyhound, or a mastiff, or a little dog, whether on the road, or at table, or in bed, always keeps near to the person from whom he takes his food, and leaves and is shy and fierce with all others; and if the dog is afar off, he always has his heart and his eye upon his master; even if his master whip him and throw stones at him, the dog follows, wagging his tail and lying down before his master, seeks to mollify him, and through rivers, through woods, through thieves and through battles follows him. . . . Wherefore for a better and stronger reason women, to whom God has given natural sense and who are reasonable, ought to have a perfect and solemn love for their husbands; and so I pray you to be very loving and privy with your husband who shall be.'[7] Patience is an essential quality in wives, and, however sorely tried they must never complain. The Ménagier tells three stories to illustrate how a wife should bear herself in order to win back the love of an unfaithful husband. One of these is the famous tale of Griselda, but the two others are drawn (so he says) from his own experience. In the first of these he tells of the wife of a famous *avocat* in the *parlement* of Paris, who saw to the nurture and marriage of her husband's illegitimate daughter; 'nor did he ever perceive it by one reproach, or one angry or ugly word.' The second is the charmingly told story of how John Quentin's wife won back her husband's heart from the poor spinner of wool to whom it had strayed.[8] All seem to show that the Ménagier's simile of the little dog was selected with care, for the medieval wife, like the dog, was expected to lick the hand that smote her. Nevertheless, while subscribing to all the usual standards of his age, the Ménagier's robust sense, his hold upon the realities of life, kept him from pushing them too far. The comment of another realist, Chaucer, on the tale of Patient Griselda will be remembered.

> Grisilde is deed and eek hire pacience,
> And bothe at ones buryed in Ytaille;
> For which I crie in open audience,
> No wedded man so hardy be t'assaille
> His wyves pacience in hope to fynde
> Grisildes, for in certein he shal faille!
>
> O noble wyves, ful of heigh prudence,
> Lat noon humylitee youre tonge naill,
> Ne lat no clerk have cause or diligence
> To write of yow a storie of swich mervaille
> As of Grisildis pacient and kynde,
> Lest Chichivache* yow swelwe in hire entraille! . . .

His creation of the Wife of Bath was an even more pointed commentary. Here is what the Ménagier has to say to his young wife on the same subject:

And I, who have put [the tale of Griselda] here only to teach you, have not put it here to apply it to you, for I am not worthy thereof, and I am not a marquis and I have not taken you as a beggar, nor am I so foolish, so conceited or so lacking in sense that I know not that 'tis not for me to assault nor to assay you thus, nor in like manner. God keep me from trying you thus under colour of false simulations. . . . And forgive me that the story speaks (in my opinion) of too great cruelty and beyond reason. And know that it never befel so, but thus the tale runs and I may nor correct nor alter it, for a wiser than I hath made it. And it is my desire that since others have read it you also may know and be able to talk about everything even as other folk do.[9]

Moreover, in spite of the ideal of submission which he sets before his wife, the Ménagier has some charming words to say about love – with a sigh, perhaps, for his own advanced though not crabbed age,

* Chichevache, the lean cow who fed on patient wives, while her mate Bicorne grew fat on humble husbands (A. W. Pollard).

and a glance at that younger husband of the future who shall one day enjoy his little bride.

In God's name (he says) I believe that when two good and honourable people are wed, all other loves are put far off, destroyed and forgotten, save only the love of each for the other. And meseems that when they are in each other's presence, they look upon each other more than upon the others, they clasp and hold each other and they do not willingly speak or make sign save to each other. And when they are separated, they think of each other and say in their hearts, 'When I see him I shall do thus and thus to him, or say this to him, I shall beseech him concerning this or that.' And all their special pleasure, their chief desire and their perfect joy is to do pleasure and obedience one to the other, if they love one another.[10]

The greater part of the Ménagier's book is concerned, however, not with the theoretical niceties of wifely submission, but with his creature comforts. His instructions as to how to make a husband comfortable positively palpitate with life; and at the same time there is something indescribably homely and touching about them; they tell more about the real life of a burgess's wife than a hundred tales of Patient Griselda or of Jehanne la Quentine. Consider this picture (how typical a product of the masculine imagination!) of the stout bread-winner, buffeted about in all weathers and amid all discomforts, nobly pursuing the task of earning his living, and fortified by the recollection of a domesticated little wife, darning his stockings at home by the fire, and prepared to lavish her attentions on the weary hero in the evening. The passage is an excellent example of the Ménagier's vivid and simple style, and of the use of incidents drawn from everyday life to illustrate his thesis, which is one of the chief charms of the book.

Fair sister, if you have another husband after me, know that you should think much of his comfort, for after a woman has lost her first husband she commonly finds it difficult to find another according to her estate, and she remains lonely and disconsolate for a long time;* and more so still, if she lose the second. Wherefore cherish the person of your husband carefully, and, I pray you, keep him in clean linen, for 'tis your business. And because the care of outside affairs lieth with men, so must a husband take heed, and go and come and journey hither and thither, in rain and wind,

---

* This seems to be contrary to experience.

in snow and hail, now drenched, now dry, now sweating, now shivering, ill-fed, ill-lodged, ill-warmed and ill-bedded; and nothing harms him, because he is upheld by the hope that he has of his wife's care of him on his return, and of the ease, the joys and the pleasures which she will do to him, or cause to be done to him in her presence; to have his shoes removed before a good fire, his feet washed and to have fresh shoes and stockings, to be given good food and drink, to be well served and well looked after, well bedded in white sheets and night-caps, well covered with good furs, and assuaged with other joys and amusements, privities, loves, and secrets, concerning which I am silent; and on the next day fresh shirts and garments. Certes, fair sister, such service maketh a man love and desire to return to his home and to see his goodwife and to be distant with other women.

And therefore I counsel you to make such cheer to your husband at all his comings and goings and to persevere therein; and also to be peaceable with him and remember the rustic proverb, which saith that there be three things which drive the goodman from home, to wit, a dripping roof, a smoking chimney and a scolding woman.[11] Wherefore, fair sister, I pray you that in order to keep yourself in love and good favour with your husband you be unto him gentle, amiable and debonair. Do unto him what the good simple women of our country say has been done unto their sons, when the lads have set their love elsewhere and their mothers cannot wean them from it. It is certain that when fathers and mothers be dead, and stepfathers and stepmothers argue with their stepsons, and scold them and repulse them, and take not thought for their sleeping, nor for their food and drink, their hose and their shirts and all their other needs and affairs, and the same children find elsewhere a good home and good counsel from some other woman, who receives them and takes thought to warm them with some poor gruel with her and to give them a bed and keep them tidy, mending their hosen, breeches, shirts, and other garments, then those lads cleave to her and desire to be with her, and to sleep warm between her breasts, and are altogether estranged from their mothers and fathers, who before took no heed of them, and now want to get them back and have them again. But it may not be, for these children hold more dear the company of strangers, who think and care for them, than that of their kinsfolk, who have no care of them. Then the parents lament and weep and say that these same women have bewitched their children and that they are spellbound and cannot leave, but are never easy save when they are with their enchantresses. But whatever may be said of it, it is no witchcraft, but it by reason of the love, the care, the intimacies, joys and pleasures, which these women do in all ways unto the lads, and on my soul there is no other enchantment. . . . Wherefore, dear sister, I pray you thus to bewitch and bewitch again your husband, and beware of dripping roof and smoking fire, and scold him not, but be unto him gentle and amiable and peaceable. Be careful that in winter he has good fire without smoke, and let him rest well and be well covered between your breasts and thus bewitch him. . . . And thus you shall preserve and guard him from all discomforts and give him all the ease that you can, and serve him and cause him to be well served in your house; and you shall look to him for outside things, for if he be a good man he will take even more care and trouble over them than you wish, and by doing as I have said, you will make him always miss you and have his heart with you and with your loving service, and he will shun all other houses, all other women, all other services and households; all will be naught to him save you alone, if you think of him as aforesaid. . . . And so on the road, husbands will think of their wives, and no trouble will be a burden to them for the hope and love they will have of their wives, whom they will long to see, even as poor hermits, penitents and fasting monks long to see the face of Christ Jesus; and husbands served thus will never desire to abide elsewhere or in other company but will withhold, withdraw and abstain themselves there-from; all the rest will seem to them but a bed of stones compared with their home.[12]

Enough has perhaps been quoted to show the Ménagier's idea of a perfect wife; his idea of the perfect housewife is contained in a mass of instructions which make excellently entertaining reading. So modern in tone is his section on the management of servants, both in his account of their ways and in his advice upon dealing with them, that one often rubs one's eyes to be sure that what one is reading is really a book written over five centuries ago by an old burgess of Paris. The Ménagier evidently had a fairly large household, and he probably owned a country as well as a town house, for he speaks several times of overseeing the farm-hands 'when you are in the village'. To assist his wife in superintending this large staff he has a *maître d'hôtel*, called Master John the Steward (*le despensier*), and a duenna, half housekeeper and half chaperon, for her young mistress, called Dame Agnes *la béguine*,* and a bailiff or

---

* The Béguines were a sort of religious order, or, more correctly, a lay sisterhood, standing half-way between the lay and the monastic life, and somewhat analogous to the Franciscan Tertiaries, or Third Order.

foreman to look after the farm. The Ménagier divides his servants and workmen into three classes – first, those engaged by the day or by the season for special work, such as porters and carriers, reapers, winnowers, coopers, and so on; secondly, those engaged on piece-work, such as tailors, furriers, bakers, and shoemakers, hired by medieval households of some wealth to make what was needed from raw material purchased at fairs or in the shops of the city; and thirdly, the ordinary domestic servants, who were hired by the year and lived in their master's house; 'and of all these,' he says, 'there is none who does not gladly seek work and a master'.

He gives an amusing account, evidently based upon bitter experience, of the wiles of the hired workman. He says that they are commonly lazy, rough, quick at 'answering back', arrogant (except on payday) and ready to break into insults if unsatisfied with their pay. He warns his wife to bid Master John always to take the peaceable ones and always to bargain with them beforehand as to the pay for which they will do the work.

For know that most often they do not want to bargain, but they want to get to work without any bargain having been made and they say gently, 'Milord, it is nothing – there is no need – you will pay me well and I shall be content with what you think fit.' And if Master John take them thus, when the work is finished they will say, 'Sir, there was more to do than I thought, there was this and that to do, and here and there,' and they will not take what is given them and will break out into shouting and angry words . . . and will spread abroad evil report concerning you, which is worst of all.[13]

We know from the various ordinances fixing wages from the time of the Black Death onwards, that labour troubles were acute in France as well as in England at the end of the fourteenth century; and the Ménagier's advice throws an interesting sidelight on the situation.

It is, however, in his observations upon the engagement and management of maidservants that the wisdom of the serpent is most apparent. Incidentally he gives an account of how servants were hired in fourteenth-century Paris, which shows that the registry office and the character are by no means modern phenomena. There

were *recommanderesses* – women holding what we should call
registry offices – in Paris at this time, and an ordinance of 1351
(fixing wages after the Black Death) allows them to take 1*s*. 6*d*.
for placing a chambermaid and 2*s*. for a nurse. A servant maid's
wage at this time was 30*s*. a year and her shoes. The Ménagier
counsels his wife thus on the delicate subject of interviewing and
engaging her domestic chambermaids and serving men:

Know, dear sister (he says), that in order that they may obey you better
and fear the more to anger you, I leave you the rule and authority to have
them chosen by Dame Agnes the béguine, or by whichever other of your
women you please, to receive them into our service, to hire them at your
pleasure, to pay and keep them in our service as you please, and to dismiss
them when you will. Nathless you should privily speak to me about it and
act according to my advice, because you are too young and might be deceived by your own people. And know that of those chambermaids who
are out of a place, many there be who offer themselves and clamour and
seek urgently for masters and mistresses; and of these take none until
you first know where their last place was, and send some of your people
to get their character, to wit whether they talked or drank too much,
how long they were in the place, what work they have been accustomed
to doing and can do, whether they have homes or friends in the town,
from what sort of people and what part of the country they come, how
long they were there and why they left; and by their work in the past
you shall find out what hope or expectation you may have of their work
in the future. And know that oft-times such women from distant parts of
the country have been blamed for some fault in their own part of the
world and that is what brings them into service at a distance. . . .

And if you find from the report of her master and mistress, neighbours
and others that a girl is what you need, find out from her, and cause Master
John to register in his account book, the day on which you engage her,
her name and those of her father, mother and any of her kinsfolk, the
place where they live and her birthplace and her references. For servants
will be more afraid to do wrong if they know that you are recording all
these things and that if they leave you without permission, or are guilty
of any offence, you will write and complain to the justice of their country
or to their friends. And not withstanding bear in mind the saying of the
philosopher called Bertrand the Old, who says that if you engage a maid or
man of high and proud answers, you shall know that when she leaves she
will miscall you if she can; and if, on the contrary, she be flattering and

full of blandishments, trust her not, for she is in league with someone else to trick you; but if she blushes and is silent and shamefast when you correct her, love her as your daughter.[14]

The Ménagier's instructions as to how to look after servants when they have been engaged are equally practical. Good order is to be maintained, quarrels and bad language[15] prevented, and morals guarded. Each is to have his or her work assigned and to do it promptly. 'If you order them to do something now and these your servants answer "There is plenty of time, it shall be done," or "It shall be done tomorrow," hold it as forgotten, it must all be begun again, it is as nought. And also when you give a general order to every one, each will wait for the other to do it, and it is the same.' Not only is the work of the servants to be carefully superintended by the mistress and by Dame Agnes, 'who is with you', the Ménagier tells his wife, 'in order to teach you wise and ripe behaviour and to serve and instruct you and to whom in particular I give the charge of this matter', but she is to show herself careful and benevolent in looking after their health and happiness. At the proper hour she is to cause them to sit down before a hearty meal of one sort of meat, avoiding rich viands, and one kind of drink, which must be nourishing but not intoxicating – 'the cup that cheers but not inebriates'; probably in this case the light ale which was the habitual drink of the Middle Ages. She is to admonish them to eat and drink their fill, but

as soon as they begin to tell stories, or to argue, or to lean on their elbows, order the béguine to make them rise and take away their table, for the common folk have a saying 'when a varlet holds forth at table and a horse grazes in the ditch, it is time to take them away, for they have had their fill.'

In the evening, after their afternoon's work, they are to have another hearty meal, and then in winter time they may warm themselves at the fire and take their ease. Then she is to lock up the house and pack them all off to bed.

And arrange first that each have beside his bed a candlestick in which to put his candle, and have them wisely taught to extinguish it with the mouth or hand before getting into bed and by no means with their shirts. And also have them admonished and taught each and all, that they must begin again the next day and that they must rise in the morning and each set to upon his own work.

The Ménagier further advises his wife that chambermaids of fifteen to twenty years of age are foolish girls who do not know the world, and that she should always cause them to sleep near her in an antechamber, or a room without a skylight or a low window looking on to the street, and should make them get up and go to bed at the same time as herself. 'And you yourself,' he adds, 'who, if God please, will be wise by this time, must keep them near to you.' Moreover, if any of her servants fall ill, 'do you yourself, laying aside all other cares, very lovingly and charitably care for him or her, and visit him and study diligently how to bring about his cure'.[16]

But it is perhaps in his capacity as Mrs Beeton that the Ménagier is most amusing. His infinite variety of household knowledge is shown in the incidental recipes which he gives when he is describing the measures which a wife must take for her lord's comfort, and the work of the servants. There are elaborate instructions concerning the costly medieval garments, worn year after year for a lifetime and often bequeathed in their owner's will, instructions for cleaning dresses and furs and for preserving them from moths, and instructions for removing stains and grease spots. The Ménagier gives seven recipes for taking out grease spots, but he is rather sceptical about one or two of them, which he has evidently copied from a book without trying them for himself. 'To get rid of stains on a dress of silk, satin, camlet, damask cloth or another,' runs one of these, 'dip and wash the stain in verjuice and the stain will go; even if the dress be faded, it will regain its colour. *This I do not believe.*' The chief impression left, however, is that the medieval housewife was engaged in a constant warfare against fleas. One of the Ménagier's infallible rules for keeping a husband happy at home is to give him a good fire in the winter and keep his bed free from fleas in the summer. He gives six recipes for getting rid of such small livestock, which must indeed have been a very common trial to our forefathers:

In summer take heed that there be no fleas in your chamber nor in your bed, which you may do in six ways, as I have heard tell. For I have heard from several persons that if the room be scattered with alder leaves the fleas will get caught therein. Item, I have heard tell that if you have at night one or two trenchers of bread covered with birdlime or turpentine and put about the room with a lighted candle set in the midst of each trencher, they will come and get stuck thereto. Another way which I have found and which is true: take a rough cloth and spread it about your room and over your bed and all the fleas who may hop on to it will be caught, so that you can carry them out with the cloth wheresoever you will. Item, sheepskins. Item, I have seen blankets placed on the straw and on the bed and when the black fleas jumped upon them they were the sooner found and killed upon the white. But the best way is to guard oneself against those which are within the coverlets and furs and the stuff of the dresses wherewith one is covered. For know that I have tried this, and when the coverlets, furs or dresses in which there be fleas are folded and shut tightly up, in a chest straitly bound with straps or in a bag well tied up and pressed, or otherwise compressed so that the said fleas are without light and air and kept imprisoned, then they will perish and die at once.[17]

A similar war had also to be waged against flies and mosquitoes, which rendered summer miserable. 'I have sometimes,' says the Ménagier, 'seen in several chambers that when one has gone to bed in them, they were full of mosquitoes, which at the smoke of the breath came to sit on the faces of those who slept and sting them so that they were fain to get up and light a fire of hay to smoke them off.' Against such pests he has also six infallible recipes – to wit, a mosquito net over the bed; sprigs of fern hung up for the flies to settle on; a bowl filled with a mixture of milk and hare's gall, or with the juice of raw onions, which will kill them; a bottle containing a rag dipped in honey, or else a string dipped in honey to hang up; fly whisks to drive them away; and closing up windows with oiled cloth or parchment.[18]

The section on cookery, which contains the Ménagier's injunctions for 'feeding the brute', is the longest in the book, and gives an extraordinarily interesting picture of the domestic economy of our ancestors.[19] The Ménagier must have been brother to Chaucer's Franklin, 'Epicurus owene sone':

An housholdere, and that a greet, was he:
Seint Julian he was in his contree;
His breed, his ale, was alwey after oon;
A bettre envyned man was nowher noon.
Withoute bake mete was never his hous,
Of fissh and flessh, and that so plenteuous
It snewed in his hous of mete and drynke.
Of alle deyntees that men koude thynke.
After the sondry sesons of the yeer,
So chaunged he his mete and his soper.
Ful many a fat partrich had he in muwe
And many a breem and many a luce in stuwe.
Wo was his cook but if his sauce were
Poynaunt and sharpe and redy al his geere.
His table dormant in his hal alway
Stood redy covered al the longe day.

In this, as in all other medieval cookery books, what strikes the
modern reader is the length and elaboration of the huge feasts, with
their many courses and dishes, and the richness of the highly spiced
viands. There are black puddings and sausages, venison and beef,
eels and herrings, fresh water fish, round sea fish and flat sea fish,
common pottages unspiced, spiced pottages, meat pottages and
meatless pottages, roasts and pastries and entremets, divers sauces
boiled and unboiled, pottages and 'slops' for invalids. Some of them
sound delicious, others would be ruin to our degenerate digestions
today. Pungent sauces of vinegar, verjuice, and wine were very
much favoured, and cloves, cinnamon, galingale, pepper, and ginger
appear unexpectedly in meat dishes. Almonds were a favourite
ingredient in all sorts of dishes, as they still are in China and other
parts of the East, and they might well be used more lavishly than
they are in modern European cookery. True to his race, the
Ménagier includes recipes for cooking frogs and snails.[20] To the
modern cook some of his directions may appear somewhat vague,
as when he bids his cook to boil something for as long as it takes to
say a paternoster or a *miserere*; yet for clockless kitchens in a pious
age what clearer indication could a man give? And, after all, it is no
worse than 'cook in a hot oven', which still finds a place in many

modern cookery books which should know better. Other instructions are detailed enough. In one valuable passage he gives a list of all the meat markets of Paris, together with the number of butchers to be found in each and the number of sheep, oxen, pigs, and calves sold there every week, adding also for interest the amount of meat and poultry consumed weekly in the households of the King, the Queen and the royal children, the Dukes of Orleans, Berry, Burgundy, and Bourbon. Elsewhere also he speaks of other markets – the Pierre-au-Lait, or milk market; the Place de Grève, where they sell coal and firewood; and the Porte-de-Paris which is not only a meat market, but the best place in which to buy fish and salt and green herbs and branches to adorn your rooms.

For his wife's further guidance the Ménagier sets out a careful specification of the catering arrangements for several great feasts – to wit, a dinner given by the Abbot of Lagny to the Bishop of Paris and the members of the King's Council, the feast, comprising dinner and supper, which one Master Elias (evidently a grave and reverend *maître d'hôtel*, like Master John *le despensier* himself) made for the wedding of Jean du Chesne, upon a Tuesday in May, and the arrangements for another wedding, 'les nopces Hautecourt', in the month of September, as to which the Ménagier observes 'that because they were widower and widow they were wed very early, in their black robes and then put on others'; he was anxious that his widow should do the correct thing at that second wedding of hers. The description of the wedding feast arranged by Master Elias is particularly detailed and valuable.[21] The careful Ménagier, perhaps because he foresaw some big entertainment which he must give to the burgesses and gentlemen of Paris, perhaps because of his delightful interest in all the details of material life, has set down at length not only the menu of the dinner and supper, but a long account of the ingredients needed, their quantities and prices, and the shops or markets where they must be bought, so that the reader can see with his eyes the *maître d'hôtel* and the cooks going round from stall to stall, visiting butcher and baker, poulterer, saucemaker, vintner, wafer maker, who sold the wafers and pastries dear to medieval ladies, and spicer whose shop was heavy with the scents of the East.

The Ménagier sets down also all the esquires and varlets and waiters who will be needed to serve such a feast as this. There was the master cook, comfortably stout and walking 'high and disposedly', as Queen Elizabeth danced, brain pan stuffed full of delectable recipes, hand of ravishing lightness with pastries, eye and nose skilled to say when a capon was done to a turn, warranted without a rival

> To boille the chiknes with the marybones,
> And poudre-marchant tart and galyngale . . .
> He koude rooste and seethe and boille and frye,
> Maken martreux and wel bake a pye . . .
> For blankmanger, that made he with the beste.

He brought his varlets with him, and in Paris he took two francs for his hire 'and perquisites' (a pregnant addition). Then there were ushers, 'stout and strong', to keep the doors, and a clerk to add up the account; bread-cutters and water-carriers, two squires to serve at the dresser in the kitchen where the plates and dishes were handed out, two others at the hall dresser to give out spoons and drinking cups and pour wine for the guests, and two others in the pantry to give out the wine which their varlet kept drawing for them. There were the two *maîtres d'hôtel* to set out the silver salt-cellars for the high table, the four great gilded goblets, the four dozen hanaps, the four dozen silver spoons, the ewers and alms mugs and sweetmeat dishes, and to usher the guests to their places; a head waiter and two servitors for each table, a flower girl to make chaplets of flowers for the guests, women to see to the linen and deck the bridal bed,[22] and a washerwoman. The floors were strewn with violets and green herbs and the rooms decked with branches of May (all bought in the market in early morning), and there was a good stock of torches and candles, small candles to stand on the supper tables, and great torches to be set in sconces on the walls, or to be carried in procession by the guests, for the supper ended with 'dancing, singing, wine and spices and lighted torches'. On this occasion eight francs were given to the minstrels, over and above the spoons and other presents made to them during the meal, and there were also acrobats and mimes to amuse the guests. If they had to prepare a great feast

Master John and his little mistress could not go far wrong after this, or fail to please the genial epicure who set it down for them. The Ménagier copied many of his recipes from other cookery books, but he must have got the details of this entertainment from Master Elias himself, and one can see their grey heads wagging with enjoyment, as one talked and the other wrote.

The cookery book ends with a section containing recipes for making what the Ménagier calls 'small things which are not necessities'. There are various sorts of jams, mostly made with honey; in the Middle Ages vegetables were evidently much prepared in this way, for the Ménagier speaks of turnip, carrot, and pumpkin jam. There is a delicious syrup of mixed spices (at least the palate of faith must believe it to have been delicious) and a powder of ginger, cinnamon, cloves, cardamom, and sugar, to be sifted over food, as sugar is sifted today; there is a recipe for hippocras, and for 'gauffres' or wafers, and for candied oranges. There are various sage pieces of advice as to the seasons for certain foods and the best ways of cooking and serving them. Most amusing of all these are a number of recipes not of a culinary nature – to wit, for making glue and marking ink, for bringing up small birds in aviaries and cages, preparing sand for hour-glasses, making rose-water, drying roses to lay among dresses (as we lay lavender today), for curing toothache, and for curing the bite of a mad dog. The latter is a charm, of the same type as the Ménagier's horse charms: 'Take a crust of bread and write what follows: ✠ *Bestera* ✠ *bestie* ✠ *nay* ✠ *brigonay* ✠ *dictera* ✠ *sagragan* ✠ *es* ✠ *domina* ✠ *fiat* ✠ *fiat* ✠ *fiat* ✠.' Let us remember, however, that the nation which produced it, some four centuries later, produced Pasteur.

Enough has been said about this entrancing book to show how vividly it brings not only the Ménagier, but the Ménagier's young wife before our eyes after these many years. In the morning she rises, much earlier than ladies rise nowadays, though not so early as nuns, who must say matins, for that, her husband tells her, is not a fitting hour for married women to leave their beds. Then she washes, much less than ladies nowadays, hands and face only perchance, and says her orisons, and dresses very neatly, for she knows whose eye is upon her, and so goes with Dame Agnes the béguine

V. THE MÉNAGIER'S WIFE HAS A GARDEN PARTY

VI. THE MÉNAGIER'S WIFE COOKS HIS SUPPER, WITH
THE AID OF HIS BOOK

to Mass, with eyes on the ground and hands folded over her painted primer. After Mass, and perhaps confession, back again to see if the servants are doing their work, and have swept and dusted the hall and the rooms, beaten the cushions and coverlets on the forms and tidied everything, and afterwards to interview Master John the steward and order dinner and supper. Then she sends Dame Agnes to see to the pet dogs and birds, 'for they cannot speak and so you must speak and think for them if you have any'. Then, if she be in her country house, she must take thought for the farm animals and Dame Agnes must superintend those who have charge of them, Robin the shepherd, Josson the oxherd, Arnoul the cowherd, Jehanneton the milkmaid, and Eudeline the farmer's wife who looks after the poultry yard. If she be in her town house she and her maids take out her dresses and furs from their great chests and spread them in the sun in the garden or courtyard to air, beating them with little rods, shaking them in the breeze, taking out spots and stains with one or other of the master's tried recipes, pouncing with lynx eyes upon the moth or sprightly flea.

After this comes dinner, the serious meal of the day, eaten by our ancestors about 10 a.m. What the Ménagier's wife gives to her lord and master will depend upon the time of year and upon whether it be a meat or a fast day; but we know that she has no lack of menus from which to choose. After dinner she sees that the servants are set to dine, and then the busy housewife may become the lady of leisure and amuse herself. If in the country she may ride out hawking with a gay party of neighbours; if in town, on a winter's day, she may romp and play with other married ladies of her tender years, exchange riddles or tell stories round the fire. But what she most loves is to wander in her garden, weaving herself garlands of flowers, violets, gilly flowers, roses, thyme, or rosemary, gathering fruit in season (she likes raspberries and cherries), and passing on to the gardeners weighty advice about the planting of pumpkins ('in April water them courteously and transplant them'), to which the gardeners give as much attention as gardeners always have given, give still, and ever shall give, world without end, to the wishes of their employers. When she tires of this, the busy one gathers together Dame Agnes and her maids, and they sit under the carved beams of the hall mending his mastership's doublet, embroidering a vestment for the priest at his family chantry, or a tapestry hanging for the bedchamber. Or perhaps they simply spin (since, in the words of the Wife of Bath, God has given women three talents – deceit, weeping, and spinning!); and all the while she awes them with that tale of Griselda, her voice rising and falling to the steady hum of the wheels.

At last it is evening, and back comes the lord and master. What a bustle and a pother this home-coming meant we know well, since we know what he expected. Such a running and fetching of bowls of warm water to wash his feet, and comfortable shoes to ease him; such a hanging on his words and admiring of his labours. Then comes supper, with a bevy of guests, or themselves all alone in the westering sunlight, while he smacks connoisseur's lips over the roast crane and the blankmanger, and she nibbles her sweet wafers. Afterwards an hour of twilight, when she tells him how she has passed the day, and asks him what she shall do with the silly young housemaid, whom she caught talking to the tailor's 'prentice through that low window which looks upon the road. There is warm affection in the look she turns up to him, her round little face puckered with anxiety over the housemaid, dimpling into a smile when he commends her; and there is warm affection and pride too in the look the old man turns down upon her. So the night falls, and they go round the house together, locking all the doors and seeing that the servants are safe abed, for our ancestors were more sparing of candlelight than we. And so to bed.

We may take our leave of the couple here. The Ménagier's wife evidently had a full life.

> Some respit to husbands the weather may send,
> But huswiues affaires haue neuer an end.

There was no room in it for the idleness of those lovely ladies, with their long fingers, whom Langland admonished to sew for the poor. Moreover, exaggerated as some of her husband's ideas upon wifely submission appear today, the book leaves a strong impression of good sense and of respect as well as love for her. The Ménagier does not want his wife to be on a pedestal, like the troubadour's lady, nor licking his shoes like Griselda; he wants a helpmeet, for, as Chaucer said, 'If that wommen were nat goode and hir conseils goode and profitable, oure Lord God of hevene wolde never han wroght hem, ne called hem "help" of man, but rather confusioun of man.'[23] Ecclesiastical Jeremiahs were often wont to use the characteristically medieval argument that if God had meant woman for a position of superiority He would have taken her from Adam's head rather than his side; but the Ménagier would have agreed with the more logical Peter Lombard, who observed that she was not taken from Adam's head, because she was not intended to be his ruler, nor from his feet either, because she was not intended to be his slave, but from his side, precisely, because she was intended to be his companion. There is something of this spirit in the Ménagier's attitude towards his little wife, and it is this which makes his book so charming and causes it to stand head and shoulders above most other medieval books of behaviour for women. But, above all, its social and historical value lies in the fact that it gives us, in hues undimmed by time, a full length portrait of a medieval housewife, who has her place (and it is a large one) in history, but concerning whom historians have almost invariably been silent.

CHAPTER VI

Thomas Betson

A MERCHANT OF THE STAPLE IN THE

FIFTEENTH CENTURY

Some men of noble stock were made, some glory in the murder blade:
Some praise a Science or an Art, but I like honourable Trade!
— JAMES ELROY FLECKER
The Golden Journey to Samarcand

THE VISITOR TO the House of Lords, looking respectfully upon that august assembly, cannot fail to be struck by a stout and ungainly object facing the throne – an ungainly object upon which in full session of Parliament, he will observe seated the Lord Chancellor of England. The object is a woolsack, and it is stuffed as full of pure history as the office of Lord Chancellor itself. For it reminds a cotton-spinning, iron-working generation that the greatness of England was built up, not upon the flimsy plant which comes to her to be manufactured from the Far East and West of the world, nor upon the harsh metal delved from her bowels, but upon the wool which generation after generation has grown on the backs of her black-faced sheep. First in the form of a raw material sought after eagerly by all the cloth-makers of Europe, then in the form of a manufacture carried on in her own towns and villages, and sent out far and wide in ships, wool was the foundation of England's greatness right up to the time of the Industrial Revolution, when cotton and iron took its place. So if you look at old pictures of the House of Lords, in Henry VIII's reign, or in Elizabeth's, you will see the woolsack before the throne,[1] as you will see it if you visit the House today. The Lord Chancellor of England is seated upon a woolsack because it was upon a woolsack that this fair land rose to prosperity.

Thomas Betson

The most remarkable body of traders in England during the Middle Ages were the Merchants of the Staple, who traded in wool. The wool trade had for long been the largest and most lucrative body of trade in the country, and it was one in which the Kings of England were particularly interested, for their customs revenue was drawn largely from wool and wool fells; and, moreover, when they desired to borrow money in anticipation of revenue it was to the wool merchants that they turned, because the wool merchants were the wealthiest traders in the country. For these and other reasons the Government adopted the custom of fixing staple towns, which acted as centres of distribution through which the export trade was forced to go. The location of the Staple was altered from time to time; sometimes it was at Bruges, sometimes at Antwerp, sometimes in England; but usually it was at Calais, where it was first fixed in 1363 and finally established in 1423. Through the Staple all wool and wool fells, hides, leather, and tin had to pass, and the organization of the system was complete when the body of wool merchants, in whose hands lay the bulk of the Staple trade, were finally incorporated in 1354, under the governance of a mayor. The system was a convenient one for Crown and merchants alike. The Crown could concentrate its customs officers in one place and collect its customs the more easily, particularly as a method was gradually developed by which the custom and subsidy on wool was paid to the Royal officials by the Fellowship of the Staple, who then collected it from the individual members. The merchants, on the other hand, benefited by the concentration in trade: they were able to travel in groups and to organize convoys to protect the wool fleets from pirates who swarmed in the narrow seas between England and France; as members of a powerful corporation they could secure both privileges and protection in Flanders. Moreover, the wool buyers also benefited by the arrangement, which rendered possible a careful surveillance by the Crown and the Company of the Staple of the quality of the wool offered for sale, and a series of regulations against fraud. It must be remembered that in days when trade stood in need of a protection which the Government was not yet able to give it, there was nothing unpopular in the idea of giving the monopoly of the staple trade to the members of a single company. 'Trade in companies is natural to Englishmen,' wrote Bacon; and for four centuries it was the great trading companies which nurtured English trade and made this country the commercial leader of the world.

The wool trade throve in England until the close of the Middle Ages, but throughout the fifteenth century the staplers were beginning to feel the competition of another company – that of the famous Merchant Adventurers, who, taking advantage of the growth in the native cloth manufacture during the previous century, had begun to do a great trade in the export of cloth. This was obnoxious to the staplers, who desired the continuance of the old system, by which they exported English wool to the Continent, where at Ypres and Ghent, Bruges and Mechlin, and the other famous cloth-working cities of the Netherlands, it was woven into fine cloth. This cloth manufacture gave to the Netherlands a sort of industrial pre-eminence in Europe throughout the Middle Ages, and it was dependent entirely upon a good supply of English wool, for the next best wool in Europe – that of Spain – was not satisfactory unless mixed with wool of English growth. Hence the close political tie between England and Flanders, the one needing a customer, the other an essential raw material; for, as a fifteenth century poet said,

> the lytelle londe of Flaundres is
> But a staple to other londes, iwys,
> And alle that groweth in Flaundres, greyn and sede,
> May not a moneth fynde hem mete and brede.
> What hath thenne Flaundres, be Flemmyngis leffe or lothe
> But a lytelle madere and Flemmyshe cloothe?
> By drapynge of our wolle in substaunce
> Lyvene here comons, this is here governaunce;
> Wythought whyche they may not leve at ease,
> Thus moste hem sterve, or wyth us most have peasse.[2]

In those days the coat on the Englishman's back was made out of English wool, indeed, but it had been manufactured in Flanders, and the staplers saw no reason why it should ever be otherwise. As to the Flemings, the political alliances which commercial necessities constantly entailed between the two countries gave rise among them to a proverb that they bought the fox-skin from the English for a groat and sold them back the tail for a guelder;[3] but it was the sheepskin which they bought, and they were not destined to go on buying it for ever. The great cloth-making cities of the Netherlands were finally ruined by the growth of the English cloth manufacture, which absorbed the English wool. However, in spite of the growing prosperity of this trade, which had by the beginning of the sixteenth century ousted that of wool as the chief English export trade, the Company of the Merchants of the Staple was still great and famous throughout the fifteenth century.

Many were the wealthy and respected staplers who were in those days to be found directing the destinies of English towns, mayors of London and provincial ports, contractors and moneylenders to an impecunious king, so rich and so powerful that they became a constitutional menace, almost, it has been said, a fourth estate of the realm, with which His Majesty was wont to treat for grants apart from Parliament. Many are the staplers' wills preserved in registries up and down England and bearing witness to their prosperity and public spirit. Many are the magnificent brasses which preserve their memory in the parish churches of the Cotswolds and other wool-growing districts of England. At Chipping Campden lies William Grevel with his wife, 'late citizen of London and flower of the wool merchants of all England', who died in 1401, and his beautiful house still stands in the village street. At Northleach lies John Fortey, who rebuilt the nave before he died in 1458; his brass shows him with one foot on a sheep and the other on a woolpack, and the brasses of Thomas Fortey, 'woolman', and of another unknown merchant, with a woolpack, lie near by. At Linwood, at Cirencester, at Chipping Norton, at Lechlade, and at All Hallows, Barking, you may see others of the great fraternity.[4] They rest in peace now, but when they lived they were the shrewdest traders of their day. Of wool, cries the poet Gower,

> O leine, dame de noblesce
> Tu est des marchantz la duesse,
> Pour toy servir tout sont enclin –

'O wool, noble dame, thou art the goddess of merchants, to serve thee they are all ready; by thy good fortune and thy wealth thou makest some mount high, and others thou bringest to ruin. The staple where thou dwellest is never free of fraud and trickery, wherewith man wounds his conscience. O wool, Christians no less than pagans and Saracens seek to have thee and confess thee. O wool, we should not be silent about thy doings in strange lands; for the merchants of all countries, in time of peace, in time of war, come to seek thee by reason of their great love, for whoever else hath enemies thou art never without good friends, who have given themselves to thy profitable service. Thou art cherished throughout the world, and the land where thou art born may do great things by reason of thee. Thou art carried throughout the world by land and sea, but thou goest to the wealthiest men; in England art thou born, but it is said that thou art but ill governed, for Trick, who hath much money, is made regent of thy staple; at his will he taketh it to foreign lands, where he purchaseth his own gain to our harm. O fair, O white, O delightful one, the love of thee stings and binds, so that the hearts of those who make merchandise of thee cannot escape. So they compass much trickery and many schemes how they may gather thee, and then they make thee pass the sea, queen and lady of their navy, and in order to have thee envy and covetousness hie them to bargain for thee.' [5]

The daily life of a Merchant of the Staple is not a difficult one to reconstruct, partly because the Golden Fleece has left so many marks upon our national life, partly because the statute book is full of regulations concerning the wool trade, but chiefly because there have come down to us many private letters from persons engaged in shipping wool from England to Calais. Of all the different sorts of raw material out of which the history of ordinary people in the Middle Ages has to be made, their letters are perhaps the most enthralling, because in their letters people live and explain themselves in all their individuality. In the fifteenth century most men and women of the upper and middle classes could read and write, although their spelling was sometimes marvellous to behold, and St Olave's Church is apt to become 'Sent Tolowys scryssche' beneath their painfully labouring goose quills, and punctuation is almost entirely to seek. But what matter? their meaning is clear enough.

Good fortune has preserved in various English archives several great collections of family letters written in the fifteenth century. Finest of all are the famous Paston Letters, written by and to a family of Norfolk gentlefolk, and crammed with information about high politics and daily life.[6] Less interesting, but valuable all the same, are the letters of the Plumptons, who were lords in Yorkshire.[7] But for our purposes the most interesting are two other collections, to wit, the correspondence of the Stonors, whose estates lay chiefly in Oxfordshire and the neighbouring counties; and the Cely papers, kept by a family of Merchants of the Staple.

These two collections give us a vivid picture of wool staplers in their public and private lives. The Cely papers cover the years 1475 to 1488, and it so happens that during that period William Stonor (he became Sir William in 1478) also became interested in the wool trade, for in 1475 he married Elizabeth Riche, the daughter and widow of wealthy city merchants. The Stonors had great sheep runs on their estates in the Chilterns and Cotswolds, and William readily perceived the advantage of his alliance with Elizabeth's family, who were interested in the wool trade. Consequently he entered into a partnership with a friend of his wife's, a Merchant of the Staple in Calais, named Thomas Betson, who is the subject of this study, and until Elizabeth's death in 1479, he took an active part in the export trade. Thomas Betson died in 1486, and was thus an exact contemporary of those other Merchants of the Staple, George and Richard Cely, whom he must have known; indeed, William Cely, their cousin and agent, writes from London to George in Calais in 1481, advising him that he has dispatched 464 fells to him in the *Thomas* of Newhithe, 'and the sayd felles lyeth nexte be afte the maste lowest under the felles of Thomas Bettson'.[8] By the aid of the 'Stonor Letters and Papers', which contain many letters from and concerning him during the years of his partnership with Sir William, and of the 'Cely Papers', which are full of information about the life of a Merchant of the Staple at Calais, Thomas Betson may be summoned before us by a kindly magic until he almost lives again. So he deserves to do, for he is one of the most delightful people revealed to us in any of the fifteenth-century letters; for honest charm he has no rival save the attractive Margery Brews, who married John Paston the younger, and shows up so pleasantly beside the hard Paston women.

Perhaps the reason why our hearts warm immediately towards Thomas Betson is that our first meeting with him plunges us immediately into a love affair. His first letter to William Stonor is dated April 12, 1476, and informs William that their wool has come in to Calais. 'Right worshipfful Syr,' it begins, 'I recomaund me unto your good maystershipe, and to my right worshipffulle may-stresse your wiffe, and yf it plese your maystershipe, to my may-stresse Kateryn.'[9] Ten days later he writes again from London, on the eve of sailing for Calais, thanking Stonor for his 'gentle cheer and faithful love, the which alway ye bear and owe unto me, and of my behalf nothing deserved,'* announcing that he has sent a present of powdered† lampreys from himself and a pipe of red wine from his brother, and adding this postscript: 'Sir, I beseech your mastership that this poor writing may have me lowly recommended to my right worshipful mistress, your wife, and in like wise to my gentle cousin and kind mistress Katherine Riche, to whom I beseech your mastership ever to be favourable and loving.'[10] Who was this Katherine Riche to whom he so carefully commends himself? Katherine Riche was William Stonor's stepdaughter, one of his wife's children by her first husband; she was Thomas Betson's affianced bride, and at this time she was about thirteen years old.

Modern opinion, which is happily in favour of falling in love, and of adult marriages, is often shocked by the air of business which pervades matchmaking in the days of chivalry, and by the many cases of grown men married to little girls not yet out of their teens. In those days it was held that a boy came of age at fourteen and a girl at twelve (a discrepancy which the great canon lawyer, Lyndwood, the son of a stapler,[11] attributed to the fact that ill weeds grow apace!). For reasons of property, or to settle family feuds, or simply to assure their own future, babies in cradles were sometimes betrothed and even married; all that the Church required was that children should be free when they came of age (at the ages of fourteen and twelve!) to repudiate the contract if they so desired.

* Henceforth I shall modernize spelling, for the reader's convenience.
† I.e. pickled.

Nothing seems to separate modern England from the good old days so plainly as the case of little Grace de Saleby, aged four, who for the sake of her broad acres was married to a great noble, and on his death two years later to another, and yet again, when she was eleven, to a third, who paid three hundred marks down for her.[12] There is an odd mixture of humour and pathos in the story of some of these marriages. John Rigmarden, aged three, was carried to church in the arms of a priest, who coaxed him to repeat the words of matrimony, but half-way through the service the child declared that he would learn no more that day, and the priest answered, 'You must speak a little more, and then go play you.' James Ballard, aged ten, was married to Jane his wife 'at x of the clocke in the night without the consent of any of his frendes, bie one Sir Roger Blakey, then curate of Colne, and the morowe after, the same James declarid vnto his Vnckle that the said Jane [beyinge a bigge damsell and mariageable at the same tyme] had intised him with two Apples, to go with her to Colne and to marry her.' Elizabeth Bridge *née* Ramsbotham, says that after her marriage to John Bridge, when he was eleven and she thirteen, he never used her 'lovinglie, insomoche that the first night they were maried, the said John wold Eate no meate at supper, and whan hit was bed tyme, the said John did wepe to go home with his father, he beynge at that tyme at her brother's house.'[13]

Sometimes, however, medieval records throw a pleasanter light on these child marriages. Such was the light thrown by the Ménagier de Paris's book for his young wife, so kindly, so affectionate, so full of indulgence for her youth; and such also is the light thrown by the charming letter which Thomas Betson wrote to little Katherine Riche on the first day of June in 1476. It is a veritable gem, and it is strange that it has not attracted more notice, for certainly no anthology of English letters should be without it. I set it down here at length, for it brings to warm life again both Thomas Betson and Katherine Riche:

Mine own heartily beloved Cousin Katherine, I recommend me unto you with all the inwardness of my heart. And now lately ye shall understand that I received a token from you, the which was and is to me right heartily welcome, and with glad will I received it; and over that I had a letter from Holake, your gentle squire, by the which I understand right well that ye be in good health of body, and merry at heart. And I pray God heartily in his pleasure to continue the same: for it is to me very great comfort that he so be, so help me Jesu. And if ye would be a good eater of your meat alway, that ye might wax and grow fast to be a woman ye should make me the gladdest man of the world, by my troth; for when I remember your favour and your sad loving dealing to me wards, for sooth ye make me even very glad and joyous in my heart; and on the tother side again, when I remember your young youth, and see well that ye be none eater of your meat, the which should help you greatly in waxing, for sooth then ye make me very heavy again. And therefore I pray you, mine own sweet Cousin, even as you love me, to be merry and eat your meat like a woman. And if ye will so do for my love, look what ye will desire of me, whatsoever it be, and by my troth, I promise you by the help of our Lord to perform it to my power. I can no more say now, but on my coming home I will tell you much more between you and me and God before. And whereas ye, full womanly and like a lover, remember me with manifold recommendation in divers manners, remitting the same to my discretion to depart them there as I love best, for sooth, mine own sweet Cousin, ye shall understand that with good heart and good will I receive and take to myself the one half of them and them will I keep by me; and the tother half with hearty love and favour I send them to you, mine own sweet Cousin, again, for to keep by you; and over that I send you the blessing that our Lady gave her dear son, and ever well to fare. I pray you greet well my horse and pray him to give you four of his years to help you withal; and I will at my coming home give him four of my years and four horse loaves till amends. Tell him that I prayed him so. And Cousin Katherine, I thank you for him, and my wife shall thank you for him hereafter; for ye do great cost upon him, as is told me. Mine own sweet Cousin, it was told me but late that ye were at Calais* to seek me, but could not see me nor find me; forsooth ye might have comen to my counter, and there ye should both find me and see me, and not have faulted of me; but ye sought me in a wrong Calais, and that ye should well know if ye were here and saw this Calais, as would God ye were and some of them with you that were with you at your gentle Calais. I pray you, gentle Cousin, commend me to the clock, and pray him to amend his unthrifty manners; for he strikes ever in undue time, and he will be ever afore, and that is a shrewd condition. Tell him without he amend his condi-

* Possibly an inn with that name (?).

tion that he will cause strangers to avoid and come no more there. I trust to you that he shall amend against mine coming, the which shall be shortly, with all hands and all feet, with God's grace. My very faithful Cousin, I trust to you that though all I have not remembered my right worshipful mistress your mother afore in this letter, that ye will of your gentleness recommend me to her mistresship as many times as it shall please you: and ye may say, if it please you, that in Whitsun week next I intend to the mart ward. And I trust you will pray for me; for I shall pray for you and, so it may be, none so well. And Almighty Jesu make you a good woman and send you many good years and long to live in health and virtue to his pleasure. At great Calais, on this side on the sea, the first day of June, when every man was gone to his dinner, and the clock smote nine, and all your household cried after me and bade me 'Come down, come down to dinner at once!' – and what answer I gave them, ye know it of old.

By your faithful Cousin and lover Thomas Betson. I send you this ring for a token.

So ending, Thomas Betson smiled, dropped a kiss on the seal and inscribed his letter, 'To my faithful and heartily beloved cousin Katherine Riche at Stonor, this letter be delivered in haste.'[14]

Henceforth there begins a charming triangular correspondence between Betson and Stonor and Dame Elizabeth Stonor, in which family news and business negotiations are pleasantly mingled. Dame Elizabeth and Betson were on the best of terms, for they had been old friends before her second marriage. A special chamber was kept for him at Stonor, and by an affectionate anticipation she often refers to him as 'My son Stonor'. Almost all her letters to her husband contain news of him – how he took his barge at 8 a.m. in the morning and God speed him, how no writing has come from him these eight days, how he has now written about the price to be paid for forty sacks of Cotswold wool, how he recommends him to Sir William and came home last Monday. Sometimes he is entrusted with the delicate business of interviewing Dame Elizabeth's mother, a difficult old lady with a tongue; 'God send her,' says Thomas, mopping his brow, after one of these interviews, 'once a merry countenance or shortly to the Minories!'* After another he writes to Dame Elizabeth: 'Sith I came home to London

---

* The convent of Minoresses, or Franciscan nuns, outside Aldgate.

I met with my lady your mother and God wot she made me right sullen cheer with her countenance whiles I was with her; methought it long till I was departed. She break out to me of her old "ffern-yeres" and specially she brake to me of the tale I told her between the vicar that was and her; she said the vicar never fared well sith, he took it so much to heart. I told her a light answer again and so I departed from her. I had no joy to tarry with her. She is a fine merry woman, but ye shall not know it nor yet find it, nor none of yours by that I see in her.'[15] It was the faithful Betson, too, who was chosen to look after his Katherine's little sister Anne when she was ill in London, and he writes home asking for her clothes – 'She hath need unto them and that knoweth our Lord' – and complaining of the old grandmother's behaviour: 'If my lady your mother meet my cousin Anne she will say no more but "God's blessing have ye and mine', and so go her way forth, as though she had no joy of her.'[16] It was Betson, too, who escorted Dame Elizabeth, when need was, from Windsor to London and wrote to her husband: 'By the way we were right merry, thanked be God, and so with his mercy we mean here to be merry for the season that my lady is here, and when your mastership is ready to come hitherwards, we here shall so welcome you that the season of your abiding shall not be noisome, with God's grace.'[17] Whereupon Sir William sends a present of capons by the carrier to assist the merriment, and Betson reports, 'Sir, I took two capons, but they were not the best, as ye counselled me by your letter to take, and indeed to say the truth I could not be suffered. My lady your wife is reasonably strong waxed, the Lord be thanked, and she took her will in that matter like as she doth in all other.'[18]

There are, indeed, a hundred evidences of the warmth of Betson's affection for the Stonors and of the simple piety of his character. Sometimes he ventures to give them good advice. Dame Elizabeth was somewhat uplifted by her elevation from the ranks of the mercantile bourgeoisie to a place among the country gentry, and was apt to be extravagant, nor was her husband entirely guiltless of running up bills. We hear of the ale brewer and the bread baker calling daily upon his agent for money, and on one occasion the Stonors owed over £12 to Betson's own brother, a vintner, for various pipes of red and white wine and a butt of Rumney.* [19] So Thomas writes to Dame Elizabeth, on his way to the mart: 'Our blessed lord Jesus Christ preserve you both in honour and worship virtuously to continue in God's pleasure and also to send you good and profitable counsel and grace to do hereafter. This is and shall be my prayer forsooth every day; your honour and worship of countenance hereafter sticketh as nigh mine heart as doth any friend, man or other about you, by my troth, our blessed Lord so help me. I will avise you, Madame, to remember large expenses and beware of them, and in likewise my master your husband; it is well done ye remember him of them, for divers considerations, as ye know both right well. And our blessed Lord be your comforter and help in all your good work. Amen.' [20] A month later he hears that William Stonor has been ill and writes to sympathize with Dame Elizabeth: 'And if I could do anything here that might be to his pleasure and yours, I would I knew it and it should be done withouten fail. Truly your discomfort is not my comfort, God knoweth it. Nevertheless your ladyship must cause him to be merry and of glad cheer, and to put away all fantasies and unthrifty thoughts, that comes no good of, but only hurtful. A man may hurt himself by riotous means; it is good to beware.' [21]

Meanwhile what of little Katherine Riche? She recurs over and over in Thomas Betson's letters. Occasionally she is in disgrace, for she was not handy with her pen. 'I am wroth with Katherine,' writes he to her mother, 'because she sendeth me no writing. I have to her divers times and for lack of answer I wax weary; she might get a secretary if she would and if she will not, it shall put me to less labour to answer her letters again.' [22] But the important thing is that she grows steadily older, though not quickly enough to please our lover. On Trinity Sunday in 1478 he writes to Dame Elizabeth: 'I remember her full oft, God know[eth] it. I dreamed once she was thirty winters of age and when I woke I wished she had been but twenty and so by likelihood I am sooner like to have my wish than my dream, the which I beseech Almighty Jesu heartily when it shall please Him' [23]; and to the lady's stepfather he writes a month later: 'I beseech you to remember my cousin

* Greek wine.

Katherine. I would she did well, God knoweth it, and ye deme, as I trow, if I had found her at home here my comfort should have been the more; but I thank God of all. My pain is the more; I must needs suffer as I have done in times past, and so will I do for God's sake and hers.'[24] However, Katherine was now fifteen years of age and was sufficiently grown up to wed, and the next letter, written a week later to Dame Elizabeth, shows us Thomas Betson beginning to set his house in order and getting exceedingly bothered about laying in her trousseau, a business with which Dame Elizabeth had, it seems, entrusted the future bridegroom.

Madam, and it like you, I understand by your writing that it will be the latter end of August or your ladyship can come here to London; and if it should be so I would be sorry, for I have much to do and I can little skill to do anything that longeth to the matter ye wot of [evidently the preparations for Katherine] . . . I must beseech your ladyship to send me [your advice] how I shall be demeaned in such things as shall belong unto my cousin Katherine, and how I shall provide for them. She must have girdles, three at the least, and how they shall be made I know not, and many other things she must have, ye know well what they be, in faith I know not; by my troth, I would it were done, liever than more than it shall cost. . . . And as for the sending hither of my Cousin Katherine, your ladyship may do therein as it shall please you. I would she knew as much as you know, forsooth, and then she should do some good and help me in many things when she come. . . . Also, madam, as ye write me the courteous dealing of my master with my Cousin Katherine, etc., truly I am very glad thereof and I pray God heartily thank him therefore, for he hath ever been lovingly disposed [unto] her, and so I beseech God ever continue him and also my Cousin Katherine to deserve it unto him by her goodly demeanour and womanly disposition, as she can do right well if her list, and so saith every body that praiseth her.[25]

The note of pride in the last words is as engaging as the impatience of the harassed male faced with the choosing of girdles. Even more charming is the letter which he wrote the same day to Sir William Stonor. He is a little incoherent with joy and gratitude, full of regrets that business keeps him from Stonor and good wishes for the health of the family. 'I fare like a sorry piper,' he says. 'When I begin I cannot leave, but yet once again our blessed Lord be your speed and your help.' Of Katherine he writes thus:

I understand by the worshipful report of your mastership the [be]-haviours of my cousin Katherine unto you, to my lady your wife and to all other, etc.; and truly it is to me right joyful and comfortable gladness to hear of her and I beseech our blessed Lord ever to preserve her in all virtue and good living to his pleasure, and to reward your mastership with heaven at your ending, for your good disposition to herwards in good ex-hortations giving. And that I wot well of old, or else truly she could not be of that disposition, virtuous and goodly, her youth remembered and excused. . . . Sir, remember your mastership well what ye have written of my Cousin Katherine; truly I shall when I speak with her, tell her every word, and if I find the contrary. Our vicar here, so God help me, shall cry out upon her* within this ten weeks and less, and by that time I shall be ready in every point, by God's grace, and so I would she were, forsooth ye may believe me of it.[26]

This letter was written on June 24, 1478, and Thomas probably married his little Katherine in August or September, for when Dame Elizabeth writes to her husband on October 5, she says, 'My son Betson and his wife recommend them to you.'[27] The poor child was to learn soon enough some of the sorrows of a wife, for a year later Thomas Betson fell dangerously ill, and she was nursing him and looking after his business for all the world as though she were a grave matron and not a bride of sixteen. Moreover, she must already have been expecting the birth of her eldest son. William Stonor's attitude towards his partner's illness is not without humour. He was torn between anxiety for the life of a friend and an even greater anxiety that Betson should not die without setting straight the business obligations between them. We hear of the illness and of Katherine's labours in a letter from one of Stonor's agents to his master:

Sir, according to the commandment of your mastership, we were at Stepney by nine of the clock; at such time as we came thither we saw the gentleman forthwith, and in good faith he made us good cheer as a sick man might by countenance notwithstanding, for in good faith we saw by his

* I.e. call the banns.

133

demeanour that he might not prosper in this world, for Mistress Bevice and other gentlewomen and his uncle were of the same opinion. And we desired and prayed him to be of good comfort and so comforted him as heartily as we could in your name and in my lady's, and so we departed from the chamber down into the hall, and he fell into a great slumbering and was busily moved in his spirits. And at eleven of the clock I called his uncle out of his bed into the gentleman's chamber, and I asked his advice and my mistress his wife, of the stock and of the demeanour thereof for the year and the half that is last past. And touching the stock he confessed that it was £1,160, wherein at the sight of your acquittance in discharging of him and all his doers that shall be behind him, the said stock shall be ready. And as for the occupation of it, as he will answer between God and devil, the book that he bought it by ye shall be privy thereto; and the book that he sold by ye shall be also privy to, which two books shall be his judges, which remain in the keeping of my mistress his wife's hands under lock and key and other bills and obligations according, concerning the surety for divers payments to be made to divers merchants, as the said lord saith. . . . And as for the plate my mistress Jane [probably Jane Riche, the younger sister of Katherine] and I have caused it to be taken up and set in surety, save that that must needs by occupied.

He sends to Sir William for information about two sums of £80 each owed by Betson to his master and mistress, and adds:

I trust to Jesu he shall endure till the messenger come again; longer the physicians have not determined. The executors be three persons, my mistress his wife, Humphrey Starkey, Recorder of London, Robert Tate, merchant of Calais; notwithstanding I moved him, between him and me and mistress Jane, that he should break this testament and make my mistress his wife sole executrix. What will be done therein as yet I cannot speak, but I shall do as I can, with God's grace.[28]

There is something unexpected and a little vulture-like about this gathering of creditors and seizing of plate about the death-bed of a man who had always, after all, shown himself exceedingly affectionate towards the Stonors and devoted to their interests, and who was now my lady's son-in-law. The attempt to make the young wife of sixteen sole executrix, so that she might be completely in her family's hands and without the counsel of two experienced and disinterested merchants, has a somewhat sinister air. The intrigues went on, and three days later the agent writes again. It is pleasant to observe that bad-tempered old Mistress Croke, Dame Elizabeth's mother, was not unmindful of Betson's forbearance during those visits when she had railed upon him with her sharp tongue:

As for the tidings that is here, I trust to God it shall be very good. On Thursday my lady Croke came to Stepney and brought with her Master Brinkley to see Betson, and in faith he was a very sick man; and ere he departed he gave him plasters to his head, to his stomach and to his belly, [so] that he all that night was in a quiet rest. And he came to him again on Friday . . . and he was well amended and so said all the people that were about him. Notwithstanding he will not determine him whether he shall live or die as yet, but he may keep him alive till Tuesday noon, he will undertake him. The cause that I write to you now rather was because I had no certainty. Sir, there hath been many special labours and secret -made, sithen mistress Jane and I were come, to the contrary disposition that we come for. I cannot write the plain[nes]s of them as yet, for my mistress Betson attendeth, all things and counsels laid apart, to abide and trust in your good fatherhood and in my lady, and furthermore if he depart the world, ye shall hear tidings of her in as goodly haste as we may purvey for her. And whether he die or live, it is necessary and behoveful that mistress Jane depart not from her into [i.e. until] such time as the certainty be knowen, for in truth divers folks, which ye shall know hereafter and my lady, both thus hath and would exhort her to a contrarier disposition, had not we been here by time. And mistress Jane is worthy of much thank.[29]

However, all the schemings were premature, for Betson happily recovered. On October 10 the 'prentice' Henham writes: 'My master Betson is right well amended, blessed be Jesus, and he is past all doubts of sickness and he takes the sustenance right well, and as for physicians, there come none unto him, for he hath no need of them.'[30] But another death was at hand to break the close association between Thomas Betson and the Stonors, for at the end of the year the kind, extravagant, affectionate Dame Elizabeth died. It is a surprising fact that her death seems to have brought to a close the business partnership between her husband and her son-in-law. Henceforth the only references to Thomas Betson in the Stonor papers are occasional notes of his debts to Stonor: doubtless he had bought Sir William's share in their joint business. On March 10, 1480, he acknowledged obligations of £2,835 9s. 0d. to Stonor, and in 1482 he still owed £1,200.[31] It is impossible to guess why the relationship, which was an affectionate personal friendship as well as a business tie, should have come to such a sudden end. As the editor of the *Stonor Letters* remarks, 'The sincerity and honesty of Betson's character as revealed in his letters, forbids one to suppose that he was to blame.'

Such was the more private and domestic side of Thomas Betson's life; but it tells us little (save in occasional references to the Fellowship of the Staple or the price of Cotswold wool) about that great company with which this chapter began; and since he stands here as a type as well as an individual, we must needs turn now to his public and business life, and try to find out from more indirect evidence how a Merchant of the Staple went about his business. The stapler, who would make a good livelihood, must do two things, and give his best attention to both of them: first, he must buy his wool from the English grower, then he must sell it to the foreign buyer. Some of the best wool in England came from the Cotswolds, and when you are a Merchant of the Staple you enjoy bargaining for it, whether you want the proceeds of the great summer clip or of the fells after the autumn sheep-killing. So Thomas Betson rides off to Gloucestershire in the soft spring weather, his good sorrel between his knees, and the scent of the hawthorn blowing round him as he goes. Other wool merchants ride farther afield – into the long dales of Yorkshire to bargain with Cistercian abbots for the wool from their huge flocks, but he and the Celys swear by Cotswold fells (he shipped 2,348 of them to London one July 'in the names of Sir William Stonor knight and Thomas Betson, in the *Jesu* of London, John Lolyngton master under God'). May is the great month for purchases, and Northleach the great meeting place of staplers and wool dealers. It is no wonder that Northleach Church is so full of woolmen's brasses, for often they knelt there and often the village hummed with the buyers and sellers, exchanging orders and examining samples. The Celys bought chiefly from two Northleach wool dealers, William Midwinter and John Busshe. The relations between dealers and sellers were often enough close and pleasant: Midwinter even occasionally tried to provide a customer with a bride as well as with a cargo, and marriageable young ladies were not unwilling to be examined over a gallon of wine and much good cheer at the inn.[32] It is true that Midwinter was apt to be restive when his bills remained for too long unpaid, but he may be forgiven for that. Thomas Betson favoured the wool fells of Robert Turbot of Lamberton,[33] and dealt also with one John Tate, with Whyte of Broadway (another famous wool village),[34] and with John Elmes, a Henley merchant well known to the Stonors. Midwinter, Busshe, and Elmes were all wool dealers, or 'broggers' – middlemen, that is to say, between the farmers who grew and the staplers who bought wool, but often the staplers dealt directly with individual farmers, buying the small man's clip as well as the great man's, and warm friendships sprang from the annual visits, looked forward to in Yorkshire dale and Cotswold valley. It strikes a pleasant note when Richard Russell, citizen and merchant of York, leaves in his will, 'for distribution among the farmers of Yorkes Walde, from whom I bought wool 20 l., and in the same way among the farmers of Lyndeshay 10 l.' (1435).[35]

The 'Cely Letters' give a mass of information about the wool buying at Northleach. In the May of the same year in which Betson's partnership with Stonor would seem to have ended, old Richard Cely was up there doing business and reporting it to his son, 'Jorge Cely at Caleys'.

I greet you well and I have received a letter from you writ at Calais the 13th day of May (1480), the which letter I have well understood of your being at the marts and of the sale of my middle wool, desired by John Destermer and John Underbay. Wherefore by the grace of God I am a-busied for to ship this foresaid 29 sarplers, the which I bought of William Midwinter of Northleach, 26 sarplers, the which is fair wool, as the wool packer Will Breten saith to me, and also the 3 sarplers of the rector's is fair wool, much finer wool nor was the year before, the which I shipped afore Easter last past. The shipping is begun at London, but I have none shipped as yet, but I will after these holy days, for the which I will ye order for the freight and other costs. This same day your brother Richard Cely is rid to Northleach for to see and cast a sort of fell for me and another sort of fell for you.[36]

On another occasion he writes: 'By your letter you avise me for to buy wool in Cotswold, for which I shall have of John Cely his gathering 30 sack, and of Will Midwinter of Northleach 40 sack. And I am avised to buy no more; wool in Cotswold is at great price, 13*s.* 4*d.* a tod, and great riding for wool in Cotswold as was any year this seven year.'[37] What a picture it calls up of merchants trotting along the roads and looking as Chaucer often saw them look:

> A Marchant was ther with a forked berd,
> In motteleye and hye on horse he sat,
> Upon his heed a Flaundryssh bever hat,
> His boots clasped faire and fetisly;
> His resons he spak ful solempnely,
> Sounynge alway thencrees of his wynnyng.

Often at Northleach Betson must have encountered his brethren of the Staple, the staid old merchant Richard Cely among the rest, and son George who rides with 'Meg', his hawk, on his wrist, and has a horse called 'Bayard' and another called 'Py'; and perhaps also John Barton of Holme beside Newark, the proud stapler who set as a 'posy' in the stained glass windows of his house this motto:

> I thank God and ever shall
> It is the sheepe hath payed for all;[38]

though indeed it is unlikely that he came as far south as the Cotswolds for his wool. Sometimes also Betson meets upon the road his rivals, stout, self-possessed Flemings and thin sleek Lombards with black eyes and gesticulating hands, who have no business in the Cotswolds at all, but ought to be buying wool in the mart at Calais. But they come, and all good Englishmen are angry at their tricks and angrier still perhaps at their successful trade. 'I have not as yet packed my wool in London,' writes old Richard Cely on October 29, 1480; 'nor have I not bought this year a lock of wool, for the wool of Cotswold is bought by Lombards, wherefore I have the less haste for to pack my wool at London';[39] and his son writes to him on November 16 from Calais: 'There is but little Cotswold wool at Calais and I understand Lombards has bought it up in England.' [40] It is true that the Celys, other English merchants too, are not unwilling to conclude private bargains from time to time with foreign buyers in England. Two years later their agent, William Cely, writes to advise them that two Flemish merchants are now trying to buy in England contrary to the ordinance, and that those in authority at Calais have got wind of it, and therefore his masters must take care and make Wyllykyn and Peter Bale pay at Calais, 'but as for your dealings knoweth no man, without they search Peter Bale's books.' [41] The upright Betson no doubt eschewed such tricks and resented particularly the clever usurious Lombards, so full of financial dodges to trick the English merchant, for did they not buy the wool in England on credit, riding about as they list in the Cotswolds?

> In Cotteswolde also they ryde aboute
> And al Englonde, and bien wythouten doute,
> What them liste, wythe fredome and fraunchise
> More then we Englisshe may getyn in any wyse.

And then did they not carry the wool to Flanders and sell it for ready money at a loss of five per cent, thereafter lending out this money at heavy usury, mostly to the English merchants themselves, so that by the time pay day came in England, they had realized a heavy profit?

> And thus they wold, if we will beleve
> Wypen our nose with our owne sleve,
> Thow this proverbe be homly and undew,
> Yet be liklynesse it is forsoth fulle trew. [42]

The next serious piece of business Thomas Betson must take in hand is the packing and shipping of his wool to Calais. Here he found himself enmeshed in the regulations of the company and the Crown, ever on the look-out for fraud in the packing or description of the staple product. The wool had to be packed in the county from which it came, and there were strict regulations against mixing hair and earth or rubbish with it. The collectors appointed by the company for the different wool-growing districts, and sworn in before the Exchequer, rode round and sealed each package, so that it could not be opened without breaking the seal. Then the great bales were carried on the backs of pack-horses 'by the ancient trackways over the Wiltshire and Hampshire Downs, which had been used before the Roman conquest, and thence through Surrey and Kent to the Medway ports by the Pilgrims' Way.' At the different ports the collectors of customs were ready to enter on their rolls the names of the merchants shipping wool, together with the quantity and description of wool shipped by each.[43] Some of the wool came to London itself, where many of the staplers had offices in Mark Lane (which is a corruption of Mart Lane) and was weighed for the assessment of the customs and subsidy at the Leadenhall.[44] In this business Thomas Betson was helped by Stonor's three assistants or 'prentices', as they call themselves, Thomas Henham, Goddard Oxbridge, and Thomas Howlake, for the last of whom he had a warm corner in his heart, because the young man was gentle to little Katherine Riche. These men were sometimes at the Stonors' London warehouse and sometimes at their house in Calais, and they saved Betson a good deal of trouble, being experienced enough to oversee both the packing of wool in London and its sale in Calais.

To Calais the wool thus packed, and weighed and marked and assessed by the customs officer, was carried in the ships of Calais itself, or of the little ports on the east or south-eastern coast of England, many of which are mere villages today. For ships put out not only from Hull and Colchester, but from Brightlingsea, Rotherhithe, Walberswick in Suffolk, Rainham in Essex, Bradwell, Maidstone, Milton, Newhithe, and Milhall. In August 1478, the Celys were paying the masters of twenty-one different ships for the freight of their sarplers of wool after the summer clip.[45] All through the summer the shipping went on, and right up to Christmas; but during the winter months the merchants were mostly sending over fells or sheepskins, after the great slaughter of sheep and cattle which took place at Martinmas, when housewives salted down their meat for the winter and farmers made delivery of the fells and hides, for which the staplers had long ago bargained. Very often merchants' letters and customs accounts give us the names of these doughty little ships and their cargoes. In the October of 1481, for instance, the Celys were shipping a consignment of fells:

Right worshipful sir, after due recommendation I lowly recommend unto you, letting you understand that my master hath shipped his fells at the port of London now at this shipping in October . . ., which fells ye must receive and pay the freight first by the grace of God, in the 'Mary' of London, William Sordyvale master, 7 packs, sum 2800, lying be aft the mast, one pack lieth up rest and some of that pack is summer fells marked with an O, and then lieth 3 packs fells of William Daltons and under them lieth the other 6 packs of my masters. Item in the 'Christopher' of Rainham, Harry Wylkyns master, 7 packs and a half Cots[wold] fell, sum 3000 pelt, lying be aft the mast, and under them lieth a 200 fells of Welther Fyldes, William Lyndys man of Northampton, and the partition is made with small cords. Item, in the 'Thomas' of Maidstone, Harry Lawson master, 6 pokes, sum 2400 pelt, whereof lieth 5 packs next before the mast under hatches, no man above them, and one pack lieth in the stern sheet; of the six packs fells be some summer fells marked with an O likewise. Item, in the 'Mary Grace' of London, John Lokyngton master 6 packs, sum 2400 pelt, lying be aft under the fells of Thomas Graunger, the partition between them is made with red; sum of the fells my master hath shipped at this time 26 packs and a half whereof be winter fells of the country 561 fells and they be marked with an C, and of summer fells there should be 600 and more, but part of them be left behind, for we have two packs we could have no appointment for them, and all the summer fells be marked with an O. Item, sir, ye shall receive of the 'Mary' of Rainham, John Danyell master, your *male* [trunk] with your gear and a Essex cheese marked with my master's mark.

And so on, with details of the number of fells shipped in like manner by the *Michael* of Hull and the *Thomas* of Newhithe, where they lay 'next the mast aftward under the fells of Thomas Betson's', over 11,000 fells in all.[46]

How invigorating is such a list of ships. Cargoes are the most romantic of topics, whether they be apes and ivory and peacocks, or 'cheap tin trays'; and since the day that Jason sailed to Colchis fleeces have ever been among the most romantic of cargoes. How they smack of the salt too, those old master mariners, Henry Wilkins, master of the *Christopher* of Rainham, John Lollington, master of the *Jesu* of London, Robert Ewen, master of the *Thomas* of Newhithe, and all the rest of them, waving their hands to their wives and sweethearts as they sail out of the sparkling little bays, with the good woolsacks abaft or under hatches – shipmen, all of them, after Chaucer's heart:

> But of his craft, to rekene wel his tydes
> His stremes and his daungers hym besides,
> His herberwe and his moone, his lodemenage,
> Ther was noon swich from Hulle to Cartage.
> Hardy he was, and wys to undertake:
> With many a tempest hadde his berd been shake;
> He knew wel alle the havenes, as they were,
> From Gootland to the Cape of Fynystere,
> And every cryke in Britaigne and in Spayne.
> His barge y-cleped was the Maudelayne.

Their ships were doubtless like the *Margaret Cely*, which the two Cely brothers bought and called after their mother, for the not excessive sum of £28, exclusive of rigging and fittings. She carried a master, boatswain, cook, and sixteen jolly sailor-men, and she kept a good look out for pirates and was armed with cannon and bows, bills, five dozen darts, and twelve pounds of gunpowder! She was victualled with salt fish, bread, wheat and beer, and she plied with the Celys' trade to Zealand, Flanders, and Bordeaux.[47] She must have been about two hundred tons, but some of the other little ships were much smaller, for, as the learned editor of the *Cely Papers* tells us, 'The ships of the little Medway ports could scarcely have been of thirty tons to navigate the river safely; the "Thomas" of Maidstone can have been only a barge, if she had to pass Aylesford Bridge.'[48] But they navigated the channel and dodged the pirates blithely enough, though often Thomas Betson at Calais was nervous about the safe arrival of the wool fleet. Like Chaucer's merchant,

> He wolde the see were kept for any thing
> Betwixe Middelburgh and Orewelle.

Side by side with George or Richard Cely he must often have strained his eyes from the quay, with the salt wind blowing out the feather in his cap, and breathed a thanksgiving to God when the ships hove in sight. 'And, Sir,' he writes once to Stonor from London, 'thanked be the good Lord, I understand for certain that our wool shipped be comen in . . . to Calais. I would have kept the tidings till I had comen myself, because it is good, but I durst not be so bold, for your mastership now against this good time may be glad and joyful of these tidings, for in truth I am glad and heartily thank God of it.'[49] The 'prentice' Thomas Henham writes likewise three weeks later: 'I departed from Sandwich the 11th day of April and so came unto Calais upon Sher Thursday* last with the wool ships, and so blessed be Jesu I have received your wools in safety. Furthermore, Sir, if it please your mastership for to understand this, I have received your wools as fair and as whole as any man's in the fleet. Moreover, Sir, if it please your mastership for to understand how your wool was housed ever deal by Easter even. Furthermore, Sir, if it please your mastership for to understand that the shipman be content and paid of their freight.'[50] The Celys write in the same strain too: 'This day the 16th of August the wool fleet came to Calais both of London and Ipswich in safety, thanked be God, and this same day was part landed and it riseth fair yet, thanked be God.'[51] Their letters tell us too what danger it was that they feared. 'I pray Jesu send you safe hither and soon,' writes Richard to his 'right well beloved brother George', on June 6, 1482. 'Robert Eryke was chased with Scots between Calais and Dover. They scaped narrow.'[52] There are many such chases recorded, and we hear too of wool burnt under hatches or cast overboard in a storm.[53]

Thomas Betson and the Celys travelled very often across the Channel in these ships, which carried passengers and letters, and they were almost as much at home in Calais as in London. When in Calais English merchants were not allowed to live anywhere they liked, all over the town. The Company of the Staple had a list of regular licensed 'hosts', in whose houses they might stay. Usually a number of merchants lived with each host, the most potent, grave, and reverend seniors dining at a high table, and smaller fry at side tables in the hall. Sometimes they quarrelled over terms, as when

* I.e. Shrove Thursday.

William Cely writes home one day to Richard and George in London:

Item. Sir, please it you to understand that here is a variance betwixt our host Thomas Graunger and the fellowship, of our lodging, for Thomas Graunger promised us at his coming in to our lodging that we should pay no more for our board but 3*s*. 4*d*. a week at the high table, and 2*s*. 6*d*. at the side table, and now he saith he will have no less than 4*s*. a week at the high table and 40*d*. at the side table, wherefore the fellowship here will depart into other lodgings, some to one place and some to another, William Dalton will be at Robert Torneys and Ralph Temyngton and master Brown's man of Stamford shall be at Thomas Clarke's and so all the fellowship departs save I, wherefore I let your masterships have knowledge, that ye may do as it shall like you best.[54]

But Thomas Betson never fell out with his hosts, whose only complaint of him must have been that he sat long over his love letters and came down late to dinner.

There was business enough for him to do at Calais. First of all, when the wool was landed, it had to be inspected by the Royal officers, to see that it had been properly labelled, and their skilled packers examined, repacked, and resealed the bales. This was an anxious moment for merchants who were conscious of inferior wool among their bulging sarplers. The honest Betson, we may be certain, never cheated, but the Celys knew more than a little about the tricks of the trade, and one year, when the Lieutenant of Calais took out sarpler No. 24, which their agent, William Cely, knew to be poor wool, in order to make a test, he privily substitutes No. 8, which was 'fair wool' and changed the labels, so that he was soon able to write home, 'Your wool is awarded by the sarpler that I cast out last.'[55] No wonder Gower said that Trick was regent of the Staple,

> Siq'en le laines maintenir
> Je voi plusours descontenir
> Du loyalté la viele usance.[56]

Then there was the custom and subsidy to be paid to the Mayor and Fellowship of the Staple, who collected it for the King. And then came the main business of every merchant, the selling of the wool. Thomas Betson preferred, of course, to sell it as quickly as possible, as the ships came in, but sometimes the market was slow and wool remained for some months on his hands. Such wool from the summer sheep shearing, shipped in or before the month of February following, and remaining unsold by April 6th, was classed as old wool, and the Fellowship of the Staple ordained that foreign buyers must take one sarpler of old wool with every three of new; and although the Flemings grumbled and wanted to take one of old to five of new, they had to put up with the regulation.[57] A great deal of Betson's business would be done at the mart of Calais itself, where he met with the dignified Flemish merchants, scions of old families with estates of their own, and the more plebeian merchants of Delft and Leyden, and the wool dealers from sunny Florence and Genoa and Venice. Among the best customers both of the Stonors and the Celys (for they are mentioned in the letters of both) were Peter and Daniel van de Rade of Bruges. Thomas Howlake on one occasion reports a sale of four sarplers of fine Cotswold wool to them at 19 marks the sack, with a rebate of $4\frac{1}{2}$ cloves on the sack of 52, and adds: 'Sir, an it please you, as for the foresaid merchants that have bought your wool, [they] be as good as any that came out of Flanders and for that I have showed them the more favour and given them the more respite of that.'[58]

The staplers, however, did not do business at Calais alone, but rode also to the great fairs at Antwerp, Bruges, and the country round. 'Thomas Betson,' writes Henham to his master, 'came unto Calais the last day of April and so he departed in good health unto Bruges mart the first day of May.'[59]

> But so bifel this marchant on a day
> Shoop hym to make redy his array
> Toward the toun of Brugges for to fare,
> To byen there a porcioun of ware – [60]

only it was to 'sellen' a portion that Betson went. He himself writes Sir William: 'Liketh it you to wit that on Trinity even I came to Calais and, thanked be the good Lord, I had a full fair passage, and, Sir, with God's might I intend on Friday next to depart to the mart-wards. I beseech the good Lord be my speed and help me in all my works. And, Sir, I trust to God's mercy, if the world be merry here, to do somewhat that shall be both to your profit and mine. As yet there cometh but few merchants here; hereafter with God's grace there will come more. I shall lose no time when the season shall come, I promise you. . . . And, Sir, when I come from the mart I shall send you word of all matters by the mercy of our Lord.'[61] At the fairs Betson would meet with a great crowd of merchants from all over Europe, though often enough political disturbances made the roads dangerous and merchants ran some risk of being robbed. The English traders were commonly reputed to be the best sellers and customers at the fairs of Flanders and Brabant, though the Flemings sometimes complained of them, and said that the staplers made regulations forbidding their merchants to buy except on the last day, when the Flemish sellers, anxious to pack and be off, let their goods go at insufficient prices.[62] The author of the *Libelle of Englyshe Polycye* boasts proudly of the custom brought by the English to these marts:

> But they of Holonde at Calyse byene oure felles,
> And oure wolles, that Englyshe men hem selles . . .
> And wee to martis of Braban charged bene
> Wyth Englysshe clothe, fulle gode and feyre to seyne,
> Wee bene ageyne charged wyth mercerye
> Haburdasshere ware and wyth grocerye,
> To whyche martis, that Englisshe men call feyres
> Iche nacion ofte makethe here repayeres,
> Englysshe and Frensh, Lumbards, Januayes [Genoese],
> Cathalones, theder take here wayes,
> Scottes, Spaynardes, Iresshmen there abydes,
> Wythe grete plente bringing of salt hydes,
> And I here saye that we in Braban lye,
> Flaunders and Seland, we bye more marchaundy
> In common use, then done all other nacions;
> This have I herde of marchaundes relacions,
> And yff the Englysshe be not in the martis,
> They bene febelle and as nought bene here partes;
> For they bye more and fro purse put owte
> More marchaundy than alle other rowte.[63]

Fairs were held at different times in different places, but there were during the year four great fair seasons corresponding to the four seasons in the year.[64] There was the Cold mart in the winter, to which Thomas Betson rode muffled in fur, with his horse's hoofs ringing on the frosty roads; there was the Pask (*Pasques*, Easter) mart in the spring, when he whistled blithely and stuck a violet in his cap; there was the Synxon (St John) mart in the summer, round about St John the Baptist's Day, when he was hot and mopped his brow, and bought a roll of tawny satin or Lucca silk for Katherine from a Genoese in a booth at Antwerp; and there was the Balms, or Bammys mart in the autumn, round about the day of St Rémy, whom the Flemings call St Bamis (October 28), when he would buy her a fur of budge or mink, or a mantle of fine black shanks from the Hansards at their mart in Bruges. It was at these marts that the Merchants of the Staple, jaunting about from place to place to meet buyers for their wool, did a hundred little commissions for their friends; for folk at home were apt to think that staplers existed to do their errands for them abroad and to send them presents. One wanted a pair of Louvain gloves, the other a sugar loaf, the other a pipe of Gascon wine ('You can get it cheaper over there, my dear'), the other a yard or two of Holland cloth; while ginger and saffron were always welcome, and could be bought from the Venetians, whom the Celys spell 'Whenysyans'. Then, of course, there were purchases to be made in the way of business, such as Calais pack-thread and canvas from Arras or Brittany or Normandy to pack the bales of wool.[65] As to the Celys, Thomas Betson was wont to say that their talk was of nothing but sport and buying hawks, save on one gloomy occasion, when George Cely rode for ten miles in silence and then confided to him that over in England his grey bitch had whelped and had fourteen pups, and then died and the pups with her.[66]

Between the counting-house in Calais and the fairs and marts of the country Thomas Betson would dispose of his wool and fells. But his labour did not end here, for he would now have to embark upon the complicated business of collecting money from his customers, the Flemish merchants, and with it paying his creditors in England, the Cotswold wool dealers. It was customary for the staplers to pay for their wool by bills due, as a rule, at six months, and Thomas Betson would be hard put to meet them if the foreign buyers delayed to pay him. Moreover, his difficulties were inconceivably complicated by the exchanges. We think we know something about the difficulty of divers and fluctuating exchanges today, but we can hardly imagine the elaborate calculations and the constant disputes which racked the brain of a Merchant of the Staple in the fifteenth century. Not only did the rates between England and the Continent constantly vary, but, as the editor of the *Cely Papers* points out, 'the number of potentates of all kinds who claimed the privilege of issuing their own coinage and the frequently suspicious character of what they uttered as gold and silver, made the matter of adjustment of values difficult for the Celys, who were evidently obliged to take what they could get.'[67] Only imagine the difficulties of poor Thomas Betson, when into his counting-house there wandered in turn the Andrew guilder of Scotland, the Arnoldus gulden of Gueldres (very much debased), the Carolus groat of Charles of Burgundy, new crowns and old crowns of France, the David and the Falewe of the Bishopric of Utrecht, the Hettinus groat of the Counts of Westphalia, the Lewe or French Louis d'or, the Limburg groat, the Milan groat, the Nimueguen groat, the Phelippus or Philippe d'or of Brabant, the Plaques of Utrecht, the Postlates of various bishops, the English Ryall (worth ten shillings), the Scots Rider or the Rider of Burgundy (so called because they bore the figure of a man on horseback), the Florin Rhenau of the Bishopric of Cologne and the Setillers.[68] He had to know the value in English money of them all, as it was fixed for the time being by the Fellowship, and most of them were debased past all reason. Indeed, English money enjoyed an enviable good fame in this respect until Henry VIII began debasing the coinage for his own nefarious ends. The letters of the Celys are full of worried references to the exchange, and much we should pity Thomas Betson. But doubtless he was like Chaucer's bearded merchant: 'Wel koude he in exchaunge sheeldes [French crowns] selle.'

To effect their payments between England and the Netherlands the staplers used to make use of the excellent banking facilities and instruments of credit (bills of exchange and so forth), which were

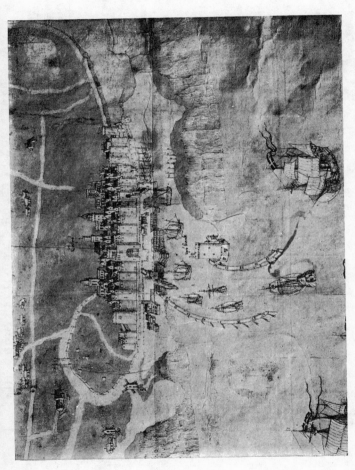

VII. CALAIS ABOUT THE TIME OF THOMAS BETSON

VIII. THOMAS PAYCOCKE'S HOUSE AT COGGESHALL

placed at their disposal by Italian and Spanish merchants and by the English mercers, all of whom combined trading with financial operations. Thus we find William Cely writing to his masters:

Please your masterships to understand that I have received of John Delowppys upon payment of the bill, the which is sent me by Adlington but £300 fleming, whereof I have paid to Gynott Strabant £84 6s. 6d. fleming. Item, I have made you over by exchange with Benynge Decasonn, Lombard, 180 nobles sterling, payable at usance. I delivered it at 11s. 2½d. fleming the noble, it amounteth £100 17s. 6d. fleming. Item, I have made you over by exchange in like wise with Jacob van de Base 89 nobles and 6s. sterling, payable at London at usuance in like wise; I delivered it at 11s. 2d. fleming for every noble sterling; it amounteth fl. – £50 fleming and the rest of your £300 remains still by me, for I can make you over no more at this season, for here is no more that will take any money as yet. And money goeth now upon the bourse at 11s. 3½d. the noble and none other money but Nimueguen groats, crowns, Andrew guilders and Rhenish guilders, and the exchange goeth ever the longer worse and worse. Item, sir, I send you enclosed in this said letter, the two first letters of the payment of the exchange above written. Benynge Decasonn's letter is directed to Gabriel Defuye and Peter Sanly, Genoese, and Jacob van de Base's is directed to Anthony Carsy and Marcy Strossy, Spaniards; in Lombard Street ye shall hear of them.[69]

A week later he writes:

I understand your masterships hath taken up by exchange of John Raynold, mercer, £60 sterling, payable the 25th day of the month and of Deago Decastron [Diego da Castro, a Spaniard] other £60 sterling, payable the 26th day of the same month, the which shall be both content at the day; and as for master Lewis More, Lombard, [he] is paid and I have the bill; his attorney is a wrangling fellow—he would none other money but Nimueguen groats.[70]

Many a letter such as this must Thomas Betson have written at his lodgings, sitting so late over his work that he must needs write to his friends when he ought to be sleeping and date his letters: 'At London, on our Lady day in the night, when I deem ye were in your bed, for mine eyne smarted, so God help me.'[71] And when he came to make up his annual accounts he had the hardest work of all to do. Here is a portrait of him at his labours:

> The thridde day this marchant up ariseth,
> And on his nedes sadly hym avyseth,
> And up into his countour-hous gooth he,
> To rekene with hymself, as wel may be,
> Of thilke yeer, how that it with hymn stood,
> And how that he despended hadde his good,
> And if that he encressed were or noon.
> His bookes and his bagges, many oon,
> He leith biform hymn on his countyng-bord.
> Ful riche was his tresor and his hord,
> For which ful faste his countour dore he shette;
> And eek he nolde that no man sholde hymn lette
> Of his accountes, for the meene tyme;
> And thus he sit til it was passed pryme.[72]

Thus was passed the life of a Merchant of the Staple: in riding to the Cotswold farms for wool; in business at the counting-houses in Marks Lane; in sailing from London to Calais and from Calais to London again; in dealing with merchant strangers at the mart in Calais, or riding to the marts of Flanders in fair time. The great company sheltered him, arranged his lodging, kept a sharp eye on the quality of his wool, made rules for his buying and selling, and saw that he had justice in its court. It was in this setting of hard and withal of interesting work that Thomas Betson's love story flowered into a happy marriage. He was not destined to live long after his recovery from the serious illness of 1479; perhaps it left him permanently delicate, for he died some six years later, in 1486. During her seven years of married life (beginning, be it remembered, at the age of fifteen), the diligent Katherine had borne him five children, two sons, Thomas and John, and three daughters, Elizabeth, Agnes, and Alice. Fortunately Thomas died very comfortably off, as his will (still preserved in Somerset House) informs us. He had become a member of the Fishmongers' Company as well as a Merchant of the Staple, for by his time the great city companies were no longer confined to persons actually engaged in the trade which each represented. In his will[73] Thomas Betson leaves money for the repair of the roof loft in his parish church of All Hallows, Barking, where he was buried, and 'thirty pounds to the garnishing of the Staple Chapel in Our Lady Church at Calais, to buy some jewel', and twenty pounds to the 'Stockfishmongers' to buy plate. He makes the latter company the guardian of his children, leaves his house to his wife, and a legacy of 40s. to Thomas Henham, his colleague in Stonor's service, and characteristically gives directions 'for the costs of my burying to be done not outrageously, but soberly and discreetly and in a mean [moderate, medium] manner, that it may be unto the worship and laud of Almighty God.' Katherine, a widow with five children at the age of twenty-two, married as her second husband William Welbech, haberdasher (the Haberdashers were a wealthy company), by whom she had another son. But her heart stayed with the husband who wrote her her first playful love-letter when she was a child, and on her death in 1510 she directed that she should be laid by the side of Thomas Betson at All Hallows, Barking, where three staplers still lie beneath their brasses, although no trace of him remains.[74] There let them lie, long forgotten, and yet worthier of memory than many of the armoured knights who sleep under carved sepulchres in our beautiful medieval churches.

> The garlands wither on your brow;
>   Then boast no more your mighty deeds!
> Upon Death's purple altar now
>   See where the victor-victim bleeds.
>   Your heads must come
>   To the cold tomb:
> Only the actions of the just
> Smell sweet and blossom in their dust.

CHAPTER VII

Thomas Paycocke of Coggeshall

AN ESSEX CLOTHIER IN THE DAYS OF HENRY VII

This was a gallant cloathier sure
Whose fame for ever shall endure.

— THOMAS DELONEY

THE GREAT AND noble trade of cloth-making has left many traces upon the life of England, architectural, literary, and social. It has filled our countryside with magnificent Perpendicular churches and gracious oak-beamed houses. It has filled our popular literature with old wives' tales of the worthies of England, in which the clothiers Thomas of Reading and Jack of Newbury rub elbows with Friar Bacon and Robin Hood. It has filled our shires with gentlemen; for, as Defoe observed, in the early eighteenth century 'many of the great families who now pass for gentry in the western counties have been originally raised from and built up by this truly noble manufacture'. It has filled our census lists with surnames – Weaver, Webber, Webb, Sherman, Fuller, Walker, Dyer – and given to every unmarried woman the designation of a spinster. And from the time when the cloth trade ousted that of wool as the chief export trade of England down to the time when it was in its turn ousted by iron and cotton, it was the foundation of England's commercial greatness. 'Among all Crafts,' says old Deloney, 'this was the only chief, for that it was the greatest merchandize, by the which our Country became famous thorowout all Nations.'[1]

Already by the end of the fourteenth century the English clothiers were beginning to rival those of the Netherlands in the making of fine cloth, as witness Chaucer's Wife of Bath:

Of clooth-making she hadde swiche an haunt
She passed hem of Ypres and of Gaunt,

and by the end of the sixteenth century all real rivalry was at an end, for the English manufacture was so clearly victorious. With the development of the manufacture a change too took place in its organization. It had never been an easy industry to organize on a gild basis, because the making of a piece of cloth entailed so many distinct processes. The preliminary processes of spinning and carding were always by-industries, performed by women and children in their cottages; but the weavers, who bought the spun yarn, had their gild; and so had the fullers, who fulled it; and the shearmen, who finished it; and the dyers who dyed it. All could not sell the finished piece of cloth, and in the group of inter-dependent crafts, each with its gild, we sometimes find the weavers employing the fullers and sometimes the fullers the weavers. Moreover, since weaving is a much quicker process than spinning, the weaver often wasted much time and found it hard to collect enough yarn to keep his loom busy; and, as the market for cloth grew wider and was no longer confined to the town of the weaver, the need was felt for some middleman to specialize in the selling of the finished cloth. So by degrees there grew up a class of men who bought wool in large quantities and sold it to the weavers, and then by a natural transition began, not to sell the wool outright, but to deliver it to the weavers to weave, to the fullers to full, and to the shearmen to finish at a wage, receiving it back again when the work was done. These men grew rich; they amassed capital; they could set many folk at work. Soon they began to set to work all the different workers who combined to make a piece of cloth; their servants carried wool to the cottages for the women to card and spin; carried the spun yarn in turn to dyers, weavers, fullers, shearers; and carried the finished piece of cloth back to the industrial middleman – the clothier, as he was called – who in his turn disposed of it to the mercantile middleman, who was called a draper. The clothiers grew rapidly in wealth and importance, and in certain parts of the country became the backbone of the middle class. They pursued their activities in country villages, rather than in the old corporate towns, for they wished to avoid the restrictions of the gilds, and gradually the cloth industry migrated almost entirely to the country. In the west of England and in East Anglia (though not in Yorkshire) it

was carried out by clothiers on this 'putting out' system, right up
to the moment when the Industrial Revolution swept it out of the
cottages into the factories and out of the south into the north. Then
the thriving villages emptied themselves, so that today we must
needs re-create again from scattered traces and old buildings, and
still older names, the once familiar figures of the East Anglian
clothier and his swarm of busy workmen.

Such a familiar figure was once old Thomas Paycocke, clothier,
of Coggeshall in Essex, who died full of years and honour in 1518.
His family originally came from Clare, in Suffolk, but about the
middle of the fifteenth century a branch settled at Coggeshall, a
village not far distant. His grandfather and father would seem to
have been grazing butchers, but he and his brother and their de-
scendants after them followed 'the truly noble manufacture' of
cloth-making, and set an indelible mark upon the village where they
dwelt. Coggeshall lies in the great cloth-making district of Essex,
of which Fuller wrote: 'This county is charactered like Bethsheba,
"She layeth her hand to the spindle and her hands hold the distaffe." . . . It will not be amiss to pray that the plough may go along
and the wheel around, that so (being fed by the one and clothed
by the other) there may be, by God's blessing, no danger of starv-
ing in our nation.'[2] All over Essex there lay villages famous for
cloth-making, Coggeshall and Braintree, Bocking and Halstead,
Shalford and Dedham, and above all Colchester, the great centre
and mart of the trade. The villages throve on the industry and there
was hardly a cottage which did not hum with the spinning wheel,
and hardly a street where you might not have counted weavers'
workshops, kitchens where the rough loom stood by the wall to
occupy the goodman's working hours. Hardly a week but the clatter
of the pack-horse would be heard in the straggling streets, bringing
in new stores of wool to be worked and taking away the pieces of
cloth to the clothiers of Colchester and the surrounding villages.
Throughout the fifteenth century Coggeshall was an important
centre, second only to the great towns of Norwich, Colchester, and
Sudbury, and to this day its two inns are called the 'Woolpack' and
the 'Fleece.' We must, as I said, build up the portrait of Thomas
Paycocke and his compeers from scattered traces; but happily such

traces are common enough in many and many an English village, and in Coggeshall itself they lie ready to our hand. Out of three things he can be brought to life again – to wit, his house in the village street, his family brasses in the aisle of the village church, and his will, which is preserved at Somerset House. A house, a brass, a will – they seem little enough, but they hold all his history. It is the greatest error to suppose that history must needs be something written down; for it may just as well be something built up, and churches, houses, bridges, or amphitheatres can tell their story as plainly as print for those who have eyes to read. The Roman villa, excavated after lying lost for centuries beneath the heel of the un- witting ploughboy – that villa with its spacious ground-plan, its floors rich with mosaic patterns, its elaborate heating apparatus, and its shattered vases — brings home more clearly than any textbook the real meaning of the Roman Empire, whose citizens lived like this in a foggy island at the uttermost edge of its world. The Nor- man castle, with moat and drawbridge, gatehouse and bailey and keep, arrow slits instead of windows, is more eloquent than a hundred chronicles of the perils of life in the twelfth century; not thus dwelt the private gentleman in the days of Rome. The country manor-house of the fourteenth century, with courtyard and chapel and hall and dovecote, speaks of an age of peace once more, when life on a thousand little manors revolved round the lord, and the great mass of Englishmen went unscathed by the Hundred Years' War which seamed the fair face of France. Then begin the mer- chants' elaborate Perpendicular houses in the towns and villages of the fifteenth century, standing on the road, with gardens behind them, and carved beams, great fire-places, and a general air of com- fort; they mark the advent of a new class in English history – the middle class, thrust between lord and peasant and coming to its own. How the spacious days of great Elizabeth are mirrored in the beautiful Elizabethan houses, with their wide wings and large rooms, their chimneys, their glass windows, looking outwards on to open parks and spreading trees, instead of inwards on to the closed courtyard. Or go into a house built or redecorated in the eighteenth century, where you will see Chippendale chairs and lacquer tables and Chinese wall-papers covered with pagodas and mandarins; and surely there will come to your mind the age of the nabobs, the age which John Company had familiarized with the products of the Far East, the age in which tea ousted coffee as the drink for a gentleman of fashion, in which Horace Walpole collected porcelain, Oliver Goldsmith idealized China in 'The Citizen of the World', and Dr Johnson was called the Great Cham of Literature. Look here upon this picture and on this: look at that row of jerry-built houses, a hundred in a row and all exactly alike, or that new-art villa, all roof and hardly any window, with false bottle glass in its panes; here is the twentieth century for you. Indeed all the social and very much of the political history of England may be reconstructed from her architecture alone; and so I make no apology for calling Thomas Paycocke's house first-rate historical evidence.

Of much the same type, though less interesting, is the evidence of monumental brasses, which are to be found in most parts of England and which abound in East Anglia, the Home Counties, and the Thames Valley.[3] Their variety is magnificent; brasses of ecclesiastics in vestments, of doctors of law and divinity and masters of arts in academic dress and of a few abbots and abbesses; brasses of knights in armour; brasses of ladies, with their little dogs at their feet and dresses which show the changes in fashion from century to century and make clear all the mysteries of kirtles and cottehardies, wimples and partlets and farthingales and the head-dresses appropriate to each successive mode. The brasses also, like the houses, bear witness to the prosperity of the middle class, for in the fourteenth century when merchants began to build themselves fine houses they began also to bury themselves under splendid brasses. Finest of all, perhaps, are the brasses of the wool staplers, with feet resting on woolpack or sheep; but there are many other merchants too. Mayors and aldermen abound; they set their merchants' marks upon their tombs as proudly as gentlemen set their coats of arms, and indeed they had as great cause for pride. You may see them at their proudest in the famous brass at Lynn, where Robert Braunch lies between his two wives, and at his feet is incised a scene representing the feast at which he entertained Edward III royally and feasted him on peacocks. There is a tailor with his shears, as glorious as the Crusader's sword, at Northleach, and a wine merchant with his feet upon a wine cask at Cirencester. There are smaller folk, too, less dowered with wealth but proud enough of the implements of their craft; two or three public notaries with penhorn and pencase complete, a huntsman with his horn, and in Newland Church one of the free miners of the Forest of Dean, cap and leather breeches tied below the knee, wooden mine-hod over shoulder, a small mattock in his right hand, and a candlestick between his teeth. This kind of historical evidence will help us with Thomas Paycocke. His family brasses were set in the north aisle of the parish church of St Peter Ad Vincula. Several of them have disappeared in the course of the last century and a half, and unluckily no brass of Thomas himself survives; but in the aisle there still lie two – the brass of his brother John, who died in 1533, and John's wife, and that of his nephew, another Thomas, who died in 1580; the merchant's mark may still be seen thereon.

Lastly, there is the evidence of the Paycocke wills, of which three are preserved at Somerset House – the will of John Paycocke (*d.* 1505), Thomas's father and the builder of the house; the will of Thomas Paycocke himself (*d.* 1518); and the will of his nephew Thomas, the same whose brass lies in the aisle and who left a long and splendidly detailed testament, full of information upon local history and the organization of the cloth industry. For social historians have as yet hardly, perhaps, made as much use as they might of the evidence of wills. The enormous amount of miscellaneous information to be derived therefrom about the life of our forefathers can hardly be believed, save by those who have turned the pages of such a collection as the great *Testamenta Eboracensia.*[4] In wills you may see how many daughters a man could dower and how many he put into a nunnery, and what education he provided for his sons. You may note which were the most popular religious houses, and which men had books and what the books were, how much of their money they thought fit to leave for charitable purposes, and what they thought of the business capacity of their wives. You may read long and dazzling lists of family plate, all the favourite cups and dishes having pet names of their own, and of rings and brooches and belts and rosaries. There are detailed descriptions of dresses and furs, sometimes splendid, sometimes ordinary, for people handed on their rich clothes as carefully as their jewels. There are even more wonderful descriptions of beds, with all their bedclothes and hangings, for a bed was a very valuable article of furniture and must often, judging from the wills, have been a brilliant and beautiful object indeed; Shakespeare has earned a great deal of unmerited obloquy for leaving Ann Hathaway his second-best bed, though it is not to be denied that he might have left her his first-best. Even more beautiful than dressings and bed or chamber hangings are the brocaded and embroidered vestments mentioned in wills, and the elaborate arrangements for funeral ceremonies are extremely interesting. The wills are of all kinds; there are even villeins' wills, though in theory the villein's possessions were his lord's, and there are wills of kings and queens, lords and ladies, bishops and parsons and lawyers and shopkeepers. Here also is more evidence for the social prosperity of the middle class, details of their trade, the contents of their shops, the inventories of their houses, their estates (sometimes) in the country, their house rents (almost always) in the town, their dressers garnished with plate and their wives' ornaments, their apprentices and their gilds, their philanthropy, their intermarriage with the gentry, their religious opinions. Such a living picture do men's wills give us of their daily lives.

These, then, are the three sources from which the life and times of Thomas Paycocke may be drawn. All three – houses, brasses, and wills – contain much evidence for the increasingly rapid growth during the last two centuries of the Middle Ages of a large and prosperous middle class, whose wealth was based not upon landed property but upon industry and trade. It is a class of whom we have already met typical examples in Thomas Betson and the anonymous Ménagier de Paris, and we must now see what his house, his will, and his family brasses tell us about the clothier Thomas Paycocke. First and foremost, they tell us a great deal about the noble industry which supported him. Paycocke's house is full of relics of the cloth industry. The merchant mark of the Paycockes, an ermine tail, looking like a two-stemmed clover leaf, is to be found on the carved beams of the chimney, on the breastsummers of the fire-places, and set in the midst of the strip of carving along the front of the house.

Thomas marked his bales of cloth thus, and what other armorial bearings did he need? The whole house is essentially middle class – the house of a man who was *nouveau riche* in an age when to be *nouveau riche* was not yet to be vulgar. His prosperity has blossomed out into exquisitely ornate decoration. A band of carving runs along the front of the house, and from the curved stem of it branch out a hundred charming devices – leaves, tendrils, strange flowers, human heads, Tudor roses, a crowned king and queen lying hand in hand, a baby diving with a kick of fat legs into the bowl of an arum lily, and in the midst the merchant's mark upon a shield and the initials of the master of the house. In the hall is a beautiful ceiling of carved oakwork, exceedingly elaborate and bearing at intervals the merchant's mark again. Upstairs in the big bedchamber is a ceiling of beams worked in bold roll mouldings; and there is an exquisite little parlour, lined with linen fold panels, with a breastsummer carved with strange animals. This elaboration is characteristic. It is all of a piece with Coggeshall Church, and with all those other spacious East Anglian churches, Lavenham, Long Melford, Thaxted, Saffron Walden, Lynn, Snettisham, lofty and spacious, which the clothiers built out of their newly won wealth. The very architecture is characteristic, *nouveau riche* again, like those who paid for it, the elaborate ornament and sumptuous detail of the Perpendicular taking the place of the simple majesty of the Early English style. It is just the sort of architecture that a merchant with a fortune would pay for. The middle class liked some show for its money; but again it was the ostentation without the vulgarity of wealth. Looking upon his beautiful house, or worshipping beside his family tombs, with the merchant's mark on the brasses, in St Katherine's aisle, Thomas Paycocke must often have blessed the noble industry which supported him.

The wills of the Paycockes tell the same story. To whom beside his family does Thomas leave legacies but the good folk of the neighbourhood, who worked for him. There is the Goodday family of cheerful name, two of whom were shearmen, or cloth finishers, and had substantial gifts. 'I bequeth to Thomas Goodday Sherman xx s. and ych of his childryn iij s. iiij d. apece. Item, I bequeth to Edward Goodday Sherman xvj s. viij d., and to his child iij s. iiij d.,

He also left money to Robert Goodday of Sampford and to Robert's brother John and to each of Robert's sisters, with something extra for Grace, who was his goddaughter; and he did not forget Nicholas Goodday of Stisted and Robert Goodday of Coggeshall and their families, nor their relative John, who was a priest and had ten shillings for a trental. All these Gooddays were doubtless bound to Thomas Paycocke by ties of work as well as of friendship. They belonged to a well-known Coggeshall family, for generations connected with the cloth industry. Thomas Paycocke's namesake and grand-nephew, whose will is dated 1580, was still in close relations with· them, and left 'to Edwarde Goodaye my godson Fourtie shillinges and to every brother and sister the saide Edwarde hath livinge at the tyme of my decease tenne shillinges a pece,' and 'unto William Gooday thelder tenne shillinges.' The hurrying, scattering generation of today can hardly imagine the immovable stability of the village of past centuries, when generation after generation grew from cradle to grave in the same houses, on the same cobbled streets, and folk of the same name were still friends, as their fathers and grandfathers had been before them.

Other friends and employees of Thomas Paycocke also had their legacies. He leaves 6s. 8d. to Humphrey Stonor, 'somtyme my prentis'. We may see Humphrey Stonor, with sleepy eyes, making his way downstairs on a frosty morning, from those huge raftered attics, where perhaps the 'prentices used to sleep. He was on terms of impudent friendship, no doubt, with the weavers and fullers whom his master set to work; withal a young man of good family, a relative perchance of those Stonors for whom Thomas Betson worked, for, as Deloney wrote, 'the yonger sons of knights and gentlemen, to whom their Fathers would leave no lands, were most commonly preferred to learn this trade, to the end that thereby they might live in good estate and drive forth their days in prosperity.' Two of his friends got substantial legacies; apparently Thomas Paycocke had lent them money and wished to wipe out the debt upon his death-bed, for, says the will, 'I bequethe to John Beycham, my weyver, v li and [i.e. if] there be so moch bitwene vs and ells to make it vp v li, and a gowne and a doublett. . . . I bequeth and forgive Robert Taylor, fuller, all that is betwixt vs, and more I give him

iij s. iiij d.' Other legacies show even more clearly that his operations
were on a larger scale. 'I bequeth to all my wevers, ffullers and sher-
men that be not afore Rehersed by name xij d. apece, And will they
that have wrought me verey moch wark have iij s. iiij d. apece.
Item, I bequethe to be distributed amonge my Kembers, Carders
and Spynners summa iiij li.' [5] Here are all the branches of the cloth
industry at a glance. It is Thomas Paycocke, clothier, round whom
the whole manufacture revolves. He gives the wool to the women
to comb it and card it and spin it; he receives it from them again
and gives it to the weaver to be woven into cloth; he gives the cloth
to the fuller to be fulled and the dyer to be dyed; and having received it when finished, he has it made up into dozens and sends it
off to the wholesale dealer, the draper, who sells it; perhaps he has
been wont to send it to that very 'Thomas Perpoint, draper'
whom he calls 'my cosyn' and makes his executor. The whole
of Thomas Paycocke's daily business is implicit in his will. In
the year of his death he was still employing a large number of
workers and was on friendly and benevolent terms with them. The
building of his house had not signalized his retirement from business,
as happened when another great clothier, Thomas Dolman, gave up
cloth-making and the weavers of Newbury went about lamenting:

> Lord have mercy upon us, miserable sinners.
> Thomas Dolman has built a new house and turned away all his
> spinners.[6]

The relations between Paycocke and his employees evinced
in his will are happy ones. Such was not always the case, for if the
clothiers of this age had some of the virtues of capitalists, they also
had many of their vices, and the age-old strife of capital and
labour was already well advanced in the fifteenth century One detail
Paycocke's will does not give us, which we should be glad to know:
did he employ only domestic weavers, working in their own
houses, or did he also keep a certain number of looms working in
his house? It was characteristic of the period in which he lived that
something like a miniature factory system was establishing itself in
the midst of the new outwork system. The clothiers were beginning to set up looms in their own houses and to work them by

journeymen weavers; as a rule the independent weavers greatly disliked the practice, for either they were forced from the position of free masters into that of hired servants, obliged to go and work in the clothier's loom shop, or else they found their payment forced down by the competition of the journeymen. Moreover, the clothiers sometimes owned and let out looms to their work-people, and then also part of the industrial independence of the weaver was lost. All through the first half of the sixteenth century the weavers in the cloth districts kept on petitioning Parliament against this new evil of capitalism. It was as though, long before it established itself in England they had a prevision of the factory system and of the worker no longer owning either his raw material, his tool, his workshop, or the produce of his industry, but only his labour; the master-weaver dwindled to a hired hand. Certainly the practice was growing in Essex, where, some twenty years after Thomas Paycocke's death, the weavers petitioned against the clothiers, who had their own looms and weavers and fullers in their own houses, so that the petitioners were rendered destitute; 'for the rich men, the clothiers, be concluded and agreed among themselves to hold and pay one price for weaving the said cloths,' a price too small to support their households, even if they worked day and night, holiday and work-day, so that many of them lost their independence and were reduced to become other men's servants. [7] Nevertheless, the outwork system remained the more common, and without doubt the majority of Paycocke's workers lived in their own cottages, though it is probable also that he had some looms in his house, perhaps in the long, low room at the back, which is traditionally supposed to have been used for weaving, perhaps in a shed or 'spinning house'.

A highly idyllic picture of work in one of these miniature factories, which we may amuse ourselves by applying to Thomas Paycocke's, is contained in Deloney's *Pleasant History of Jack of Newbery*. Jack of Newbury was an historical character, a very famous clothier named John Winchcomb who died at Newbury only a year later than Paycocke himself, and of whom Paycocke must certainly have heard, for his kersies were famous on the Continent, and old Fuller, who celebrates him among his *Worthies of England* calls him 'the most considerable clothier (without fancy or fiction) England ever beheld'.[8] The tales of how he had led a hundred of his own 'prentices to Flodden Field, how he had feasted the King and Queen in his house at Newbury, how he had built part of Newbury Church, and how he had refused a knighthood, preferring 'to rest in his russet coat a poor clothier to his dying day,' spread about England, growing as they spread. In 1597 Thomas Deloney, the forefather of the novel, enshrined them in a rambling tale, half prose and half verse, which soon became extremely popular. It is from this tale that we may take an imaginary picture of work in a clothier's house, being wary to remember, however, that it is an exaggeration, a legend, and that the great John Winchcomb certainly never had as many as two hundred looms in his own house, while our Thomas Paycocke probably had not more than a dozen. But the poet must have his licence, for, after all, the spirit of the ballad is the thing, and it is always a pleasant diversion to drop into rhyme:

> Within one roome, being large and long
> There stood two hundred Loomes full strong.
> Two hundred men, the truth is so,
> Wrought in these Loomes all in a row.
> By every one a pretty boy
> Sate making quilts with mickle joy,
> And in another place hard by
> A hundred women merrily
> Were carding hard with joyfull cheere
> Who singing sate with voyces cleere,
> And in a chamber close beside
> Two hundred maidens did abide,
> In petticoats of Stammell red,
> And milk white kerchers on their head.
> Their smocke-sleeves like to winter snow
> That on the Westerne mountaines flow,
> And each sleeve with a silken band
> Was featly tied at the hand.
> These pretty maids did never lin
> But in that place all day did spin,
> And spinning so with voyces meet
> Like nightingales they sang full sweet.
> Then to another roome came they

Where children were in poore aray;
And every one sate picking wool
The finest from the course to cull:
The number was sevenscore and ten
The children of poore silly men:
And these their labours to requite
Had every one a penny at night,
Beside their meat and drinke all day,
Which was to them a wondrous stay.
Within another place likewise
Full fifty proper men he spies
And these were sheremen everyone,
Whose skill and cunning there was showne:
And hard by them there did remaine
Full four-score rowers taking paine.
A Dye-house likewise had he then,
Wherein he kept full forty men:
And likewise in his Fulling Mill
Full twenty persons kept he still.
Each weeke ten good fat oxen he
Spent in his house for certaintie,
Beside good butter, cheese and fish
And many another wholesome dish.
He kept a Butcher all the yeere,
A Brewer eke for Ale and Beere;
A Baker for to bake his Bread,
Which stood his hushold in good stead.
Five Cookes within his kitchin great
Were all the yeare to dress his meat.
Six Scullion boyes vnto their hands,
To make clean dishes, pots and pans,
Beside poore children that did stay
To turne the broaches every day.
The old man that did see this sight
Was much amaz'd, as well he might:
This was a gallant Cloathier sure,
Whose fame forever shall endure.[9]

The private life of Thomas Paycocke, no less than his business,
can be made to live again. Of his family the invaluable will tells us

a little. His first wife was that Margaret whose initials, together with his own, decorate the woodwork of the house, and indeed it is probable that old John Paycocke built the house for the young couple on their wedding. Gay, indeed, must have been the sights which it witnessed on that happy day, for our ancestors knew how to put their hearts into a wedding, and Merry England was never merrier then when the bridegroom led home the bride. We may borrow once again from Deloney's idyll, to recreate the scene:

The Bride being attyred in a gowne of sheepes russet and a kertle of fine woosted, her head attyred with a billiment of gold and her haire as yeallow as gold hanging downe behinde her, which was curiously combed and pleated, according to the manner in those dayes; shee was led to Church betweene two sweete boyes, with Bridelaces and Rosemary tied about their silken sleeves. Then was there a fair Bride-cup of silver and gilt carried before her, wherein was a goodly branch of Rosemary gilded very faire, hung about with silken Ribands of all colours; next was there a noyse of Musicians that played all the way before her; after her came all the chiefest maydens of the Country, some bearing great Bride Cakes and some Garlands of wheate finely gilded and so she past unto the Church. It is needlesse for mee to make any mention here of the Bridegroome, who being a man so well beloued, wanted no company and those of the best sort, beside diuers Marchant strangers of the Stillyard that came from London to the wedding. The marriage being solemnized, home they came in order as before and to dinner they went where was no want of good cheare, no lack of melody. . . . The wedding endured ten dayes, to the great reliefe of the poore that dwelt all about.[10]

Much dancing the house doubtless saw under the beautiful carved roof of the hall, with much song, games, kissing, and general abandon. Even when the bride and groom retired to the bridal chamber with its roll-moulded beams the merry-making was not done; they must hold a levee to their nearest friends in the bedchamber itself, enthroned in the great four-poster bed. There was no false delicacy about our ancestors. Indeed, as Henry Bullinger says (he was a very different person from jovial Deloney, but he was a contemporary of Paycocke's, and Coverdale translated him, so let him speak): 'After supper must they begynne to pype and daunce agayne of the new. And though the yonge parsones, beynge weery of the bablyng noyse and inconuenience, come ones towarde theyer rest, yet can they haue no quietnesse. For a man shall fynd unmanerly and restlesse people, that will first go to theyr chambre dore, and there syng vycious and naughtie balates that the deuell maye haue his triumphe now to the vttermost.'[11] What would we not give for one of those 'naughty ballads' today?

The bride Margaret, who was somewhat after this merry fashion brought home to Coggeshall, came from Clare, the ancient home of the Coggeshall Paycockes. She was the daughter of one Thomas Horrold, for whose memory Paycocke retained a lively affection and respect, for in founding a chantry in Coggeshall Church he desired specially that it should be for the souls of himself and his wife, his mother and father, and his father-in-law, Thomas Horrold of Clare. He also left five pounds, with which his executors were 'to purvey an oder stone to be hade to Clare chirch and layd on my ffader in lawe Thomas Horrold w^t his pycture and his wife and childryn thereon' (i.e. a memorial brass), and also five cows or else three pounds in money to Clare Church 'to kepe and mayntene my ffader in lawe Thomas Horrold his obitt'. He also left money to his wife's brother and sisters. Margaret Paycocke died before her husband and without children; and the only young folk of his name whom Thomas ever saw at play in his lofty hall, or climbing upon his dresser to find the head, as small as a walnut, hidden in the carving of the ceiling, were his nephews and nieces, Robert and Margaret Uppcher, his sister's children; John, the son of his brother John; and Thomas, Robert, and Emma, the children of his brother Robert; perhaps also his little godchild Grace Goodday. It was perhaps in the hope of a son to whom he might leave his house and name that Thomas Paycocke married again a girl called Ann Cotton. She was the wife of his old age, 'Anne my good wif', and her presence must have made bright the beautiful house, silent and lonely since Margaret died. Her father, George Cotton, is mentioned in the will, and her brothers and sister, Richard, William, and Eleanor, have substantial legacies. But Thomas and Ann enjoyed only a short term of married life; she brought him his only child but death overtook him before it was born. In his will he provide carefully for Ann; she is to have five hundred marks sterling, and as long as she lives the beautiful house is to be hers; for to his elaborate arrangements for its inheritance he adds, 'provided alwey that my wif Ann haue my house that I dwell in while she lyvyth at hir pleyser and my dof house [dove-house] with the garden y^t stoundeth in.' A gap in the Paycocke records makes it difficult to say whether Thomas Paycocke's child lived or died; but it seems probable that it either died or was a girl, for Paycocke had bequeathed the house, provided that he had no male heirs, to his nephew John (son of his eldest brother John), and in 1575 we find it in the hands of this John Paycocke, while the house next door was in the hands of another Thomas Paycocke, his brother Robert's son. This Thomas died about 1580, leaving only daughters, and after him, in 1584, died John Paycocke, sadly commemorated in the parish register as 'the last of his name in Coxall'. So the beautiful house passed out of the hands of the great family of clothiers who had held it for nearly a hundred years.[12]

Of Thomas Paycocke's personal character it is also possible to divine something from his will. He was obviously a kind and benevolent employer, as his thought for his work-people and their children shows. He was often asked to stand godfather to the babies of Coggeshall, for in his will he directs that at his burial and the ceremonies which were repeated on the seventh day and 'month mind' after it there were to be 'xxiiij or xij smale childryn in Rochettes with tapers in theire hands and as many as may be of them lett them be my god childryn and they to have vj s. viij d. apece and euery oder child iiij d. apece . . . and also euery god chyld besyde vj s. viij d. apece.' All these children were probably little bread-winners, employed at a very early age in sorting Thomas Paycocke's wool. 'Poore people,' says Thomas Deloney, 'whom God lightly blessed with most children, did by meanes of this occupation so order them, that by the time they were come to be sixe or seven yeeres of age, they were able to get their owne bread';[13] and when Defoe rode from Blackstone Edge to Halifax, observing the cloth manufacture, which occupied all the villages of the West Riding, it was one of his chief grounds for admiration that 'all [were] employed from the youngest to the oldest; scarce any thing above four years old, but its hands were sufficient for its own support.'[14] The employment of children at what we should regard as an excessively early age was by no means a new phenomenon introduced with the Industrial Revolution.

That Thomas Paycocke had many friends, not only in Coggeshall but in the villages round, the number of his legacies bears witness. His will also shows that he was a man of deep religious feeling. He was a brother of the Crutched Friars of Colchester and left them on his death five pounds to pray 'for me and for them that I am bound to pray fore'. It was customary in the Middle Ages for monastic houses to give the privilege of the fraternity of the house to benefactors and persons of distinction; the reception took place at a long and elaborate ceremony, during which the *confrater* received the kiss of peace from all the brethren. It is a mark of the respect in which Thomas Paycocke was held in the countryside that he should have been made a brother by the Crutched Friars. He seems to have had a special kindness for the Order of Friars; he left the Grey Friars of Colchester and the Friars of Maldon, Chelmsford, and Sudbury each ten shillings for a trental and 3*s.* 4*d.* to repair their houses; and to the Friars of Clare he left twenty shillings for two trentals, 'and at Lent after my deceste a kade of Red heryng'. He had great interest in Coggeshall Abbey; it lay less than a mile from his house, and he must often have dined in state with the abbot at his guest table on feast days and attended Mass in the abbey church. He remembered the abbey as he lay dying, and the sound of its bells ringing for vespers came softly in at his window on the mellow September air; and he left 'my Lord Abbot and Convent' one of his famous broadcloths and four pounds in money 'for to have a dirige and Masse and their belles Ryngyng at my buriall when it is doon at Chirche, lykewyse the vij[th] day and mounth day, with iij tryntalls upon the same day yf they can serve them, orells when they can at more leasur, Summa x li.'

His piety is shown also in his bequests to the churches of Bradwell, Pattiswick, and Markshall, parishes adjacent to Coggeshall, and to Stoke Nayland, Clare, Poslingford, Ovington, and Beauchamp St Pauls, over the Essex order, in the district from which the Paycockes originally came. But his greatest care was naturally for Coggeshall Church. One of the Paycockes had probably built the north aisle, where the altar was dedicated to St Katherine, and all the Paycocke tombs lay there. Thomas Paycocke left instructions in his will that he should be buried before St Katherine's altar, and made the following gifts to the church: 'Item, I bequeth to the high aulter of Coxhall Chirche in recompence of tithes and all oder thyngs forgoten, Summa iiij li. Item, I bequethe to the Tabernacle of the Trenyte at the high awlter and an other of Seint Margarete in seint Katryne Ile, there as the great Lady stands, for carvyng and gildyng of them summa c. marcs sterlinge. Item, to the reparacons of the Chirch and bells and for my lying in the Chirche summa c. nobles.' He founded a chantry there also and left money to be given weekly to six poor men to attend Mass in his chantry thrice a week.

Of piety and of family pride these legacies to religious houses and to churches speak clearly. Another series of legacies, which takes a form characteristic of medieval charity, bears witness perhaps to Thomas Paycocke's habits. He must often have ridden abroad, to see the folk who worked for him or to visit his friends in the villages round Coggeshall; or farther afield to Clare, first to see the home of his ancestors, then to court Margaret Horrold, his bride, and then, with Margaret beside him, to visit his well-loved father-in-law. Certainly, whether he walked to church in Coggeshall, or whether he rode along the country lanes, he often sighed over the state of the road as he went; often he must have struggled through torrents of mud in winter or stumbled among holes in summer; for in the Middle Ages the care of the roads was a matter for private or ecclesiastical charity, and all except the great highways were likely to be but indifferently kept. Langland, in his *Piers Plowman*, mentions the amending of 'wikked wayes' (by which he means not bad habits but bad roads) as one of those works of charity which rich merchants must do for the salvation of their souls. Thomas Paycocke's choice of roads no doubt reflects many a wearisome journey, from which he returned home splashed and testy, to the ministrations of 'John Reyner my man' or 'Henry Briggs my servant', and of Margaret, looking anxiously from her oriel window for his return. In his own town he leaves no less than forty pounds, of which twenty pounds was to go to amend a section of West Street (where his house stood), and the other twenty was 'to be layde on the fowle wayes bitwene Coxhall and Blackwater where as moost nede ys'; he had doubtless experienced the evils of this road on his way to the abbey. Farther afield, he leaves twenty pounds for the 'fowle way' between Clare and Ovington, and another twenty for the road between Ovington and Beauchamp St Pauls.

As his life drew to its close he doubtless rode less often afield. The days would pass peacefully for him; his business flourished and he was everywhere loved and respected. He took pride in his lovely house, adding bit by bit to its beauties. In the cool of the evening he must often have stood outside the garden room and seen the monks from the big abbey fishing in their stewpond across the field, or lifted his eyes to where the last rays of sun slanted on to the lichened roof of the great tithebarn, and on to the rows of tenants, carrying their sheaves of corn along the road; and he reflected, perhaps, that John Mann and Thomas Spooner, his own tenants, were good, steady friends, and that it was well to leave them a gown or a pound when he died. Often also, in his last year or two, he must have sat with his wife in his garden with the dove-house and watched the white pigeons circling round the apple-trees, and smiled upon her bed of flowers. And in winter evenings sometimes he would take his furred cloak and stroll to the Dragon Inn, and Edward Aylward, mine host, would welcome him with bows; and so he would sit and drink a tankard of sack with his neighbours, very slow and dignified, as befitted the greatest clothier of the town, and looking benevolently upon the company. But at times he would frown, if he saw a truant monk from the abbey stolen out for a drink in spite of all the prohibitions of bishop and abbot, shaking his head, perhaps, and complaining that religion was not what it had been in the good old days; but not meaning much of it, as his will shows, and never dreaming that twenty years after his death abbot and monks would be scattered and the King's servants would be selling at auction the lead from off the roof of Coggeshall Abbey; never dreaming that after four hundred years his house would still stand, mellow and lovely, with its carved ceiling and its proud merchant's mark, when the abbey church was only a shadow on the surface of a field in hot weather and all the abbey buildings were shrunk to one ruined ambulatory, ignobly sheltering blue Essex hay wagons from the rain.

So Thomas Paycocke's days drew to a close amid the peace and beauty of the most English of counties, 'fatt, frutefull and full of profitable thinges,'[15] whose little rolling hills, wych elms, and huge clouded skies Constable loved to paint. There came a day in September when gloom hung over the streets of Coggeshall, when the spinning-wheels were silent in the cottages, and spinners and weavers stood in anxious groups outside the beautiful house in West Street; for upstairs in his bridal chamber, under its noble ceiling, the great clothier lay dying, and his wife wept by his bedside, knowing that he would never see his child. A few days later the cottages were deserted again, and a concourse of weeping people followed Thomas Paycocke to his last rest. The ceremony of his burial befitted his dignity: it comprised services, not only on burial day itself, but on the seventh day after it, and then again after a month had passed. It is given best in the words of his will, for Thomas Paycocke followed the custom of his time, in giving his executors elaborate injunctions for his funeral rites: 'I will myne executors bestowe vpon my buryng daye, vij day and mounthe daye after this manner: At my buriall to have a tryntall of prests and to be at dirige, lawdis, and comendacons as many of them as may be purveyed that day to serve the tryntall, and yf eny lack to make it vpp the vij^th daye. And at the Mounthe daye an oder tryntall to be purveyed hoole of myne executors and to kepe dirige, lawdis and commendacons as is afore reherssed, with iij high massis be note [by note, i.e. with music], oon of the holy gost, an other of owre lady, and an other of Requiem, both buriall, seuenth day and Mounthe daye. And prests beyng at this obseruance iiij d. at euery tyme and childryn at euery tyme ij d., w^t torches at the buriall xij, and vj at the vij^th day and xij at the mounthe daye, with xxiij^ti or xij smale childryn in Rochettes with tapers in theire honds, and as many as may be of them lett them be my god Childryn, and they to haue vj s. viij d. apece; and euery oder child iiij d. apece; and euery man that holdith torches at euery day he to have ij apece; and euery man, woman and child that holdeth upp hound [hand] at eny of thes iij days to haue j d. apece; And also euery god chyld besyde vj s. viij d. apece; and to the Ryngars for all iij dayes x s.; and for mete, drynke, and for twoo Semones of a doctor, and also to haue a dirige at home, or I be borne to the Chirche summa j li.'

Here is something very different from the modest Thomas Betson's injunction: 'The costes of my burying to be don not outrageously, but sobrely and discretly and in a meane maner, that it may be unto the worship and laude of Almyghty God.' The worthy old clothier was not unmindful of the worship and laud of Thomas Paycocke also, and over £500 in modern money was expended upon his burial ceremonies, over and above the cost of founding his new chantry. Well indeed it was that his eyes were closed in death, ere the coming of the Reformation abolished all the chantries of England, and with them the Paycocke chantry in St Katherine's aisle, which had provided alms for six poor men weekly. Thomas Paycocke belonged to the good old days; in a quarter of a century after his death Essex was already changing. The monks were scattered from the abbey, which stood roofless; the sonorous Latin tongue no longer echoed in the church, nor priests prayed there for the souls of Thomas and his wife and his parents and his father-in-law. Even the cloth industry was changing, and the county was growing more prosperous still with the advent of finer kinds of cloth, brought over there by feat-fingered aliens, the 'new drapery', known as 'Bays and Says'. For as the adage says:

> Hops, reformation, bays and beer
> Came into England all in a year,

and Coggeshall was destined to become more famous still for a new sort of cloth called 'Coxall's Whites', which Thomas Paycocke's nephews made when he was in his grave.[16] One thing, however, did not change; for his beautiful house still stood in West Street, opposite the vicarage, and was the delight of all who saw it. It stands there still, and looking upon it today, and thinking of Thomas Paycocke who once dwelt in it, do there not come to mind the famous words of Ecclesiasticus?

Let us now praise famous men and our fathers that begat us.

The Lord hath wrought great glory by them through His great power from the beginning. . . .

Rich men furnished with ability, living peaceably in their habitations:

All these were honoured in their generations and were the glory of their times.

Notes and Sources

CHAPTER II

THE PEASANT BODO

A. Raw Material

1. The Roll of the Abbot Irminon, an estate book of the Abbey of St Germain des Prés, near Paris, written between 811 and 826. See *Polyptyque de l'Abbaye de Saint-Germain des Prés*, pub. Auguste Longnon, t. I, *Introduction*; t. II, *Texte* (Soc. de l'Hist. de Paris, 1886–95).

2. Charlemagne's capitulary, *De Villis*, instructions to his stewards on the management of his estates. See Guerard, *Explication du Capitulaire 'de Villis'* (Acad. des Inscriptions et Belles-Lettres, *Mémoires*, t. XXI, 1857), pp. 165–309, containing the text, with a detailed commentary and a translation into French.

3. *Early Lives of Charlemagne*, ed. A. J. Grant (King's Classics, 1907). Contains the lives by Einhard and the Monk of St Gall, on which see Halphen, cited below.

4. Various pieces of information about social life may be gleaned from the decrees of Church Councils, Old High German and Anglo-Saxon charms and poems, and Aelfric's *Colloquium*, extracts from which are translated in Bell's Eng. Hist. Source Books, *The Welding of the Race*, 449–1066, ed. J. E. W. Wallis (1913). For a general sketch of the period see Lavisse *Hist. de France*, t. II, and for an elaborate critical study of certain aspects of Charlemagne's reign (including the *Polyptychum*) see Halphen, *Études critiques sur l'Histoire de Charlemagne* (1921); also A. Dopsch, *Wirtschaftsentwicklung der Karolingerzeit, Vornehmlich in Deutschland*, 2 vols. (Weimar, 1912–13), which Halphen criticizes.

B. Notes to the Text

1. 'Habet Bodo colonus et uxor ejus colona, nomine Ermentrudis, homines sancti Germani, habent secum infantes III. Tenet mansum ingenuilem I, habentem de terre arabili bunuaria VIII et antsingas II, de

vinea aripennos II, de prato aripennos VII. Solvit ad hostem de argento solidos II, de vino in pascione modios II; ad tertium annum sundolas C; de sepe perticas III. Arat ad hibernaticum perticas III, ad tramisem perticas II. In unaquaque ebdomada corvadas II, manuoperam I. Pullos III, ova XV; et caropera ibi injungitur. Et habet medietatem de farinarium, inde solvit de argento solidos II.' *Op. cit.*, II, p. 78. 'Bodo a *colonus* and his wife Ermentrude a *colona*, tenants of Saint-Germain, have with them three children. He holds one free manse, containing eight *bunuaria* and two *antsinga* of arable land, two *aripenni* of vines and seven *aripenni* of meadow. He pays two silver shillings to the army and two hogsheads of wine for the right to pasture his pigs in the woods. Every third year he pays a hundred planks and three poles for fences. He ploughs at the winter sowing four perches and at the spring sowing two perches. Every week he owes two labour services (*corvées*) and one handwork. He pays three fowls and fifteen eggs, and carrying service when it is enjoined upon him. And he owns the half of a windmill, for which he pays two silver shillings.'

2. *De Villis*, c. 45.

3. *Ibid.* cc. 43, 49.

4. From 'The Casuistry of Roman Meals,' in *The Collected Writings of Thomas De Quincey*, ed. D. Masson (1897), VII, p. 13.

5. Aelfric's *Colloquium* in *op. cit.* p. 95.

6. The Monk of St Gall's *Life* in *Early Lives of Charlemagne*, pp. 87–8.

7. Einhard's *Life* in *op. cit.*, p. 45.

8. Anglo-Saxon charms translated in Stopford Brook, *English Literature from the Beginning to the Norman Conquest* (1899), p. 43.

9. Old High German charm written in a tenth-century hand in a ninth-century codex containing sermons of St Augustine, now in the Vatican Library. Brawne, *Althochdeutsches Lesebuch* (fifth edition, Halle, 1902), p. 83.

10. Another Old High German charm preserved in a tenth-century codex now at Vienna. Brawne, *op. cit.*, p. 164.

11. From the ninth-century *Libellus de Ecclesiasticis Disciplinis*, art. 100, quoted in Ozanam, *La Civilisation Chrétienne chez les Francs* (1849), p. 312. The injunction however, really refers to the recently conquered and still half-pagan Saxons.

12. *Penitential* of Haligart, Bishop of Cambrai, quoted *ibid.* p. 314.

13. *Documents relatifs à l'Histoire de l'Industrie et du Commerce en France*, ed. G. Faigniez, t. I, pp. 51–2.

14. See references in Chambers, *The Medieval Stage* (1913), I, pp. 161–3.

15. For the famous legend of the dancers of Kölbigk, see Gaston Paris, *Les Danseurs Maudits, Légende Allemande du XIe Siècle* (Paris 1900, reprinted from the *Journal des Savants*, Dec., 1899), which is a *conte rendu* of Schröder's study in *Zeitschrift für Kirchengeschichte* (1899). The poem occurs in a version of English origin, in which one of the dancers, Thierry, is cured of a perpetual trembling in all his limbs by a miracle of St Edith at the nunnery of Wilton in 1065. See *loc. cit.*, pp. 10, 14.

16. 'Swete Lamman dhin are,' in the original. The story is told by Giraldus Cambrensis in *Gemma Ecclesiastica*, pt. I, c. XLII. See *Selections from Giraldus Cambrensis*, ed. C. A. J. Skeel (S.P.C.K. *Texts for Students*, No. XI), p. 48.

17. Einhard's *Life* in *op. cit.* p. 45. See also *ibid.*, p. 168 (note).

18. The Monk of St Gall's *Life* in *op. cit.*, pp. 144–7.

19. Einhard's *Life* in *op. cit.*, p. 39.

20. *Ibid.*, p. 35.

21. Beazley, *Dawn of Modern Geography* (1897), I, p. 325.

22. The Monk of St Gall's *Life* in *op. cit.*, pp. 78–9.

23. See the description in Lavisse, *Hist. de France* II, pt. I, p. 321; also G. Monod, *Les mœurs judiciaires au VIIIe Siècle*, Revue Historique, t. XXXV (1887).

24. See Faigniez, *op. cit.*, pp. 43–4.

25. See the Monk of St Gall's account of the finery of the Frankish nobles: 'It was a holiday and they had just come from Pavia, whither the Venetians had carried all the wealth of the East from their territories beyond the sea, – others, I say, strutted in robes made of pheasant-skins and silk; or of the necks, backs and tails of peacocks in their first plumage. Some were decorated with purple and lemon-coloured ribbons; some were wrapped round with blankets and some in ermine robes.' *Op. cit.*, p. 149. The translation is a little loose: the 'phœnix robes' of the original were more probably made out of the plumage, not of the pheasant but of the scarlet flamingo, as Hodgson thinks (*Early Hist. of Venice*, p. 155), or possibly silks woven or embroidered with figures of birds, as Heyd thinks (*Hist. du Commerce du Levant*, I, p. 111).

26. The Monk of St. Gall's *Life* in *op. cit.*, pp. 81–2.

27. This little poem was scribbled by an Irish scribe in the margin of a copy of Priscian in the monastery of St Gall, in Switzerland, the same from which Charlemagne's highly imaginative biographer came. The

Notes and Sources

original will be found in Stokes and Strachan, *Thesaurus Palæohibernicus* (1903) II, p. 290. It has often been translated and I quote the translation by Kuno Meyer, *Ancient Irish Poetry* (2nd ed., 1913), p. 99. The quotation from the *Triads of Ireland* at the head of this chapter is taken from Kuno Meyer also, *ibid.* pp. 102–3.

CHAPTER III

MARCO POLO

A. Raw Material

1. *The Book of Ser Marco Polo the Venetian concerning the Kingdoms and Marvels of the East*, trans. and ed. with notes by Sir Henry Yule (3rd edit., revised by Henri Cordier, 2 vols., Hakluyt Soc., 1903). See also H. Cordier, *Ser Marco Polo: Notes and Addenda* (1920). The best edition of the original French text is *Le Livre de Marco Polo*, ed. G. Pauthier (Paris, 1865). The most convenient and cheap edition of the book for English readers is a reprint of Marsden's translation (of the Latin text) and notes (first published, 1818), with an introduction by John Masefield, *The Travels of Marco Polo the Venetian* (Everyman's Library, 1908; reprinted, 1911); but some of the notes (identifying places, etc.) are now out of date, and the great edition by Yule and Cordier should be consulted where exact and detailed information is required. It is a mine of information, geographical and historical, about the East. I quote from the Everyman Edition as Marco Polo, *op. cit.*, and from the Yule edition as Yule, *op. cit.*

2. *La Cronique des Veneciens de Maistre Martin da Canal.* In *Archivo Storico Italiano*, 1st ser., vol. VIII (Florence, 1845). Written in French and accompanied by a translation into modern Italian. One of the most charming of medieval chronicles.

B. Modern Works

1. For medieval Venice see –

    F. C. Hodgson: *The Early History of Venice from the Foundation to the Conquest of Constantinople* (1901); and *Venice in the Thirteenth and Fourteenth Centuries, A Sketch of Venetian History, 1204–1400* (1910).

    P. G. Molmenti: *Venice, its Growth to the Fall of the Republic*, vols.

I and II (*The Middle Ages*), trans. H. F. Brown (1906); and *La Vie Privée à Venise*, vol. I (1895).

H. F. Brown: *Studies in the History of Venice*, vol. I (1907).

Mrs Oliphant: *The Makers of Venice* (1905) is pleasant reading and contains a chapter on Marco Polo.

2. For medieval China, the Tartars, and European intercourse with the far East see –

Sir Henry Yule's introduction to his great edition of Marco Polo (above).

Cathay and the Way Thither: Medieval Notices of China, trans. and ed. by Sir Henry Yule, 4 vols. (Hakluyt Soc., 1915–16). Contains an invaluable introduction and all the best accounts of China left by medieval European travellers. Above all, Oderic of Pordenone (*d.* 1331) should be read as a pendant to Marco Polo.

R. Beazley: *The Dawn of Modern Geography*, vols. II and III (1897–1906).

R. Grousset: *Histoire de l'Asie*, t. III (3rd edit., 1922), Chap. I. A short and charmingly written account of the Mongol Empires from Genghis Khan to Timour.

H. Howarth: *History of the Mongols* (1876).

3. For medieval trade with the East the best book is –

W. Heyd: *Histoire du Commerce du Levant au Moyen-Âge*, trans., F. Raynaud; 2 vols. (Leipzig and Paris, 1885–6, reprinted 1923).

C. Notes to the Text

1. To be exact, the Flanders galleys which sailed via Gibraltar to Southampton and Bruges were first sent out forty years after 1268 – in 1308. Throughout the fourteenth and fifteenth centuries they sailed every year, and Southampton owes its rise to prosperity to the fact that it was their port of call.

2. The occasion of the speech quoted was when the imperial representative Longinus was trying to get the help of the Venetians against the Lombards in 568 and invited them to acknowledge themselves subjects of the Emperor. The speech is quoted in *Encyclop. Brit.*, Art. *Venice* (by H. F. Brown), p. 1002. The episode of the loaves of bread belongs to the attempt of Pipin, son of Charlemagne, to starve out the Rialto in the winter of 809–10. Compare the tale of Charlemagne casting his sword into the sea, with the words, 'Truly, even as this brand which I

have cast into the sea shall belong neither to me nor to you nor to any other man in all the world, even so shall no man in the world have power to hurt the realm of Venice; and he who would harm it shall feel the wrath and displeasure of God, even as it has fallen upon me and my people.' – See Canale, *Cron.*, c. VIII. These are, of course, all legends.

3. 'Voirs est que la mer Arians est de le ducat de Venise.' – Canale, *op. cit.*, p. 600. Albertino Mussato calls Venice 'dominatrix Adriaci maris.' – Molmenti, *Venice*, I, p. 120.

4. See some good contemporary accounts of the ceremony quoted in Molmenti, *Venice*, I, pp. 212–15.

5. During the fatal war of Chioggia between the two republics of Venice and Genoa, which ended in 1381, it was said that the Genoese admiral (or some say Francesco Carrara), when asked by the Doge to receive peace ambassadors, replied, 'Not before I have bitted the horses on St Mark's.' – H. F. Brown, *Studies in the Hist. of Venice*, I, p. 130.

6. Canale, *op. cit.*, p. 270.

7. 'The weather was clear and fine . . . and when they were at sea, the mariners let out the sails to the wind, and let the ships run with spread sails before the wind over the sea' – See, for instance, Canale, *op. cit.*, pp. 320, 326, and elsewhere.

8. Canale, *op. cit.*, cc. I and II, pp. 268–72. Venice is particularly fortunate in the descriptions which contemporaries have left of her – not only her own citizens (such as Canale, Sanudo and the Doge Mocenigo) but also strangers. Petrarch's famous description of Venetian commerce, as occasioned by the view which he saw from his window in the fourteenth century, has often been quoted: 'See the innumerable vessels which set forth from the Italian shore in the desolate winter, in the most variable and stormy spring, one turning its prow to the east, the other to the west; some carrying our wine to foam in British cups, our fruits to flatter the palates of the Scythians and, still more hard of credence, the wood of our forests to the Egean and the Achaian isles; some to Syria, to Armenia, to the Arabs and Persians, carrying oil and linen and saffron, and bringing back all their diverse goods to us. . . . Let me persuade you to pass another hour in my company. It was the depth of night and the heavens were full of storm, and I, already weary and half asleep, had come to an end of my writing, when suddenly a burst of shouts from the sailors penetrated my ear. Aware of what these shouts should mean from former experience, I rose hastily and went up to the higher windows of this house, which look out upon the port. Oh, what a spectacle, mingled with feelings of pity, of wonder, of fear and of delight! Resting on their

anchors close to the marble banks which serve as a mole to the vast palace which this free and liberal city has conceded to me for my dwelling, several vessels have passed the winter, exceeding with the height of their masts and spars the two towers which flank my house. The larger of the two was at this moment – though the stars were all hidden by the clouds, the winds shaking the walls, and the roar of the sea filling the air – leaving the quay and setting out upon its voyage. Jason and Hercules would have been stupefied with wonder, and Tiphys, seated at the helm, would have been ashamed of the nothing which won him so much fame. If you had seen it, you would have said it was no ship but a mountain, swimming upon the sea, although under the weight of its immense wings a great part of it was hidden in the waves. The end of the voyage was to be the Don, beyond which nothing can navigate from our seas; but many of those who were on board, when they had reached that point, meant to prosecute their journey, never pausing till they had reached the Ganges or the Caucasus, India and the Eastern Ocean. So far does love of gain stimulate the human mind.' – Quoted from Petrarch's *Lettere Senili* in Oliphant, *Makers of Venice* (1905), p. 349; the whole of this charming chapter, 'The Guest of Venice', should be read. Another famous description of Venice occurs in a letter written by Pietro Aretino, a guest of Venice during the years 1527 to 1533, to Titian, quoted in E. Hutton, *Pietro Aretino, the Scourge of Princes* (1922), pp. 136–7; compare also his description of the view from his window on another occasion, quoted *ibid.*, pp. 131–3. The earliest of all is the famous letter written by Cassiodorus to the Venetians in the sixth century, which is partly translated in Molmenti, *op. cit.*, I, pp. 14–15.

9. The account of the march of the gilds occupies cc. CCLXIII–CCLXXXIII of Canale's Chronicle, *op. cit.*, pp. 602–26. It has often been quoted.

10. Canale, *op. cit.*, c. CCLXI, p. 600.

11. This account of Hangchow is taken partly from Marco Polo, *op. cit.*, bk. II, c. LXVIII: 'Of the noble and magnificent city of Kinsai'; and partly from Odoric of Pordenone, *Cathay and the Way Thither*, ed. Yule, pp. 113–20.

12. Oderic of Pordenone, who was a man before he was a friar, remarks: 'The Chinese are comely enough, but colourless, having beards of long straggling hair like mousers, cats I mean. And as for the women, they are the most beautiful in the world.' Marco Polo likewise never fails to note when the women of a district are specially lovely, in the same way that that other traveller Arthur Young always notes the

looks of the chambermaids at the French inns among the other details of the countryside, and is so much affronted if waited on by a plain girl. Marco Polo gives the palm for beauty to the women of the Province of Timochain (or Damaghan) on the north-east border of Persia, of which, he says, 'The people are in general a handsome race, especially the women, who, in my opinion, are the most beautiful in the world.' – Marco Polo, *op. cit.*, p. 73. Of the women of Kinsai he reports thus: 'The courtesans are accomplished and are perfect in the arts of blandishment and dalliance, which they accompany with expressions adapted to every description of person, insomuch that strangers who have once tasted of their charms, remain in a state of fascination, and become so enchanted by their meretricious arts, that they can never divest themselves of the impression. Thus intoxicated with sensual pleasures, when they return to their homes they report that they have been in Kin-sai, or the celestial city, and pant for the time when they may be enabled to revisit paradise.' Of the respectable ladies, wives of the master craftsmen he likewise says: 'They have much beauty and are brought up with languid and delicate habits. The costliness of their dresses, in silks and jewellery, can scarcely be imagined.' – *op. cit.*, pp. 296, 297–8.

13. Yule, *op. cit.*, II, p. 184.

14. For Prester John see Sir Henry Yule's article 'Prester John' in the *Encyclopædia Britannica*, and Lynn Thorndike, *A History of Magic and Experimental Science* (1923), II, pp. 236–45. There is a pleasant popular account in S. Baring Gould, *Popular Myths of the Middle Ages* (1866–8).

15. For their accounts see *The Journal of William of Rubruck to the Eastern Parts, 1253–5, by himself, with two accounts of the Earlier Journey of John of Pian da Carpine*, trans. and ed. with notes by W. W. Rockhill (Hakluyt Soc., 1900). Rubruck especially is a most delightful person.

16. This, together with the whole account of the first journey of the elder Polos, the circumstances of the second journey, and of their subsequent return occurs in the first chapter of Marco Polo's book, which is a general introduction, after which he proceeds to describe in order the lands through which he passed. This autobiographical section is unfortunately all too short.

17. As a matter of fact, William of Rubruck had seen and described it before him.

18. For Marco Polo's account of this custom in the province which he calls 'Kardandan', see *op. cit.*, p. 250. An illustration of it from an album belonging to the close of the Ming dynasty is reproduced in S. W. Bushell, *Chinese Art* (1910), fig. 134.

19. Marco Polo, *op. cit.*, pp. 21–2.

20. A certain *Poh-lo* was, according to the Chinese annals of the Mongol dynasty, appointed superintendent of salt mines at Yangchow shortly after 1282. Professor Parker thinks that he may be identified with our Polo, but M. Cordier disagrees. See E. H. Parker *Some New Facts about Marco Polo's Book* in *Imperial and Asiatic Quarterly Review* (1904), p. 128; and H. Cordier, *Ser Marco Polo*, p. 8. See also Yule, *Marco Polo*, I, Introd., p. 21.

21. P. Parrenin in *Lett. Edif.*, xxiv, 58, quoted in Yule, *op. cit.*, I, Introd., p. 11.

22. On Marco Polo's omissions see Yule, *op. cit.*, I, Introd., p. 110.

23. Marco Polo, *op. cit.*, p. 288.

24. On Chao Mêng-fu see S. W. Bushell, *Chinese Art* (1910), II, pp. 133–59; H. A. Giles, *Introd. to the History of Chinese Pictorial Art* (Shanghai, 2nd ed., 1918), pp. 159 ff.; the whole of c. VI of this book on the art which flourished under the Mongol dynasty is interesting. See also L. Binyon, *Painting in the Far East* (1908), pp. 75–7, 146–7. One of Chao Mêng-fu's horse pictures, or rather a copy of it by a Japanese artist, is reproduced in Giles, *op. cit.*, opposite p. 159. See also my notes on illustrations for an account of the famous landscape roll painted by him in the style of Wang Wei.

25. Bushell, *op. cit.*, p. 135.

26. *Ibid.*, pp. 135–6, where the picture is reproduced.

27. For the episode of the mangonels constructed by Nestorian mechanics under the directions of Nicolo and Maffeo see Marco Polo, *op. cit.*, pp. 281–2.

28. Marco Polo, *op. cit.*, bk. III, c. I, pp. 321–3.

29. Ramusio's preface, containing this account, and also the story of how Rusticiano came to write the book at Marco Polo's dictation at Genoa, is translated in Yule, *op. cit.*, I, Introd., pp. 4–8.

30. He mentions these in Marco Polo, *op. cit.*, pp. 136, 138, 344.

31. Yule, *op. cit.*, I, Introd., p. 79.

32. On Rusticiano (who is mistakenly called a Genoese by Ramusio), see *ibid.*, Introd., pp. 56 ff.

33. Paulin Paris, quoted *ibid.*, Introd., p. 61.

34. *Ibid.*, Introd., pp. 67–73.

35. Extract from Jacopo of Acqui's *Imago Mondi*, quoted *ibid.*, Introd., p. 54.

36. M. Ch.-V. Langlois in *Hist. Litt. de la France*, XXXV (1921), p. 259. For tributes to Marco Polo's accuracy see Aurel Stein, *Ancient*

Khotan (1907) and *Ruins of Desert Cathay* (1912); Ellsworth Huntington, *The Pulse of Asia* (1910); and Sven Hedin, *Overland to India* (1910).

37. Yule, *op. cit.*, I, Introd., pp. 106–7.

38. For these later missions and traders see Yule, *Cathay and the Way Thither*, Introd., pp. cxxxii–iv, and text, *passim*.

39. *Ibid.*, II, p. 292; and App., p. lxv.

40. Concerning the marginal notes by Columbus see Yule, *op. cit.*, II, App. H, p. 558. The book is preserved in the Colombina at Seville. I must, however, frankly admit that modern research, iconoclastic as ever, not content with white-washing Lucrezia Borgia and Catherine de Medicis, and with reducing Catherine of Siena to something near insignificance, is also making it appear more and more probable that Columbus originally set sail in 1492 to look for the islands of the Antilles, and that, although on his return after his great discovery in 1493 he maintained that his design had always been to reach Cipangu, this was a *post hoc* story, the idea of searching for Cipangu having probably come from his partner, Martin Pinzon. It is a pity that we do not know *when* he made his notes in the edition (the probable date of publication of which was 1485) of Marco Polo's book, which might settle the matter. On the whole question see Henry Vignaud, *Études critiques sur la vie de Colomb avant ses découvertes* (Paris, 1905) and *Histoire de la Grande Enterprise de 1492*, 2 vols. (Paris, 1910), and the summary and discussion of his conclusions by Professor A. P. Newton in *History*, VII (1922), pp. 38–42 (*Historical Revisions* XX. – 'Christopher Columbus and his Great Enterprise.') The idea that a new road to the East was being sought at this time, primarily because the Turks were blocking the old trade routes, has also been exploded. See A. H. Lybyer, *The Ottoman Turks and the Routes of Oriental Trade* in *Eng. Hist. Review*, XXX (1915), pp. 577–88.

CHAPTER IV

MADAME EGLENTYNE

A. Raw Material

1. Chaucer's description of the Prioress in the Prologue to the *Canterbury Tales*.

2. Miscellaneous visitation reports in episcopal registers. On these registers, and in particular the visitation documents therein, see R. C. Fowler, *Episcopal Registers of England and Wales* (S.P.C.K. Helps for

Students of History, No. I), G. G. Coulton, *The Interpretation of Visitation Documents* (Eng. Hist. Review, 1914), and c. XII of my book, cited below. A great many registers have been, or are being, published by learned societies, notably by the Canterbury and York Society, which exists for this purpose. The most important are the Lincoln visitations, now in the course of publication, by Dr A. Hamilton Thompson. *Visitations of Religious Houses in the Diocese of Lincoln*, ed. A. Hamilton Thompson (Lincoln Rec. Soc. and Canterbury and York Soc., 1915 ff.); two volumes have appeard so far, of which see especially vol. II, which contains part of Bishop Alnwick's visitations (1436–49); each volume contains text, translation, and an admirable introduction. See also the extracts from Winchester visitations trans. in H. G. D. Liveing, *Records of Romsey Abbey* (1912). Full extracts from visitation reports and injunctions are given under the accounts of religious houses in the different volumes of the Victoria County Histories (cited as V.C.H.).

3. The monastic rules. See *The Rule of St Benedict*, ed. F. A. Gasquet (Kings Classics, 1909), and F. A. Gasquet, *English Monastic Life* (4th ed., 1910).

4. For a very full study of the whole subject of English convent life at this period see Eileen Power, *Medieval English Nunneries c. 1275 to 1535* (1922).

B. *Notes to the Text*

1. *The Register of Walter de Stapeldon, Bishop of Exeter* (1307–26), ed. F. Hingeston Randolph (1892), p. 169. The passage about Philippa is translated in G. G. Coulton, *Chaucer and His England* (1908), p. 181.

2. See the account of expenses involved in making Elizabeth Sewardby a nun of Nunmonkton (1468) in *Testamenta Eboracensia*, ed. James Raine (Surtees Soc., 1886), III, p. 168; and Power, *op. cit.*, p. 19.

3. *Year Book of King Richard II*, ed. C. F. Deiser (1904), pp. 71–7; and Power, *op. cit.*, pp. 36–8.

4. G. J. Aungier, *Hist. of Syon* (1840), p. 385.

5. As at Gracedieu (1440–1), *Alnwick's Visit*, ed. A. H. Thompson, pp. 120–3.

6. G. J. Aungier, *op. cit.*, pp. 405–9.

7. Translated from John de Grandisson's Register in G. G. Coulton, *A Medieval Garner* (1910), pp. 312–14.

8. *Rule of St Benedict*, c. 22.

9. *V. C. H. Lincs.*, II, p. 131.

10. Translated in G. G. Coulton, *A Medieval Garner*, p. 423.

11. *Myroure of Oure Ladye*, ed. J. H. Blunt (E.E.T.S., 1873), p. 54. On Tittivillus see my article in *The Cambridge Magazine* (1917), pp. 158–60.

12. *Linc. Visit.*, ed. A. H. Thompson, II, pp. 46–52; and Power, *op. cit.*, pp. 82–7.

13. *V. C. H. Oxon*, II, p. 77.

14. *Linc. Visit.*, ed. A. H. Thompson, I, p. 67.

15. On these gaieties see Power, *op. cit.*, pp. 309–14.

16. *Linc. Visit.*, II, pp. 3–4; and see Power, *op. cit.*, pp. 75–7, 303–5, on gay clothes in nunneries.

17. *Linc. Visit.*, II, p. 175.

18. Power, *op. cit.*, p. 307. On pet animals see *ibid.*, pp. 305–9, and Note E (' Convent Pets in Literature'), pp. 588–95.

19. Power, *op. cit.*, p. 77.

20. *Ibid.*, pp. 351–2; and see Chap. IX *passim* on the Bull *Periculoso* and the wandering of nuns in the world.

21. *Linc. Visit.*, II, p. 50.

22. *V. C. H. Yorks.*, III, p. 172.

CHAPTER V

THE MÉNAGIER'S WIFE

A. Raw Material

1. *Le Ménagier de Paris, Traité de Morale et d'Economie Domestique, compose vers 1393 par un Bourgeois Parisien . . . publié pour la première fois par la Société des Bibliophiles Francois* (Paris, 1846). 2 vols., edited with an introduction by Jérôme Pichon. There is a notice of it by Dr F. J. Furnivall, at the end of his edition of *A Booke of Precedence* (Early English Text Soc., 1869 and 1898), pp. 149–54. It was a book after his own heart, and he observes that it well deserves translation into English.

2. On the subject of medieval books of deportment for women see A. A. Hentsch, *De la littérature didactique du moyen âge s'addressant spécialement aux femmes* (Cahors, 1903), an admirably complete collection of analyses of all the chief works of this sort produced in western

Europe from the time of St Jerome to the eve of the Renaissance. It is full of plums for adventurous Jack Horners.

3. With the Ménagier's cookery book there may profitably be compared *Two Fifteenth Century Cookery Books*, ed. by Thomas Austin (E.E.T.S., 1888).

B. Notes to the Text

1. Pp. 1–2.

2. These long moral treatises on the seven deadly sins and the even deadlier virtues were very popular in the Middle Ages. The best known to English readers occurs in the *Parson's Tale* in Chaucer's *Canterbury Tales*, and is taken from the *Somme de Vices et de Vertus* of Frère Lorens, a thirteenth-century author. The sections on the deadly sins are usually, however, well worth reading, because of the vivid illustrative details which they often give about daily life. The Ménagier's sections are full of vigour and colour, as one would expect. Here, for instance, is his description of the female glutton: 'God commands fasting and the glutton says: "I will eat". God commands us to get up early and go to church and the glutton says: "I must sleep. I was drunk yesterday. The church is not a hare; it will wait for me." When she has with some difficulty risen, do you know what her hours are? Her matins are: "Ha! what shall we have to drink? is there nothing left over from last night?" Afterwards she says her lauds thus: "Ha! we drank good wine yesterday." Afterwards she says thus her orisons: "My head aches, I shan't be comfortable until I have had a drink." Certes, such gluttony putteth a woman to shame, for from it she becomes a ribald, a disreputable person and a thief. The tavern is the Devil's church, where his disciples go to do him service and where he works his miracles. For when folk go there they go upright and well spoken, wise and sensible and well advised, and when they return they cannot hold themselves upright nor speak; they are all foolish and all mad, and they return swearing, beating and giving the lie to each other.' – *Op. cit.*, I, pp. 47–8. The section on Avarice is particularly valuable for its picture of the sins of executors of wills, rack-renting lords, extortionate shopkeepers, false lawyers, usurers, and gamblers. – See *ibid.*, I, pp. 44–5.

3. *Prudence and Melibeus* is worth reading once, either in Chaucer's or in Renault de Louens' version, because of its great popularity in the Middle Ages, and because of occasional vivid passages. Here, for instance, is the episode in Chaucer's version, in which Melibeus, the sages, and the young men discuss going to war, and the sages advise against it:

'Up stirten thanne the yonge folk at ones, and the mooste partie of that compaignye scorned the wise olde men, and bigonnen to make noyse, and seyden that "Right so as, whil that iren is hoot, men sholden smyte, right so men sholde wreken hir wronges while that they been fresshe and newe"; and with loud voys they criden, "Werre! werre!" Up roos tho oon of thise olde wise, and with his hand made contenaunce that men sholde holden hem stille, and yeven hym audience. "Lordynges," quod he, "ther is ful many a man that crieth 'Werre! werre!' that woot ful litel what werre amounteth. Werre at his bigynnyng hath so greet an entryng and so large, that every wight may entre whan hym liketh and lightly fynde werre; but certes, what ende that shal ther-of bifalle it is nat light to knowe; for soothly, whan that werre is ones bigonne ther is ful many a child unborn of his mooder that shal sterve yong by cause of that ilke werre, or elles lyve in sarwe, and dye in wrecchednesse; and therefore, er that any werre bigynne, men moste have greet conseil and greet deliberacioun." – Chaucer, *Tale of Melibeus*, § 12; and see the French version, *op. cit.*, I, p. 191.

4. II, p. 72–9.

5. I, pp. 71–2. These medieval games are very difficult to identify. The learned editor remarks that *bric*, which is mentioned in the thirteenth century by Rutebeuf was played, seated, with a little stick; *qui féry* is probably the modern game called by the French *main chaude*; *pince merille*, which is mentioned among the games of Gargantua, was a game in which you pinched one of the players' arms, crying 'Mérille' or 'Morille'. Though the details of these games are vague, there are many analagous games played by children today, and it is easy to guess the kind of thing which is meant.

6. I, pp. 13–15.

7. I, 92, 96.

8. The story of Jeanne la Quentine is reproduced in the *Heptameron* of Margaret of Navarre (the 38th tale, or the 8th of the 4th day), where it is attributed to a *bourgeoise* of Tours, but it is probable that the Ménagier's is the original version, since he says that he had it from his father; although, knowing the ways of the professional raconteur, I should be the first to admit that this is not proof positive.

9. I, pp. 125–6.

10. I, p. 139.

11. This was a favourite saying. It occurs in the story of Melibeus, 'Trois choses sont qui gettent homme hors de sa maison, c'est assavoir la fumée, la goutière et la femme mauvaise.' – *Ibid.*, I, p. 195. Compare

Chaucer's use of it: 'Men seyn that thre thynges dryven a man out of his hous, – that is to seyn, smoke, droppyng of reyn and wikked wyves.' – *Tale of Melibeus*, § 15; and

> 'Thou seyst that droppying houses, and eek smoke,
> And chidyng wyves, maken men to flee
> Out of hir owene hous.'
> —*Wife of Bath's Prologue*, LL, 278–80.

12. I, pp. 168–71, 174–6.

13. II, p. 54. The Ménagier also warns against running up long bills on credit. 'Tell your folk to deal with peaceable people and to bargain always beforehand and to account and pay often, without running up long bills on credit by tally or on paper, although tally or paper are better than doing everything by memory, for the creditors always think it more and the debtors less, and thus are born arguments, hatreds, and reproaches; and cause your good creditors to be paid willingly and frequently what is owed to them, and keep them in friendship so that they depart not from you, for one cannot always get peaceable folk again.'

14. II, pp. 56–9.

15. It is curious here to note the antiquity of the term 'bloody' as an expletive. The Ménagier says: 'Forbid them . . . to use ugly oaths, or words which are bad or indecent, as do certain evil or ill bred persons who swear at bad bloody fevers, the bad bloody week, the bad bloody day ('de males sanglantes fièvres,' 'de male sanglante sepmaine,' 'de male sanglante journée'), and they know not, nor should they know, what a bloody thing is, for honest women know it not, since it is abominable to them to see the blood but of a lamb or a pigeon, when it is killed before them.' – *Ibid.*, II, p. 59.

16. The section on household management described above occupies sec. II, art. 2, of the Ménagier's book (II, pp. 53–72).

17. I, pp. 171–2.

18. I, pp. 172–3.

19. The cookery book occupies sec. II, arts. 4 and 5 (II, pp. 80–272).

20. II, pp. 222–3. Translated by Dr Furnivall in *A Booke of Precedence* (E.E.T.S.), pp. 152–3.

21. II, pp. 108–18, 123. The feast was still a thing of the future when the Ménagier thus gathered all the details. He calls it 'L'ordenance de nopces que fera maistre Helye en May, à un mardy . . . l'ordonnance du souper que fera ce jour.'

22. 'The office of the woman is to make provision of tapestries, to order and spread them, and in especial to dight the room and the bed

which shall be blessed. . . . And *nota* that if the bed be covered with cloth, there is needed a fur coverlet of small vair, but if it be covered with serge, or broidery, or pinwork of cendal, not.' – II, p. 118. The editor quotes the following ceremony for blessing the wedding bed: '*Benedictio thalami ad nuptias et als*, Beredic, Domine, thalamum hunc et omnes habitantes in eo, ut in tua voluntate permaneant, requiescant et multiplicentur in longitudinem dierum. Per Christum, etc. *Tunc thurificet thalamum in matrimonio, postea sponsum et sponsam sedentes vel jacentes in lecto suo. Benedicentur dicendo*: Benedic, Domine, adolescentulos istos; sicut benedixisti Thobiam et Sarram filiam Raguelis, ita benedicere eos digneris, Domine, ut in nomine tuo vivant et senescant, et multiplicentur in longitudinem dierum. Per Christum, etc. Benedictio Dei omnipotentis, Patris et Filii et Spiritus sancti descendat super vos et maneat super vobiscum. In nomine Patris, etc.' – *Ibid.*, I, *Introd.*, p. lxxxvi.

23. Chaucer, *Tale of Melibeus*, § 15.

CHAPTER VI

THOMAS BETSON

A. Raw Material

1. *The Stonor Letters and Papers*, 1290–1483, ed. C. L. Kingsford (Royal Hist. Soc., Camden, 3rd Series), 2 vols., 1919. The Betson correspondence is in vol. II.

2. *The Cely Papers, selected from the Correspondence and Memoranda of the Cely Family, Merchants of the Staple*, 1475–88, ed. H. E. Malden (Royal Hist. Soc., Camden 3rd series), 1900.

I am much beholden to the excellent introductions to these two books, which are models of what editorial introductions should be.

3. The best introduction to the history of the Company of the Staple is to be found in Mr Malden's aforesaid introduction to *The Cely Papers*, which also contains a masterly account of the political relations of England, France and Burgundy during the period. I have constantly relied upon Mr Malden's account of the working of the Staple system. Other useful short accounts of the wool trade and the Stapler's Company may be found in the following works: Sir C. P. Lucas, *The Beginnings of English Overseas Enterprise* (1917), c. II; and A. L. Jenckes, *The Staple of England* (1908).

Medieval People

B. Notes to the Text

1. Four interesting contemporary illustrations of Parliament in 1523, 1585, some date during the seventeenth century, and 1742 respectively, are reproduced in Professor A. F. Pollard's stimulating study of *The Evolution of Parliament* (1920).

2. *The Lybelle of Englyshe Polycye*, in *Political Poems and Songs*, ed. Thos. Wright (Rolls Ser., 1861), II, p. 162. This remarkable poem was written in 1436 or 1437, in order to exhort the English 'to kepe the see enviroun and namelye the narowe see' between Dover and Calais, since in the author's opinion the basis of England's greatness lay in her trade, for the preservation of which she needed the dominion of the seas. Its chief value lies in the very complete picture which it gives of English import and export trade with the various European countries. There is a convenient edition of it in *The Principal Navigations Voyages Traffiques and Discoveries of the English Nation by Richard Hakluyt* (Everyman's Lib. Edition, 1907), I, pp. 174–202.

3. G. W. Morris and L. S. Wood, *The Golden Fleece* (1922), p. 17.

4. For accounts of these brasses see H. Druitt, *A Manual of Costume as Illustrated by Monumental Brasses* (1906), pp. 9, 201, 205, 207, 253. John Fortey's brass and William Greville's brass are conveniently reproduced in G. W. Morris and L. S. Wood, *op. cit.*, pp. 28, 32, together with several other illustrations, pertinent to the wool trade.

5. Gower, *Mirour de l'Omme* in *The Works of John Gower*. I. *The French Works*, ed. G. C. Macaulay (1899), p. 280–1.

6. *The Paston Letters*, ed. J. Gairdner (London, 1872–5); Supplement 1901. See also H. S. Bennett, *The Pastons and their England* (1922).

7. *Plumpton Correspondence*, ed. T. Stapleton (Camden Soc., 1839).

8. *Cely Papers*, p. 72; and compare below p. 134.

9. *Stonor Letters*, II, p. 2.

10. *Ibid.*, II, pp. 2–3.

11. The brasses of his father 'John Lyndewode, woolman', and of his brother, also 'John Lyndewode, woolman' (*d.* 1421), are still in Linwood Church. They both have their feet on woolpacks, and on the son's woolpack is his merchant's mark. See H. Druitt, *op. cit.*, pp. 204–5.

12. See *Magna Vita S. Hugonis Episcopi Lincolniensis*, ed. J. F. Dimock (Rolls Series, 1864), pp. 170–7.

13. For these extracts see a vastly entertaining book, *Child Marriages and Divorces in the Diocese of Chester*, 1561–6, ed. F. J. Furnivall (E.E.T.S., 1897), pp. xxii, 6, 45–7.

14. *Stonor Letters*, II, pp. 6–8.

15. *Ibid.*, II, pp. 28, 64.

16. *Ibid.*, II, p. 64.

17. *Ibid.*, II, pp. 42–43.

18. *Ibid.*, II, p. 44.

19. *Ibid.*, II, pp. 61, 64–5.

20. *Ibid.*, II, pp. 46–8.

21. *Ibid.*, II, p. 53.

22. *Ibid.*, II, p. 28.

23. *Ibid.*, II, p. 47.

24. *Ibid.*, II, p. 53.

25. *Ibid.*, II, pp. 54–5.

26. *Ibid.*, II, pp. 56–7.

27. *Ibid.*, II, p. 69.

28. *Ibid.*, II, pp. 87–8.

29. *Ibid.*, II, pp. 88–9.

30. *Ibid.*, II, p. 89.

31. *Ibid.*, II, pp. 102–3, 117.

32. See Richard Cely's amusing account of the affair in a letter to his brother George, written on May 13, 1482, *Cely Papers*, pp. 101–4. For other references to the wool dealer William Midwinter see *ibid.*, pp. 11, 21, 28, 30, 32, 64, 87, 89, 90, 105, 124, 128, 157, 158.

33. *Stonor Letters*, II, p. 3.

34. *Ibid.*, II, p. 64.

35. *Testamenta Eboracensia* (Surtees Soc.), II, p. 56. He was a well-known wool merchant of York, at different times member of the town council of twelve, sheriff and mayor, who died in 1435. He is constantly mentioned in the city records; see *York Memorandum Book*, ed. Maud Sellers (Surtees Soc., 1912 and 1915), vols. I and II, *passim*.

36. *Cely Papers*, pp. 30–1.

37. *Ibid.*, p. 64.

38. See his will (1490) in *Test. Ebor.*, IV, p. 61, where he is called 'Johannes Barton de Holme juxta Newarke, Stapulæ villæ Carlisiæ marcator,' and ordains 'Volo quod Thomas filius meus Johannem Tamworth fieri faciat liberum hominem Stapulæ Carlis,' *ibid.*, p. 62.

39. *Ibid.*, p. 45.

40. *Ibid.*, p. 48.

41. *Ibid.*, pp. 154–5.

42. *The Lybelle of Englysche Polycye* in *loc. cit.*, pp. 174–7, *passim*.

Compare Gower's account of the machinations of the Lombards, *op. cit.*, pp. 281–2.

43. See the clear account of all these operations in Mr Malden's introduction to the *Cely Papers*, pp. xi–xiii, xxxviii.

44. *Ibid.*, p. vii.

45. *Cely Papers*, pp. 194–6; and see *Introd.*, pp. xxxvi–viii.

46. *Ibid.*, pp. 71–2.

47. *Ibid.*, pp. 174–88, a book entitled on the cover 'The Rekenyng of the Margett Cely,' and beginning, 'The first viage of the Margaret of London was to Seland in the yere of our Lord God m iiij^{c}iiij^{xx}v. The secunde to Caleis and the thrid to Burdews ut videt. M^d to se the pursers accomptes of the seide viages. G. Cely.'

48. *Ibid.*, p. xxxviii.

49. *Stonor Letters*, II, p. 2.

50. *Ibid.*, II, p. 4.

51. *Cely Papers*, pp. 112–13.

52. *Ibid.*, p. 106; compare *ibid.*, p. 135.

53. 'Sir, the wool ships be come to Calais all save three, whereof two be in Sandwich haven and one is at Ostend, and he hath cast over all his wool overboard.' – *Ibid.*, p. 129. 'Item, sir, on Friday the 27 day of February came passage from Dover and they say that on Thursday afore came forth a passenger from Dover to Calais ward and she was chased with Frenchmen and driven in to Dunkirk haven.' – *Ibid.*, p. 142. (There are many records of similar chases; see *Introd.*, pp. xxxiv–v.)

54. *Ibid.*, p. 135.

55. 'Sir, I cannot have your wool yet awarded, for I have do cast out a sarpler, the which is [ap]pointed by the lieutenant to be casten out toward the sort by, as the ordinance now is made that the lieutenant shall [ap]point the [a]warding sarplers of every man's wool, the which sarpler that I have casten out is No. 24, and therein is found by William Smith, packer, a 60 middle fleeces and it is a very gruff wool; and so I have caused William Smith privily to cast out another sarpler No. 8, and packed up the wool of the first sarpler in the sarpler of No. 8, for this last sarpler is fair wool enough, and therefore I must understand how many be of that sort and the number of the[m], for they must be packed again' (12 Sept., 1487). – *Ibid.*, p. 160. 'Item, sir, your wool is awarded by the sarpler that I cast out last, etc. Item, sir, this same day your mastership is elected and appointed here by the Court one of the 28, the which shall assist the Master of the Staple now at this parliament time.' – *Ibid.*, p. 162.

56. Gower, *op. cit.*, p. 281.
57. *Cely Papers*, pp. xii, xxiv–v.
58. *Stonor Letters*, II, pp. 62–3; see also *Cely Papers*, pp. 1, 10, 13.
59. *Stonor Letters*, II, p. 4.
60. Chaucer, *Canterbury Tales* (*Shipman's Tale*) LL, 1243–6.
61. *Stonor Letters*, II, p. 48.
62. *Cely Papers*, p. xxiii.
63. *Lybelle of Englysshe Polycye* in *loc. cit.*, pp. 179–81.
64. With deference, I think that Mr Malden in his introduction to the *Cely Papers*, App. II, pp. lii–iii, is mistaken in seeking to identify Synchon Mart with a particular fair at Antwerp on St John's Day, Bammes mart with the fair at St Rémy (a Flemish name for whom is Bamis) on August 8, and Cold Mart with Cortemarck near Thourout. The names simply refer to the seasons in which there were fairs in most of the important centres, though doubtless in one place the winter and in another the spring, summer, or autumn fair was the more important. That the names refer to seasons and not to places appears quite clearly in various letters and regulations relating to the Merchant Adventurers of York. See *The York Mercers and Merchant Adventurers*, 1356–1917, ed. M. Sellers (Surtees Soc., 1918), pp. 117, 121–5, 147, 160, 170–1; see Miss Sellers' note, *ibid.*, p. 122, quoting W. Cunningham: 'The ancient Celtic fairs . . . were a widespread primitive institution and appear to have been fixed for dates marked by the change of seasons.' – *Scottish Hist. Review*, xiii, p. 168. For instance, a document of 1509 ('For now att this cold marte last past, holdyn at Barow in Brabond,' *loc. cit.* p. 121) disposes of the idea that the Cold mart was the mart at Cortemarck, while another document refers to merchants intending to ship 'to the cold martes' and 'to the synxon martes' in the plural. *Ibid.*, p. 123. The identification of Balms mart with the fair at St Rémy on August 8 is, moreover, belied by the same document (1510–11), which runs, 'Whereas this present marte . . . we have lycensed and set you at libertie to shipp your commodities to the balmes marte next coming. Nevertheless . . . we thinke it good . . . that upon the recepte of these our letters ye . . . assemble and consult together, and if ye shall thinke good amongest yourselffs . . . discretly to withdraw and with holde your hands from shippyng to the said balmes marte. . . . Wryten at Andwarp the xvij day of August.' *Ibid.*, p. 124. The Balms mart was obviously the autumn fairtide, and Mr Malden is no doubt right in identifying Balms (Bammys, Bammes) with Bamis, the local Flemish name of St Rémy; St Rémy's Day was October 28, and the Balms mart was not the mart held on August 8 at

St Rémy, but the mart held on and round about St Rémy's Day. Another document of 1552 gives interesting information about the shippings for three of the marts: 'The last daye of shippinge unto the fyrst shippinge beinge for the pasche marte is ordeyned to be the laste of Marche nexte ensuyinge; and the seconde shippinge which is appointed for the sinxon marte the laste day to the same is appoynted the laste of June then nexte followinge; and unto the colde marte the laste day of shippinge is appoynted to be the laste of November then nexte insuyinge.' – *Ibid.*, p. 147. The Merchant Adventurers tried sometimes to restrict merchants to the Cold and the Synxon marts, which were the most important.

65. *Cely Papers*, p. xl, and *passim*.

66. *Ibid.*, p. 74. Richard Cely the younger to George: 'I understand that ye have a fair hawk. I am right glad of her, for I trust to God she shall make you and me right great sport. If I were sure at what passage ye would send her I would fetch her at Dover and keep her till ye come. A great infortune is fallen on your bitch, for she had 14 fair whelps, and after that she had whelped she would never eat meat, and so she is dead and all her whelps; but I trust to purvey against your coming as fair and as good to please that gentleman.' – *Ibid.*, p. 74.

67. *Ibid.*, p. xlix.

68. *Ibid.*, App. I., pp. xlix–lii, a very interesting note on contemporary coinage, identifying all the coins mentioned in the letters.

69. *Ibid.*, p. 159.

70. *Ibid.*, p. 161.

71. *Stonor Letters*, II, p. 43. So Dame Elizabeth Stonor ends a letter to her husband: 'Written at Stonor, when I would fain have slept, the morrow after our Lady day in the morning.' – *Ibid.*, p. 77.

72. Chaucer, *Canterbury Tales* (*Shipman's Tale*), LL, 1265–78, in *Works* (Globe Ed., 1903), p. 80.

73. The will is P.C.C. 24 Logge at Somerset House. For this analysis of its contents and information about the life of Thomas Betson after his breach with the Stonors see *Stonor Letters*, I, pp. xxviii–ix.

74. They are (1) John Bacon, citizen and woolman, and Joan, his wife (*d.* 1437); (2) Thomas Gilbert, citizen and draper of London and merchant of the Staple of Calais (*d.* 1483), and Agnes, his wife (*d.* 1489); (3) Christopher Rawson, mercer of London and merchant of the Staple of Calais, Junior Warden of the Mercers' Company in 1516 (*d.* 1518), and his two wives. Thomas Betson was doubtless acquainted with Gilbert and Rawson.

CHAPTER VII

THOMAS PAYCOCKE OF COGGESHALL

A. Raw Material

1. The raw material for this chapter consists of Paycocke's House, presented to the Nation in 1924 by the Right Hon. Noel Buxton, M.P., which stands in West Street, Coggeshall, Essex (station, Kelvedon); the Paycocke brasses, which lie in the North aisle of the parish church of St Peter ad Vincula at Coggeshall; and the wills of John Paycocke (*d.* 1505), Thomas Paycocke (*d.* 1518), and Thomas Paycocke (*d.* 1580), which are now preserved at Somerset House (P.C.C. Adeane 5, Ayloffe 14, and Arundell 50, respectively), and of which that of the first Thomas has been printed in Mr Beaumont's paper, cited below, while I have analysed fully the other two in my book, *The Paycockes of Coggeshall* (1920), which deals at length with the history of the Paycockes and their house. See also G. F. Beaumont, *Paycocke's House, Coggeshall, with some Notes on the Families of Paycocke and Buxton* (reprinted from Trans. Essex Archæol. Soc., IX, pt. V) and the same author's *History of Coggeshall* (1890). There is a beautifully illustrated article on the house in *Country Life* (June 30, 1923), vol. LIII, pp. 920–6.

2. For an apotheosis of the clothiers, see *The Pleasant History of John Winchcomb, in his younger days called Jack of Newbery, the famous and worthy Clothier of England* and *Thomas of Reading, or the Six Worthy Yeomen of the West,* in *The Works of Thomas Deloney,* ed. F. O. Mann (1912), nos. II and V. The first of these was published in 1597 and the other soon afterwards and both went through several editions by 1600.

3. On the cloth industry in general see G. Morris and L. Wood, *The Golden Fleece* (1922); E. Lipson, *The Woollen Industry* (1921); and W. J. Ashley, *Introd. to English Economic History* (1909 edit.). For the East Anglian woollen industry see especially the *Victoria County Histories* of Essex and Suffolk. For a charming account of another famous family of clothiers see B. McClenaghan, *The Springs of Lavenham* (Harrison, Ipswich, 1924).

B. Notes to the Text

1. *Deloney's Works,* ed. F. O. Mann, p. 213.
2. Thomas Fuller, *The Worthies of England* (1622), p. 318.
3. A convenient introduction to the study of monumental brasses,

with illustrations and a list of all the surviving brasses in England, arranged according to counties, is W. Macklin, *Monumental Brasses* (1913). See also H. Druitt, *Costume on Brasses* (1906). These books also give details as to the famous early writers on the subject, such as Weaver, Holman, and A. J. Dunkin.

4. *Testamenta Eboracensia, a selection of wills from the Registry at York*, ed. James Raine, 6 vols. (Surtees Soc., 1836–1902). The Surtees Society has also published several other collections of wills from Durham and elsewhere, relating to the northern counties. A large number of wills have been printed or abstracted. See, for instance, *Wills and Inventories from the Registers of Bury St Edmunds*, ed. S. Tymms (Camden Soc., 1850); *Calendar of Wills Proved and Enrolled in the Court of Hastings, London*, ed. R. R. Sharpe, 2 vols. (1889); *The Fifty Earliest English Wills in the Court of Probate, London*, ed. F. J. Furnivall (E.E.T.S., 1882); *Lincoln Wills*, ed. C. W. Foster (Lincoln Record Soc., 1914); and *Somerset Medieval Wills*, 1383–1558, ed. F. W. Weaver, 3 vols. (Somerset Record Soc., 1901–5).

5. The will of the other Thomas Paycocke 'cloathemaker', who died in 1580, also refers to the family business. He leaves twenty shillings 'to William Gyon my weaver'; also 'Item, I doe give seaven poundes tenne shillinges of Lawful money of Englande to and amongest thirtie of the poorest Journeymen of the Fullers occupacion in Coggeshall aforesaide, that is to every one of them fyve shillinges.' William Gyon or Guyon was related to a very rich clothier, Thomas Guyon, baptized in 1592 and buried in 1664, who is said to have amassed £100,000 by the trade. Thomas Paycocke's son-in-law Thomas Tyll also came of a family of clothiers, for in a certificate under date 1577 of wool bought by clothiers of Coggeshall during the past year there occur the names of Thomas Tyll, William Gyon, John Gooddaye (to whose family the first Thomas Paycocke left legacies), Robert Lytherland (who receives a considerable legacy under the will of the second Thomas), and Robert Jegon (who is mentioned incidentally in the will as having a house near the church and was father of the Bishop of Norwich of that name). See Power, *The Paycockes of Coggeshall*, pp. 33–4.

6. Quoted in Lipson, *Introd. to the Econ. Hist. of England* (1905), I, p. 421.

7. Quoted *ibid.*, p. 417.

8. On John Winchcomb see Power, *op. cit.*, pp. 17–18; and Lipson, *op. cit.*, p. 419.

9. Deloney's Works, ed. F. C. Mann, pp. 20–1.

10. *Ibid.*, p. 22.

11. Quoted in C. L. Powell, *Eng. Domestic Relations*, 1487–1563 (1917), p. 27.

12. The house subsequently passed, it is not quite clear at what date, into the hands of another family of clothiers, the Buxtons, who had intermarried with the Paycockes some time before 1537. William Buxton (*d.* 1625) describes himself as 'clothyer of Coggeshall' and leaves 'all my Baey Lombs [Looms]' to his son Thomas. Thomas was seventeen when his father died and lived until 1647, also carrying on business as a clothier, and the house was certainly in his possession. He or his father may have bought it from John Paycocke's executors. By him it was handed down to his son Thomas, also a clothier (*d.* 1713), who passed it on to his son Isaac, clothier (*d.* 1732). Isaac's two eldest sons were clothiers likewise, but soon after their father's death they retired from business. He apparently allowed his third son, John, to occupy the house as his tenant, and John was still living there in 1740. But Isaac had left the house by will in 1732 to his youngest son, Samuel, and Samuel, dying in 1737, left it to his brother Charles, the fourth son of Isaac. Charles never lived in it, because he spent most of his life in the pursuit of his business as an oil merchant in London, though he is buried among his ancestors in Coggeshall Church. In 1746 he sold the house to Robert Ludgater and it passed completely out of the Paycocke–Buxton connexion, and in the course of time fell upon evil days and was turned into two cottages, the beautiful ceilings being plastered over. It was on the verge of being destroyed some years ago when it was bought and restored to its present fine condition by Mr Noel Buxton, a direct lineal descendant of the Charles Buxton who sold it. See Power, *op. cit.*, pp. 38–40.

13. *Deloney's Works*, ed. F. O. Mann, p. 213.

14. Defoe, *Tour through Great Britain*, 1724 (1769 edit.), pp. 144–6.

15. 'This shire is the most fatt, frutefull and full of profitable thinges, exceeding (as far as I can finde) anie other shire for the general commodities and the plentie, thowgh Suffolk be more highlie comended by some (wherewith I am not yet acquainted). But this shire seemeth to me to deserve the title of the Englishe Goshen, the fattest of the lande, comparable to Palestina, that flowed with milk and hunnye.' – Norden, *Description of Essex* (1594), (Camden Soc.), p. 7.

16. According to Leake, writing about 1577, 'About 1528 began the first spinning on the distaffe and making of Coxall clothes. . . . These Coxall clothes weare first taught by one Bonvise, an Italian.' – Quoted *V. C. H. Essex*, II, p. 382.

Notes on Illustrations

PLATE I. *Bodo at his work*

From an eleventh-century Anglo-Saxon calendar in the British Museum (MS. Tit., B. V., pt. I), showing the occupations of Bodo, or of his masters, for each month of the year. The months illustrated are January (ploughing with oxen), March (breaking clods in a storm), August (reaping), and December (threshing and winnowing). The other pictures represent February (pruning), April (Bodo's masters feasting), May (keeping sheep), June (mowing), July (woodcutting), September (Bodo's masters boar-hunting), October (Bodo's masters hawking), and November (making a bonfire).

PLATE II. *Embarkation of the Polos at Venice*

From the magnificent MS. of Marco Polo's book, written early in the fifteenth century and now preserved at the Bodleian Library, Oxford (MS. no. 264, f. 218). The artist gives an admirable view of medieval Venice, with the Piazetta to the left, and the Polos embarking on a rowing boat to go on board their ship. In the foreground are depicted (after the medieval fashion of showing several scenes of a story in the same picture) some of the strange lands through which they passed. Note the Venetian trading ships.

PLATE III. *Part of a landscape roll by Chao Mêng-fu*

This very beautiful scene is taken from a roll painted by Chao Mêng-fu in 1309 in the style of Wang Wei, a poet and artist of the T'ang dynasty (A.D. 699–759). A fine description of it is given by Mr Laurence Binyon: 'In the British Museum collection is a long roll, over seventeen feet long, painted almost entirely in blues and greens on the usual warm brown silk. . . . It is one continuous landscape, in which the scenes melt into one another. Such rolls are not meant to be exhibited or looked at all at once, but enjoyed in small portions at a time, as the painting is slowly unrolled and the part already seen rolled up again. No small mastery is requisite, as may be imagined, to contrive that wherever the spectator pauses an harmonious composition is presented. One has the sensation, as the roll unfolds, of passing through a delectable country. In the foreground water winds, narrowing and expanding, among verdant knolls and lawns, joined here and there by little wooden bridges; and the water is fed by torrents that plunge down among pine-woods from crags of fantastic form, glowing with hues of lapis-lazuli and jade; under towering peaks are luxuriant valleys, groves with glimpses of scattered deer, walled parks, clumps of delicate bamboo, and the distant roofs of some nestling village. Here and there is a pavilion by the water in which poet or sage sits contemplating the beauty round him. These happy and romantic scenes yield at last to promontory and reed-bed on the borders of a bay where a fisherman's boat is rocking on the swell. It is possible that a philosophic idea is intended to be suggested – the passage of the soul through the pleasant delights of earth to the contemplation of the infinite.' – Laurence Binyon, *Painting in the Far East* (1908), pp. 75–6. The section of the roll which has been chosen for reproduction here has already been reproduced in S. W. Bushell, *Chinese Art* (1910), II, Fig. 127, where it is thus described: 'A lake with a terraced pavilion on an island towards which a visitor is being ferried in a boat, while fishermen are seen in another boat pulling in their draw-net; the distant mountains, the pine-clad hills in the foreground, the clump of willow opposite, and the line of reeds swaying in the wind along the bank of the water are delightfully rendered, and skilfully combined to make a characteristic picture.' – *Ibid.*, II, p. 134. Other sections of the same roll are reproduced in H. A. Giles, *Introd. to the Hist. of Chinese Pictorial Art* (2nd ed., 1918) facing p. 56; and in L. Binyon, *op. cit.*, plate III (facing p. 66). It is exceedingly interesting to compare this landscape roll with the MS of Marco Polo, illuminated about a century later, from which the scene of the embarkation at Venice has been taken; the one is so obviously the work of a highly developed and the other of an almost naïve and childish civilization.

PLATE IV. *Madame Eglentyne at home*

This is a page from a fine manuscript of *La Sainte Abbaye*, now in the British Museum (MS. Add. 39843, f. 6 v⁰). At the top of the picture a priest with two acolytes prepares the sacrament; behind them stands the abbess, holding her staff and a book, and accompanied by her chaplain and the sacristan, who rings the bell; behind them is a group of four nuns, including the cellaress with her keys, and nuns are seen at the windows of the dorter above. At the bottom is a procession of priest, acolytes and nuns in the choir; notice the big candles carried by the young nuns (perhaps novices) in front, and the notation of the music books.

PLATE V. *The Ménagier's wife has a garden party*

This beautiful scene is taken from a fifteenth-century manuscript of the *Roman de la Rose* (Harl. MS. 4425), which is one of the greatest treasures of the British Museum.

PLATE VI. *The Ménagier's wife cooks his supper with the aid of his book*

From MS. Royal, 15 D. I, f. 18, in the British Museum which is part of a *petite bible historiale*, or biblical history, by Guyart des Moulins, expanded by the addition of certain books of the Bible, in French. It was made at Bruges by the order of Edward IV, King of England by one J. du Ries and finished in 1470, so that it is about eighty years later than the Ménagier's book. The illustration represents a scene from the story of Tobias; Tobit, sick and blind, is lying in bed, and his wife Anna is cooking by the fire, with the help of a book and a serving maid. The right-hand half of the picture, which is not reproduced here, shows the outside of the house, with Tobias bringing in the angel Raphael. The illuminated border of the page from which this scene is taken contains the arms of Edward IV, with the garter and crown.

PLATE VII. *Calais about the time of Thomas Betson*

This plan of Calais in 1546 is reproduced from a 'Platt of the Lowe Countrye att Calleys, drawne in October, the 37th Hen. VIII, by Thomas Pettyt,' now in the British Museum. (Cott. MS. Aug. I, vol. II, no. 70). There is only room to show the top corner of the plan, with the drawing of Calais itself, but the whole plan is charming, with its little villages and great ships riding in the channel.

PLATE VIII. *Thomas Paycocke's house at Coggeshall*

From a photograph of the front of the house, standing on the street' Note the long carved breastsummer that supports the overhanging upper story. On the left can be seen, much foreshortened, the archway and double doors of linen fold panels. The windows are renovations on the original design, flat sash windows having been put in in the eighteenth century.

Index

Index